Geoffrey Ashe, F.R.S.L., the editor, was co-founder and Secretary of the Camelot Research Committee and a well-known writer on Arthurian themes and dark-age history. His books include *King Arthur's Avalon* and *From Caesar to Arthur*. He has lectured and broadcast widely in Britain and America and written books in other mythological and religious fields, together with one novel, *The Finger and the Moon*.

Leslie Alcock, F.S.A., F.R.S.E., is a Professor of Archaeology at the University of Glasgow. He was Director of Excavations at Dinas Powys Glamorgan, Degannwy Gwynedd and Cadbury Castle on behalf of the Camelot Research Committee. He is the author of *Arthur's Britain* and *Cadbury/Camelot*.

C. A. Ralegh Radford, D.Litt., F.B.A., F.S.A., F.R.Hist.S., was co-founder and Chairman of the Camelot Research Committee. A former President of the Royal Archaeological Institute and a leading figure in British archaeology, Dr Radford directed excavations at Tintagel, Castle Dore, Whithorn and Glastonbury Abbey.

Philip Rahtz, M.A., F.S.A., is a Professor of Archaeology, and heads the Archaeology Department at the University of York. He was a member of the Camelot Research Committee and was Director of Excavations at Glastonbury Tor.

Jill Racy is a designer of costumes and masks for theatre, cinema and television. She lectures on The History of Costumes, is a television and film actress and has collaborated on the writing of four musicals, including the lyrics.

GEOFFREY ASHE
LESLIE ALCOCK
C. A. RALEGH RADFORD
PHILIP RAHTZ

The Quest For Arthur's Britain

Published in 1987 by

Academy Chicago Publishers
425 North Michigan Avenue
Chicago, Illinois 60611

Copyright © Geoffrey Ashe 1968

Printed and bound in the USA

Library of Congress Cataloging-in-Publication Data

Ashe, Geoffrey.
     The quest for Arthur's Britain.

     Reprint. Originally published: New York : Praeger,
1968.
     Bibliography: p.
     Includes index.
     1. Arthur, King.   2. Arthurian romances–History and
criticism.   3. Great Britain–History–Anglo-Saxon
period, 449-1066.   4. Great Britain–Antiquities.
I. Title.
DA152.5.A7A827   1987   942   87-19424
ISBN 0-89733-287-3 (pbk.)

Contents

Introduction

FOR A LONG TIME NOW, the story of Arthur and his knights has been the chief myth of the island of Britain. It is far more than a medley of fireside tales. Only a theme answering to some deep sense of national character and need could have flourished for so long, or exerted such an influence on literature, art, and occasionally even politics. Nor is it purely insular in its power. During the Middle Ages, if you had asked any well-read audience on the continent–at least an audience of layfolk–what the name of England evoked in their minds, they would very likely have mentioned King Arthur. They might have gone on to tell you that England was specially famous as a home of the kind of love exemplified by Lancelot and Guinevere, Tristram and Iseult; and to assure you that Camelot was a noble and joyous city, even if they were not quite sure where it was. An audience of clerics, less familiar with the world of romance, might still have recalled Joseph of Arimathea, Glastonbury, the Holy Grail.

How far, factually, was the Arthurian Legend true? Most of those medieval readers would have taken it for granted that King Arthur did rule in Britain at some date between the Romans and Normans, presiding over an order of knighthood, a brilliant court, a sort of chivalric Utopia. That confidence eventually waned. By the Age of Reason, historians were more than doubtful whether Arthur ever existed. Then a slow reaction began. In a memorable aside in *The Decline and Fall of the Roman Empire*, Edward Gibbon cast his massive vote for Arthur's reality. By the middle of the twentieth century, for most people who studied the matter, Arthur had become once more a probably-real figure, if a rather different one from the majestic monarch of the romancers. While renewed scepticism presently revived the doubts, it remains more likely than not that the Legend has its source in an actual person. Some of the evidence once thought to substantiate him is no longer esteemed so highly, but, on the other hand, new light has been shed from other directions.

The Quest for Arthur's Britain was first published in 1968. It reflected a phase in the evolution of opinion. To quote my own words in the original introduction, it had been assumed that "while Arthur probably lived, we would never know much about him or the milieu he lived in." But, I continued, fresh approaches had recently aroused a fresh public interest.

That interest had unleashed a squadron of new investigators, a stream of funds to support investigations by others. Solid facts had begun to emerge through the labours of archaeologists. The book itself was conceived soon after a trial dig at Cadbury Castle, the reputed site of Camelot,which had disclosed at least enough basis for that idea to justify a larger project. I described *The Quest* as "an interim attempt to draw all the threads together and show how matters stand; or rather, how they stood in the year 1968, because the one certainty is that they will not stand still."

On the last point I was right. *The Quest* contains many passages which, in the 1980s, would need to be re-thought, re-stated, even drastically amended. Not only has scholarship progressed, but the wave of modern creative writing surveyed in the final chapter has rolled much further—one could name Mary Stewart, John Arden, John Heath-Stubbs and many more, conspicuously now in America. Yet it would be a mistake to try to re-write this book. It has acquired a certain status over the years, and deserves to be left untouched, not as an authoritative text but as a kind of document in its own right. For the later bibliography and a general update, I would mention a book of my own, *The Discovery of King Arthur*, published in 1985; and the far more important *Arthurian Encyclopedia*, edited by Norris J. Lacy and published in 1986. *The Quest for Arthur's Britain* is best read today in conjunction with these and, on particular topics, with works of scholarship to which they refer.

Some specific points may be noted here.

After the opening chapter, sketching the fortunes of the Arthurian Legend, I attempted in chapter 2 an account of what I called "The Arthurian Fact." By this I meant the historical struggle of post-Roman Britain (or parts of it) against the encroaching barbarians, which supplied the context of Arthur as patriotic leader,whether or not he actually existed. Further research, archaeological findings, and a tougher criticism of sources, have since affected prevailing views of this period and, among much else, have suggested a modified chronology, with some of the main events happening earlier. There has been a trend towards greater scepticism about texts that were formerly treated with respect as the chief evidence. However, I see no reason to drop the essential scheme. As to this, I remarked in *The Quest* that "historically speaking, the Arthurian Fact is far clearer than Arthur himself." Some might urge that even the "Fact" is less clear than I thought; but the contrast remains valid. Perhaps I ought to have drawn attention to the book's title. During preliminary talks, one suggestion, as I recall, was that it should be called *The Quest for Arthur*. On that I was adamant. It was not, and it could not be.

After *The Quest* appeared, Leslie Alcock, one of its leading contributors, wrote a book of his own entitled *Arthur's Britain*. In the course of this he presented the case for the "historical Arthur" as then conceived, on the basis of early Welsh writings, and more or less as outlined in chapter 2. A few years later, that case was savaged by the eminent Celticist David Dumville, and while I have never thought that his refutation of it was total, I accept that the search for a "historical Arthur" by way of Welsh matter is inconclusive.

My belief is that the proper question to ask is not precisely "Did Arthur exist?" but rather "How did his Legend originate, what facts is it rooted in?" Following that line, and pursuing hints which I (and a few others) had noticed long before, I made, after Dr Dumville's onslaught, a new study of certain continental records. The results appeared in *Speculum*, the journal of the Medieval Academy of America, in April 1981. I have expanded the thesis in the aforesaid book *The Discovery of King Arthur*, and elsewhere.

I would now suggest that the primary Arthur-figure was a leader referred to overseas as "the King of the Britons," who led the expedition mentioned in *The Quest* on page 38 as an ally of the Emperor Anthemius. This would shift the Legend's starting-point a generation or so back. The more locatable "Arthurian" battles, and the "Arthurian" refortification of Cadbury, can likewise be shifted back and fitted in here. Other data, admittedly, cannot. It looks to me as if the Arthur of Welsh storytellers and Geoffrey of Monmouth may be a composite, annexing real or fictitious exploits of real or fictitious heroes to traditions about a British king who was undoubtedly real, who flourished in the last twilight of the Western Empire, and who was the original Arthur so far as anyone was. But I would not pretend to have reached a full solution.

To pass to subsequent chapters....Here I was fortunate enough to enlist several members of the Camelot Research Committee, whose names gave weighty authority to the material they supplied. The Committee–which I was instrumental in founding, and of which I had the honour to be secretary–was the body in charge of the excavations at Cadbury. Three of its members consented to describe some of their own work, and discoveries made by colleagues.

C.A. Ralegh Radford, the major pioneer in the archaeology of post-Roman Britain, wrote on his findings at Tintagel, Arthur's supposed birthplace; at Castle Dore, linked with the romance of Sir Tristram and King Mark; and at Glastonbury Abbey, the site of Arthur's reputed grave. His contributions comprised chapters 3 and 5, and they remain as written. However, it must be said that Dr Radford's interpretation of Tintagel has been challenged. When he examined the site, so little was known about fifth-century British antiquities that there were no trustworthy guidelines for interpreting the results. He explained Tintagel as a Celtic monastery. It has been argued in recent years that the imported pottery by which he dated the site came from a princely stronghold which he never found or never identified. Tintagel may well have had a large non-monastic establishment. Geoffrey of Monmouth's choice of it for the scene of Arthur's begetting suggests that he knew a Cornish tradition, perhaps not of individuals, but of the place's importance at more or less the right time. Obviously a stronghold would be more appropriate than a monastery.

Arthur's grave at Glastonbury remains a matter of dispute. A frequent allegation that it was faked by the monks to enhance their Abbey's prestige, and thereby raise funds, was at least partly refuted by Dr Radford's excavation. They did find an early burial. The question is whether it was Arthur's, and this turns on the inscribed cross illustrated on page 101. The assumption that the cross was forged in 1190 has been criticized on other grounds besides Dr Radford's. A fair summing-up would be that the dogmatic assertion of fraud is not quite as general as it once was.

Little need be added to chapter 6, concerning Glastonbury Tor. Its author Philip Rahtz has re-affirmed his belief that Russell's maze theory should be taken seriously, and the same view is now taken by the National Trust, which owns the Tor. Professor Rahtz's inference from meat bones that the early settlement was not a monastic one has been queried, because, it seems, the meat bones are inconclusive, and its nature is still doubtful.

Chapter 7, on Cadbury, was strictly provisional. The excavations went on till 1970. Professor Alcock published an account of them two years later, and supplemented this in a British Academy lecture in 1982. A point that may be thought to need clearer statement is the justification for speaking here of Camelot, since the Camelot of romance is a fantasy place that never existed anywhere. What is significant, I would urge, is that the romancers who created Camelot did not portray it as Britain's capital city but as the personal headquarters of Arthur. There could, in the background, have been a tradition of a real Arthur possessing such a headquarters. That is the sense in which Cadbury Castle could have been the real Camelot.

Its claim rests mainly on the refortification, datable to the decades from the 460s on. To what was already known when *The Quest* appeared, Alcock was able to add a gate-house of the same period at the south-west entrance. He also unearthed foundations of a contemporary hall on the summit plateau. The gate-house resembled Roman structures, and thus modified the judgement that the refortification was purely Celtic in character. Excavation of other hill-forts has since lengthened the list of reoccupations at about this time, but nothing like the huge stone-and-timber rampart has emerged anywhere else in England or Wales, and a few partial parallels in Scotland are much smaller and have no gate-houses. Cadbury therefore implies a British leader (a king, perhaps, after all) with resources of manpower unequalled, so far as we know, in the Britain of his day.

When Leland picked out this hill as Camelot, he picked out the most appropriate one, so far as we know, throughout ex-Roman Britain. Since even a modern archaeologist could not have detected the buried 'Arthurian' rampart by inspection without digging, it seems out of the question that Leland, in 1542, merely guessed. Somehow he got hold of an authentic tradition about the hill, though it need not have included the actual romantic name, since "Camelot" was familiar as Arthur's home, and he may have simply applied it to a hill where he understood that home to have been.

Conclusions about Cadbury can be extended to Tintagel and Glastonbury. In all three instances, the personal presence of a real Arthur could be wholly legend. No specific and reliable trace of him has been found. Yet in all three instances, with no adequate surface clues to go on, the legend-weavers connected him with places which archaeology has established as inhabited centres at about the right time: the Tintagel headland, Glastonbury (the Tor certainly, the Abbey site possibly), and Cadbury Castle. With Arthur legends in other parts of Britain—in Wales, in the north—nothing equivalent can be claimed. The legends are attached to locations which have not, so far, turned out to fit in with them. I find it hard to believe that the triple score in the West Country was pure luck. Whatever we may infer about Arthur as an individual, the West Country's stories of him reflect valid traditions about the principal places where they locate him, reaching right back to his supposed lifetime. *The Quest* was attacked in some quarters for not giving enough weight to the theory that Arthur was a northerner. But the judgment that his northern links are literary rather than historical (pages 50-1) seems to have been borne out.

The following acknowledgments, at the end of the 1968 introduction, may be appended here without change. Besides the archaeologists' chapters, I am happy to include a section on Costume by Jill Racy, who brings the specialist knowledge of a theatrical designer. The account of the Bath Festival events of 1967 is based on a helpful note furnished by Barbara Robertson, who organized the events in question and wrote the script of the play.

My thanks are due to Dr Fanni Bogdanow and Dr Frederick Whitehead of Manchester University, for their assistance with the first chapter; to Miss Margaret Scherer of the Metropolitan Museum of Art, New York, for information about Arthurian pictures; to Mrs Rachel Bromwich, Dr Nora K. Chadwick, and Professor Lewis Thorpe, for their encouragement at various times. The publishers join with me in thanking Mrs Susan Bakker for her work in advising on and procuring illustrations.

I should like to thank the publishers of the following works for permission to quote from them: Kenneth Jackson, *A Celtic Miscellany*, Routledge and Kegan Paul, London 1951; Ifor Williams, "The Gododdin Poems," *Transactions of the Anglesey Antiquarian Society and Field Club*; and T.H. White, *The Once and Future King*, Collins, London 1958, Fontana paperback edition, London 1962.

Geoffrey Ashe
August 1987

General Chronological Chart

NEOLITHIC	5000
	4000
	3000
	2000
BRONZE AGE	1000
IRON AGE	500
PRE-ROMAN IRON AGE	400
	300
	200
	100
	BC 0 AD
ROMAN BRITAIN	100
	200
	300
	400
SUB-ROMAN or DARK AGE (Arthurian)	500
	600
EARLY MEDIEVAL	700
	800
	900
	1000
	1100
MEDIEVAL	1200
	1300
	1400
	1500
	1600

The chart opposite shows the periods ▶
of occupation of the main archaeological sites mentioned in the text.
The hatched horizontal band, demar-
cating the sub-Roman or dark-age
period, shows graphically that these
sites were all inhabited during the
years which range from eighty years
before the conjectural date of
Arthur's birth to one hundred years
after the date at which he is believed
to have died.

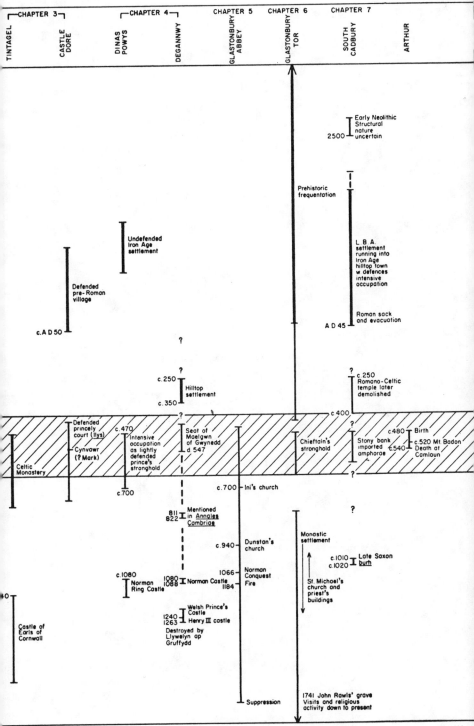

1   *The Visionary Kingdom*

Geoffrey Ashe

WHEN A MEDIEVAL STORY-WRITER was looking for themes and inspiration, there were three major sources he could go to. They were not the only sources, but they were the ones held in general respect. He could tap what was called the Matter of France; or the Matter of Rome; or the Matter of Britain.

The first of these meant the cycle of tales about Charlemagne and his peers, headed by the dauntless Roland, and their battles with the Saracens around the year AD 800. The second meant the literary legacy of the classical world, not only Roman but Greek: the siege of Troy, the adventures of Aeneas, the fortunes of the City itself. The third meant the legendary history of Britain. Above all, it meant the deeds of King Arthur and the Knights of the Round Table.

Each 'Matter' had its own geography, and to some extent its political undertones. The king of France was the heir of Charlemagne, and claimed the glory of his legend. The eastern part of Charlemagne's former realm was now a distinct state miscalled the Holy Roman Empire; this included Rome, and kept at least a trace of its glamour. But the country of King Arthur was England. Indeed, Arthur was what England stood for in many continental minds. The Matter of Britain was a more complex, elusive thing than the Matters of France and Rome, and could not be pinned down with the same historical confidence. Yet it was just as haunting and just as durable; in some ways more so.

From the twelfth century onward, the visionary kingdom of Arthur hovered behind the real kingdom of his supposed successors who wore the English crown: a presence counterpointed to it, moulding its literature, colouring its ideas, even affecting its politics. Arthur's Britain rooted itself in the national imagination. It was destined to remain rooted there for a long time, not only through the Middle Ages but afterwards.

What, in fact, was it? Where did this vision come from? Let us begin by examining the legend and what it has meant.

The Matter of Britain was a later growth than its French counterpart, and, indeed, originally took shape as a retort to it. When William the Conqueror advanced against Harold, the minstrel Taillefer rode with the Norman army singing of Charlemagne and Roland. No warrior in the English force replied with a song of Arthur. To all but a handful, the name would probably have meant nothing. But the Normans owed feudal allegiance to the French king, spoke his language, and knew the lays about his forebears.

These early ingredients of the Matter of France were known as *chansons de geste*. The most famous, the *Song of Roland*, gave epic form to a legend that had grown round a rearguard action in the Pyrenees. All this French poetry was martial, masculine, straightforward. Its prevailing motif was the warfare of Christendom against the Saracen paynim. One side was 'right' and the other 'wrong'. During the Crusades this tone suited the times. The kings of France enjoyed higher dignity because of the Charlemagne mystique. In 1147, Louis VII did what was expected of him by going on the Second Crusade in person, as Eldest Son of the Church and hereditary champion of the faith.

Ills. 1, 2. Pages from two of the earliest histories of England, in both of which King Arthur is mentioned. *Ill. 1*, is from William of Malmesbury's *Gesta Regum Anglorum*, written *c.* 1125. William mentions Arthur as 'a man clearly worthy to be proclaimed in true histories'. The manuscript illustrated here is from a twelfth-century edition, perhaps from William's own lifetime (*c.* 1090– *c.* 1143). *Ill. 2* shows a page from Geoffrey of Monmouth's *History of the Kings of Britain*. Arthur's reign was the climax of Geoffrey's history which became one of the most important books of the Middle Ages, and is the chief source for the Arthur of medieval literature.

The young monarchy founded in England by the French king's nominal vassals, the dukes of Normandy, already possessed a character of its own. But it had no equivalent legend, no sense of a pedigree or vocation. For some years, the quarrels of King Stephen and Empress Matilda threatened to tear it apart. A fortifying mythos became a psychological need. In civil war the Matter of Britain was born; and, after peace returned, the Anglo-Norman monarchy found itself equipped to confront France with a rival mystique and a counterpoise to Charlemagne.

The birth was a strange one. On the Celtic fringe of the Anglo-Norman lands, in Wales and Cornwall and Brittany, a medley of popular lore was current about a mysterious 'King Arthur'. His fame was already spreading outside these regions, through Breton minstrels descended from the British migrants who had long ago colonised the Armorican peninsula and changed its name. Welshmen supplied obscure notes on his career. He was said to have led the sixth-century Britons, who were the ancestors of all these assorted Celts, against the Saxons and Angles from across the North Sea, who were the ancestors of the English. Victorious over Britain's invaders as long as he reigned, he was killed at an unlocated Battle of Camlaun *Ill. 5* or Camlann, where a British opponent called Medraut also fell. Confusingly, he was also said to be still alive. In 1113, some French priests visited Bodmin with holy relics, and a man with a withered arm, who came to be healed, assured them that King Arthur lived. When they laughed at him, the bystanders took his side and a fight broke out.

The literary reconstitution of this cloudy figure began at Glastonbury Abbey in Somerset, an ancient foundation dating from before the Saxons. According to tradition, Christians had come there in Roman times and built a small church of wattle-work which was still standing. Between 1125 and 1130, William of Malmesbury visited the abbey. Born in Somerset of mixed Norman and Anglo-Saxon blood, William was England's first notable historian after the Con- *Ill. 1* quest. He was librarian at his own monastery of Malmesbury, and at Glastonbury his fellow-Benedictines introduced him to such legends and traditions as remained for British history in the dim age between the Roman and Saxon, when their community already existed and Arthur was alleged to have flourished. In that context William caught a glimpse of a fairly credible Arthur: a Christian warrior who, it seemed, had temporarily broken the Saxons at the 'siege of Mount Badon', wherever that was. This warrior (William realised, and re-

3

marked when he came to write about him) must be the person of whom the Cornish and others talked such nonsense; 'a man clearly worthy', he urged, 'to be proclaimed in true histories' instead of in fables.

William worked under the patronage of Empress Matilda's half-brother Robert, earl of Gloucester. Robert had a Welsh mother and a Welsh wife. His patronage extended to two other authors, Henry of Huntingdon and Caradoc of Llancarfan, who retrieved a little more from British antiquity. Stephen's brother Henry de Blois, who was abbot of Glastonbury from 1126, took an interest in the process. The disputed royal succession of 1135 brought the Norman magnates into conflict with each other. But a year or two later, the group of writers was joined by a fourth, who followed up William's hint with amazing results.

Geoffrey of Monmouth was a minor ecclesiastic and at least partly Ill. 2 Welsh. His father's name was Arthur: a fact which may have given a bias to nursery story-telling. Now Geoffrey produced a complete *History of the Kings of Britain* in Latin, with Arthur's reign as its climax.

Geoffrey's *History* is one of the key books of the Middle Ages. It purports to be based on an ancient original 'in the British language' (Welsh or Breton?) given him by 'Walter, archdeacon of Oxford'. His source has never been run to earth, and his archdeacon, though identifiable, is unenlightening. To be fair, Geoffrey is certainly not such a shameless fabricator as used to be thought. He draws on Welsh monastic writing, on Breton folklore, on poems and legends. Once or twice he has been oddly supported by archaeology. But, on the whole, he is more creative artist than historian; and the realm of Arthur, as known to literature, is his chief creation.

He traces the ancient Britons in Virgilian style to a settlement of wandering Trojans, led by Brutus, Aeneas's great-grandson. The royal line descends through such doubtful monarchs as Lud, founder of London, and Bladud, founder of Bath Spa. In due course the Romans arrive. Geoffrey reduces their rule to a vague protectorate. At the end of it stands a sovereign named Constantine. He, at least, is a real person: the emperor or pretender Constantine III, who was proclaimed in Britain in 407 and took the last legionaries out to fight on the continent. But Geoffrey prolongs the line through him to a series of post-Roman princes. During the fifth century, the heathen Angles and Saxons come to Britain, first as auxiliary troops invited by the usurper King Vortigern, then as would-be conquerors. Two sons of Ill. 26 Constantine, Ambrosius and Uther Pendragon, reassert the claims of

4

the rightful dynasty.

Ill. 6   Arthur enters the scene as the child of Uther by Ygerne, whose husband he impersonates with the aid of the wizard Merlin. Their son is born at Tintagel in Cornwall. After the husband's death in battle, Uther marries Ygerne and Arthur is legitimised. Succeeding to the throne as a youth, he launches a raid on the Saxon settlers in Britain which broadens into a full-scale campaign. With a sword called Caliburn, forged in the fairy island of Avalon, he reduces the heathen to subjection at a battle near Bath—Geoffrey's interpretation of the

Ill. 25   traditional 'Badon'.

King Arthur marries Ganhumara, a lady of Roman family, and extends his sway to Ireland, the Orkneys and Iceland. Twelve years of peace ensue. Then he conquers Norway and Gaul. His viceroys include the British noblemen Kay, Bedevere and Lot, the last of whom has a son named Gawain. Arthur holds court at Caerleon-upon-Usk, ruling over a Britain which is the wealthiest, most Christian and most civilised land in Europe. There is no Round Table in Geoffrey's story, but there is an order of knighthood. The ladies of the court, he says, 'would not deign to have the love of any till he had thrice proved himself in the wars. Wherefore did the ladies wax chaste, and knights the nobler for their love.'

Demands for tribute come from Rome, and Arthur leads an army
Ill. 3   to Gaul. The Emperor Lucius brings allies against him from the east.
Ill. 21   (Here Geoffrey is almost certainly interweaving the exploits of Maximus, who was proclaimed emperor in Britain in 383, and held Western Europe for several years with a largely British army.) Arthur presses toward Rome. But he is recalled by the rebellion of his nephew Modred—the 'Medraut' of the older Welsh annals. In the resulting civil war, this upstart and most of the nobility perish. Arthur himself
Ill. 5   receives a deadly wound at the final battle in Cornwall, and is borne away to Avalon to be healed, leaving his crown to a kinsman and dropping out of the story. The year of his disappearance is 542. Geoffrey goes on to the Anglo-Saxon recovery as a result of British dissensions and vices, and the Britons' downfall under their last king, Cadwallader. Here the *History* closes. Later Geoffrey added some *Prophecies of Merlin* and a long poem on the enchanter's life, adapted in part from genuine Welsh poetry of the dark ages. This gives a fuller account of Arthur's retirement to Avalon, described as an Isle of the Blest in distant seas. Its name means, literally, the Place of Apples.

Though Geoffrey became bishop of St Asaph, his literary public grew only slowly. But in 1154, Stephen died and Matilda's able son Henry II restored the stability of England. Henry and those around him found in the *History* the mystique they needed. If the Plantagenets were the heirs of the mighty Arthur, by adoption at any rate, they could claim an equal dignity—indeed a senior dignity—to the heirs of Charlemagne. Legendary Britain was quite as potent as legendary France. Geoffrey's own object had perhaps been merely to glorify the Welsh, who were the principal remnants of whatever Arthurian Britain had ever existed; but the Anglo-Saxons were his villains, and the Normans, having conquered the Anglo-Saxons, could feel that there was a spiritual pedigree. As they assimilated their conquest, becoming less and less like foreigners in the island, they were restoring Britain's ancestral majesty after a disruptive intrusion. The *History*, already translated into Norman-French, was accordingly believed by all but a few sceptics. The name Arthur was given to Henry II's grandson, born in 1187, whose accession as King Arthur II was a natural expectation. His uncle, John, however, removed him; tradition has it he was murdered at Rouen or Cherbourg in 1203.

Mutterings still came from the unsubdued Celts of Wales. They wanted to keep Arthur for themselves, not resign him to any self-styled heirs in London, and they prophesied his return from Avalon as their avenging chieftain. Henry, however, astutely checkmated the Welsh and confirmed his annexation of the entire legend. While passing through Wales, he learned from an imprudent bard that Arthur was, in fact, dead and buried, and that the secret of his grave was known. Seemingly, it was between two pillars in the cemetery of Glastonbury Abbey. Glastonbury, almost surrounded by marshes and lagoons, was then more or less an island in wet weather, and some said it was the actual Isle of Avalon. Henry suggested to the monks that they should look for the body. For several years nothing was done. Then, in 1184, the abbey burned down. The king organised its rebuilding, and in 1190, soon after his death, the ground between the pillars was probed.

Ill. 75

Ill. 74

Seven feet down (according to the report given out) the diggers found a slab of stone and a lead cross inscribed HIC IACET SEPULTUS INCLITUS REX ARTURIUS IN INSULA AVALONIA: Here lies buried the renowned King Arthur in the Isle of Avalon. Nine feet below these objects, they unearthed a huge coffin made of a hollowed oak log, embedded in the soil at a slight angle. Inside was the skeleton of a tall man, the skull damaged, and also some slighter bones with a scrap of yellow hair, presumably the remains of Arthur's queen.

Ill. 73

6

Thus it was proved that Arthur was really dead, and that his heritage belonged to the Plantagenets, in whose kingdom Glastonbury lay. The bones were ceremoniously gathered into a casket and deposited with the abbey's treasures. In 1191, Richard 1, on his way to the Third Crusade, presented Tancred of Sicily with a sword which he said was Ill. 4   Excalibur—the name now preferred for Arthur's sword—and had also been dug up in the abbey.

Geoffrey of Monmouth was not the only source of the Matter of Britain, or the only architect of the visionary kingdom. Once he had given King Arthur substance and value, the Celtic tales which he did not use himself acquired a fresh interest. Even before his time, bits and pieces of Arthurian lore had spread surprisingly far. Minstrels may have accompanied early Breton crusaders who travelled through Italy. Whether they did or not, it is a fact that Modena Cathedral has carvings dating from the first decade of the twelfth century, which portray Arthur rescuing his queen from an abducter. In a mosaic at Otranto he rides (for reasons unknown) on a goat*. A poet, Bleheris, can be dimly discerned recounting his deeds.

What this disjointed saga was like before Geoffrey of Monmouth, nobody knows in any detail. Apart from one Welsh story which lies outside the main stream, very little survives but names and hints. Only after Geoffrey—after him and because of him—did the now familiar body of romance begin to crystallise. It drew both on him and on the popular lore, which his *History* enabled other writers to unify and develop in a better defined setting. In 1155, the prolific Wace, born in Jersey, produced a French verse chronicle dedicated to Queen Eleanor, Henry 11's consort. It covered Geoffrey's ground from the reign of 'Constantine' onward, but with poetic amplifications and additions. The most important was the Round Table, said to have been devised by King Arthur so that no knight should have

*R. S. Loomis has put forth one conjectural suggestion. Legends of Arthur living on in supernatural form were preserved in Sicily and similar traditions may have persisted in Apulia. There is a Welsh legend of a pygmy king who rode a large goat. This pygmy king resembles the conception of an immortal Arthur in that he has infinite wealth and lives in a mysterious palace which is entered through a cave. Conceivably Arthur, in taking on the traits of various other immortal kings, acquired the Welsh king's goat. Furthermore, as the goat was the medieval symbol of lechery it is easy to understand why its association with Arthur would have been suppressed and have left no trace except at Otranto. Another theory, proposed by Arthur Rynders is that the king was believed to have been born under the sign of Capricorn. Indications of his birth date in Geoffrey of Monmouth are compatible with this view.

precedence. An adaptation of Wace by a cleric, Layamon, was the first long poem in English.

With the advent of frankly imaginative writers under royal aegis, the Matter of Britain outgrew both folklore and pseudo-history. Wace did little more than embroider a narrative which he believed to be true in substance. But his successors shifted the balance and made the throne of Arthur the starting point of a new mythology. It's popularity was rapid and immense. In the 1170s, a commentator on Geoffrey of Monmouth exclaims:

> What place is there within the bounds of the empire of Christendom to which the winged praise of Arthur the Briton has not extended? Who is there, I ask, who does not speak of Arthur the Briton, since he is but little less known to the peoples of Asia than to the Bretons, as we are informed by our palmers who return from the countries of the East? The Eastern peoples speak of him as do the Western, though separated by the breadth of the whole earth. Egypt speaks of him, and the Bosphorus is not silent. Rome, queen of cities, sings his deeds, and his wars are not unknown to her former rival Carthage. Antioch, Armenia and Palestine celebrate his ?ats.

Royal sponsorship could account for some of this literary explosion, though obviously not for the whole of it. Walter Map, an official of the Plantagenet household, was credited with composing several tales about Arthur's knights. While the ascription is almost certainly false, the fact that it could be made in such a quarter, and be accepted until modern times, is significant. For a while, the meeting-place of the new school was Queen Eleanor's private court in Poitou. Its most formative genius, however, had as his patroness not Eleanor herself but her daughter by a previous marriage to Louis VII of France: the Countess Marie de Champagne.

The countess's protégé was Chrétien de Troyes. He was busy with his long verse-romances during the third quarter of the twelfth century. The five which have survived as fairly complete works by him are *Eric et Enide*, *Cligés*, *Yvain*, *Perceval* and *Lancelot*. A special point of interest about the last of these is that it locates Arthur's court at Camelot. Chrétien told the two famous love-stories which, for many continental readers, came almost to sum up the Matter of Britain. Henceforward Arthur's queen, now called Guinevere, was everlastingly linked with Sir Lancelot, the most splendid of the knights; while from Lyonesse, a legendary sunken land off the coast

Ill. 27

of Cornwall, came Sir Tristram* as the lover of Iseult (though Chrétien's poem on them is lost).

Chrétien, of course, wrote in French, the language of the educated on both sides of the Channel, in France and England and the continental domains of the English kings. So did most of the romancers who followed him. But Arthurian tales were also written in English, Italian, German and Spanish. The international cycle gave Arthur's Britain an audience unthinkable for Geoffrey of Monmouth alone. In this context, the king himself receded somewhat. He simply presided over a court which was the scene or point of departure for adventures that supplied the main interest. Yet, for this very reason, his knights—Kay, Bedevere, Gawain and the rest—could shine with their own lustre, as could the female characters like Guinevere, Elaine and the Lady of the Lake. The Matter of Britain was more richly populated than the Matter of France. However slow and verbose by modern standards, the romances were varied enough to offer something for every taste: jousts and quests, combats and rescues, magic and heraldry and religion and love.

To many readers, love was the main attraction. As expounded by the troubadours of the day, it was an aristocratic game or cult with a set of rules, supposed to have been worked out at 'courts of love' with Queen Eleanor in the chair. The courts were a literary fiction: the cult was more or less serious. It exalted women. It also exalted extra-marital affairs. Love in the courtly sense was held to be actually impossible between married couples because it depended on distant worship and on favours and obligations of an unmatrimonial kind. The male epics of Charlemagne had no place for it. But the Arthur literature was offering hints as far back as Geoffrey himself. With the advent of such heroes as Lancelot, the mythology of courtly love became one of the principal British contributions to European culture.

A second distinctive feature of the Matter of Britain was its religious aspect. It lacked the crusading spirit of the Matter of France. The few Saracen characters were not made evil in the same way as the foes of Charlemagne. Arthur's kingdom, however, acquired a spiritual aura of its own from the Holy Grail. As the fervour of the Crusades died away, the subtler atmosphere of the Quest grew

*This name is variously spelt. 'Tristram' is the most familiar form and will be used here, except in direct quotation of texts where the spelling is different.

9

more potent.

The Grail is a bewildering concept. It seems to have begun as a sacred vessel in pagan Celtic myth. A Welsh poem cryptically portrays Arthur and his warriors as going over water in quest of a magic cauldron, which is in Annwn, a Celtic Otherworld like Avalon. In the *Conte du Graal*, partly the work of Chrétien de Troyes, the vessel which the knights go to seek has Christian associations: a Host is carried in it. Later, Robert de Borron and others make it out to be the dish or chalice of the Last Supper, conveyed to Britain and to the 'Vales of Avalon' by Joseph of Arimathea or companions of his, with drops of the Saviour's blood. By Arthur's time, the precious object has been lost. It is still in Britain, but in a mysterious castle surrounded by a waste land. Its keeper, the Fisher King, is wounded and immobile. If the Grail-seeking knight reaches the castle and asks a certain question, the Fisher King is healed and the waste land revives. Visions of Christ and the Blessed Virgin accompany this experience, and the Grail is the vehicle of a special sacrament and a special revelation. In early versions, such as the *Queste*, composed soon after 1200, it stands for an ascetic ideal opposed to the norms of knighthood and courtly love. Sir Perceval partially succeeds in the Quest, but the knight who succeeds most fully is Galahad, who is a model of chastity.

Ill. 9

Behind these riddles is an imperfect fusion of ideas, to which the key is no longer extant. The Grail has several further guises. In the German *Parzival* by Wolfram von Eschenbach, it is not a vessel at all but an oracular stone. Elsewhere it appears with three other objects: a lance, a sword and a dish. This is a combination which recurs with magical import in contexts that seem totally unconnected. The Church mistrusted the Grail stories, perhaps with reason. Several names of characters (such as Brons and Evalake) and the fertility symbolism suggest a considerable survival from pagan myth. So does the repeated motif of an otherworldly journey by water. It has been maintained that the romancers are transmitting confused notions about an initiation ritual, blending Christian and pre-Christian ideas, which was actually performed by some occult sect.

Ill. 9

At least one romancer, the author of the quest-tale *Perlesvaus* composed about 1225, seems to have drawn on a lost document at Glastonbury Abbey. Glastonbury's direct contribution to the Grail cycle was very likely no more, at most, than a legend that Joseph of Arimathea came to Britain and lived in or near the abbey precinct. But Glastonbury's mere existence—with its long Celtic tradition, its tomb of

Arthur, its claim to be Avalon—gave this bizarre Christianity a focus. The spell of Arthur's Britain was spiritual as well as secular. Under the pressure of orthodox Catholicism, the later Grail romancers dropped most of the bold and baffling imagery and declined into allegory; but the spell was not destroyed.

Having captured the aristocracy, King Arthur went on at a slower tempo to win a public in the literate middle class. Socially, that was the limit of his impact till much later times. To the popular ballad-makers he was little more than one name among many, and not a name to hold in great reverence—witness the song "King Arthur Had Three Sons". English peasants preferred Robin Hood and his merry men.

At the levels where Arthur counted—which were the powerful and articulate levels—how far did people literally believe in him? In England, at any rate, Geoffrey of Monmouth was commonly accepted, or at least not widely questioned. As for the romances, a medieval reader's assent was probably like the assent given today to the saga of the Wild West. There is a vague understanding that the place and period are real, however falsely presented. Names like Wyatt Earp and Billy the Kid refer to men who existed, however little we know of them. That vague understanding is enough. The Wild West is 'there', so to speak. The convention is valid, the responses are evoked.

But King Arthur was such an asset to English monarchs that some of them took him more seriously than any adult takes the Wild West. Royal faith affected literature, politics, customs and institutions. While in Italy, Edward I met the poet Rusticiano of Pisa and lent him a book of romances which inspired much of the Italian Arthur cycle. In 1278, Edward was busy conquering the Welsh. To make it clear once more that Arthur would not return to help them, he visited Glastonbury with his queen and the archbishop of Canterbury, and had the bones removed from the casket and put on show. Afterwards he reinterred them in the centre of the great abbey church before the high altar, where they remained till the Dissolution. As the British sovereign's successor, he asserted his right to annex Wales and proclaim his son Prince of Wales, the first English heir-apparent to hold that title. Later he invoked Geoffrey of Monmouth to prove that he was overlord of the Scots. His regalia included what was alleged to be Arthur's crown.

Ill. 64

In 1331, the young Edward III also made a state visit to Glastonbury with his queen, Philippa: a visit which cost the abbot £800. Some years later he authorised a would-be seer named John Blome to search in the abbey precincts for the body of St Joseph of Arimathea. Edward III's attempt to conquer France was all too probably influenced by the fictitious wars in Geoffrey of Monmouth. About this time he contemplated refounding the Round Table, and in 1348 he did found the Order of the Garter, in succession to Arthur's knighthood. During those sanguine decades, a recognised form of noble entertainment was a sort of dramatic pageant called a Round Table. The performers took the roles of Arthurian characters. At least eight were staged in England between 1252 and 1345.

The Black Death, defeat in France, the Peasants' Revolt, clouded the sky. By Chaucer's time, the Matter of Britain seemed out of key, dwindling away into ineffectual fable. Chaucer himself saluted Henry IV as 'conqueror of Brutus' Albion': an echo of Geoffrey. But his sole Arthurian tale is the anecdote assigned to the Wife of Bath, which is overshadowed by its highly un-Arthurian prologue.

Then, however, the fifteenth century repeated the twelfth. Again the visionary kingdom pressed in to meet the needs of the real one. Arthur had made his entry during the civil turmoil under Stephen, and helped to strengthen the morale of the English monarchy. Under Henry VI the horrors of renewed civil turmoil led to his second manifestation, with similar results.

Among the knights in the period of the Wars of the Roses was Sir Thomas Malory. Doubt overhangs Malory's career. He was long identified with a very disreputable Warwickshire Malory. Recently, however, Dr William Matthews has argued that he was a much more knightly person who came from Yorkshire. On his own showing, the Malory who matters spent a good deal of time in custody, perhaps as a criminal, perhaps as a prisoner of war—according to Dr Matthews, in the château of the duke of Nemours, who owned a collection of relevant romances. In the course of his obscure adventures, Malory managed to produce a complete Arthurian cycle in English, which was issued from the pioneer English press of Caxton. Underlying all his work was a yearning for realisable ideals of kingship and aristocracy: a yearning alien to the irresponsible troubadours, and doubtless prompted in some degree by the infamies of Yorkist and Lancastrian.

Ill. 6. A page from the first illustrated edition of Malory's *Morte d'Arthur*, published by Wynkyn de Worde in 1498. The woodcut shows Tintagel Castle and an episode in Uther Pendragon's romance with Igraine (Ygerna), the wife of the duke of Tintagel.

To judge from a manuscript found at Winchester College as lately as 1934, what Malory composed was a series of romances. Most, but not all, were free versions of French originals. The so-called *Morte d'Arthur* as a single volume is a product of Caxton's editing. But whatever Malory's precise aim, his translations and adaptations, as they grew under his hand, gave the legend a coherence it had never previously attained.

His books are bound together by linkages and cross-references; by consistency of spirit and continuity of moral concern; and also by a time-scheme that lends an air of history. One of the sources of unity, in fact, is Malory's belief in the basic truth of his subject-matter. His attitude is not so very remote from Shakespeare's in the history plays. He reworks the element of magic and marvel, generally cutting it down. That cutting heightens the effect of what he retains, giving it more point, and helping to integrate romance and supposed history. Merlin, who is prominent in Geoffrey of Monmouth but less so after him, reappears in Malory with dramatic force as the prime sponsor of the Arthurian regime. From the dubious birth through the episode of the sword in the stone to the forming of the Round Table at Camelot, the Quest of the Grail, the clash with Modred, the casting-away of Excalibur by Bedevere and the equivocal end at Glastonbury or Elsewhere, Malory traces a sequence of events which carries an impact that no random collection could.

Significantly, he changes the order. Geoffrey's Arthur reaches his apogee in the unfinished Roman campaign and declines swiftly.

Malory's Arthur marches on Rome earlier, gets there, and returns to peace. Between the triumph and the collapse, a noble way of life does fitfully flourish in Britain. An ideal of Christian knighthood is at least glimpsed in action. All the chivalric trappings are there, but underlying them is a graver morality. Malory enlarges the ethics. In the French stories, normal knighthood means essentially violence and courtly love—'open manslaughter and bold bawdry', in the words of the censorious Roger Ascham. The Grail brings a holier vision to some, but this is purely divisive: a summons to quit the court altogether for a monastery or hermitage. There is no clear middle ground for a layman with a conscience. Malory keeps much of the manslaughter and bawdry. But like other medieval Englishmen— such as Langland of *Piers Plowman*—he believes that each social order has a duty of its own, a proper path of fulfilment and salvation. His implied message to the corrupt English nobility is not to retreat into the cloister, but to turn from knighthood as it is to knighthood as it was meant to be and, under King Arthur, occasionally was.

He has three levels of virtue where most of his predecessors have two. When they are ethically concerned at all, they simply oppose the holiness of religion to the amorality of lay life. Malory too has his holy monks, his amoral or wicked laymen; but, in between, he asserts the claims of a lay life which can be good, and to some extent holy, after its own fashion. In that spirit he tones down the love theme, injecting ideas of constancy and even marriage. His Tristram is hero as well as lover. He depicts Lancelot's affair with Guinevere as a failure to live up to a true and possible chivalric ideal, a failure that dooms the Table.

Caxton printed the *Morte d'Arthur* in 1485. He tightened Malory's text and often improved it. In his preface he speaks of the publication as a request performance: Arthur's fame is still very much alive. Various relics confirm his historical existence. Winchester, for instance, has the Round Table, and Dover Castle has Gawain's skull.

Ill. 7

Thus the legend took its definitive English form, endowed with Malory's sense of authenticity and relevance to real life. On the continent, in the absence of a Malory, it faded away. No more romances were written.

To Caxton's readers, King Arthur seemed securely enshrined, but as a hero of literature or at most a moral example. Few could have foreseen the guise he began to assume almost immediately after the *Morte* was published.

Ill. 7. An eighteenth-century engraving of the Round Table in Winchester Castle (*cf. Ill. 8*). Around the Tudor rose in the centre is the legend 'Thys is the rownde table of Kyng Arthur *with* xxiv of hys namyde knygttes'. Among the knights are 'launcelot deu lake', 'gauen', 'percivale', 'trystram de lyens', 'bedwere', 'kay', 'mordrede', and, at Arthur's left hand, which was the Siege Perilous, 'galahallt'. (*Ill. 9*).

He had one feature with subtle potentialities: the strangeness of his death, or passing. The Celts themselves had never agreed about this. Though the Welsh poet who spoke to Henry II had said Arthur's grave was at Glastonbury, an earlier Welsh poet had said it was a mystery, and others always insisted that he had no grave because he was not dead. In the later Middle Ages, Geoffrey's dark statement, that after the last fight he was taken to Avalon for the healing of his wounds, could be construed in two ways.

Avalon might be Glastonbury, as the monks maintained. In that case, the healing presumably did not take effect. Arthur died after the Battle of Camlann and was buried like anybody else. But Avalon could also be a Celtic Otherworld or Isle of the Blest away in the sunset, and there Arthur might still live. If so, his prophesied return could be thought of. He was, in Malory's words, *rex quondam rexque futurus*: the Once and Future King. There were local variants of the same folklore motif, which asserted that Arthur or his knights lay asleep in a cave with a hoard of treasure. Caves of which such tales have been told exist—or have been alleged to exist—at Cadbury Castle in Somerset, at Caerleon, at Marchlyn Mawr in Caernarvon, in Snowdonia and near Melrose in Scotland.

Despite the tomb at Glastonbury, which Malory mentions, a passage toward the end of his work shows the doubt that lingered. The fifteenth-century poet Lydgate had described Arthur as 'a king y-crowned in Fairye' who would reappear to reign in Britain. Even if he really was dead, he might reappear in some symbolic manner. The belief that he could, and perhaps would, went deeper than nationalistic fancy. His legend made him a messiah, answering to an ancient pattern of the imagination. He was like the dying-and-reviving gods of so many cults, whose careers followed the seasonal cycle.

While several countries possessed legendary monarchs who were not dead but sleeping (a famous instance was Frederick Barbarossa of Germany), the supernatural glamour surrounding Arthur gave him an unrivalled magic. With England's unification, the old partisan hope of his expelling the Saxon had ceased to count. The return, if it occurred, would be a reinstatement of his kingdom, a reawakening of the majesty of his Britain.

In 1485, the very year when Caxton published the *Morte d'Arthur*, a political accident seemed to fulfil the prophecy. The Wars of the Roses ended with the triumph of Henry Tudor, who became Henry VII and married the Yorkist heiress. Though only fractionally a Welshman by blood, he regarded himself as Welsh, and marched from Wales to oust Richard III under the standard of the Red Dragon: an emblem derived through Geoffrey from Welsh writers of the dark ages. As an autocratic and highly capable ruler, Henry promoted two linked ideas which together made up the myth of the House of Tudor.

One was that his marriage had united the Roses and brought eighty-six years of strife, caused by public crimes, to a happy conclusion blessed by heaven. This view was taken up by the chroniclers and Shakespeare. The other was that, through his grandfather Owen Tudor, he had a claim to the throne independent of York and Lancaster. It could be traced via Cadwallader, Geoffrey's last 'British' king, to the Arthurian family itself. In the Welsh Tudors, Arthur actually had returned to save his realm. Britain was restored.

Henry's wedding with the heiress of York translated his mission into practice. He named their first son Arthur and groomed him to reign as Arthur II. The prince was baptised at Winchester, which Malory said was Camelot. A tapestry, probably woven for the occasion (though later used as a mat in the Warden's bedroom at Winchester College), contains the 'arms' of Belinus, one of the legendary monarchs of Britain. Prince Arthur was married to Catherine of Aragon. Unfortunately for the plan, he died young; as in John's time, the expected reign of King Arthur II failed to materialise.

But the myth went on. Geoffrey's *History* now became a vital political document. Its truthfulness now mattered as it had not mattered before. Attacked by Polydore Virgil, a sceptical Italian, the book was warmly defended by Tudor patriots. Among its upholders in a debate that dragged on for years was John Leland, the chief antiquary of his time, who was attached to the court of Henry VIII. The king had taken over his dead brother's wife, and to some extent his role. Leland defended Geoffrey in principle if not in detail, and wrote verses hailing Henry as 'Arturius Redivivus'. Although the king's name was wrong, he was willing enough to play the part. The decorations put up for him at the Field of Cloth of Gold in 1520, where he conferred with the king of France, included suitable motifs. State papers of his reign recall the Arthurian inspiration of the Order of the Garter. The Emperor Charles v's ambassador thought these pretensions interesting enough to merit mention, if not to take seriously. Alleged prophecies of Merlin supplied a mystical-magical touch, though Arthurian romance, as distinct from Geoffrey, tended to be played down as confusing the issue.

After a lapse of interest during the religious and economic upheavals, Elizabeth I brought all this back with renewed vigour. Cadwallader was said to have foretold her in person. Pageants at Kenilworth and elsewhere included such characters as the Lady of the Lake. The queen's astrologer John Dee, an early champion of the concept of a British Empire, inspired debates as to whether Arthur's subjects had colonised the New World. Several dramatists contemporary with Shakespeare drew on Geoffrey for plots. Shakespeare himself took Lear and Cymbeline from him, but avoided Arthur, although he used the other part of the Tudor myth, about the Wars of the Roses and their providential end. It is an intriguing question why England's greatest poet should have virtually ignored England's national legend. But whatever the cause of Shakespeare's neglect, another great poet was very far from ignoring it. Leland's romanticisation of Henry VIII was elaborately transferred to Elizabeth by Edmund Spenser.

In 1582, Leland's Latin writings appeared in translation. The translator, Richard Robinson, dedicated his work to Lord Grey, Sir Henry Sidney and the Society of Archers in London 'yearly celebrating the renowned memory of the magnificent Prince Arthur'. Spenser, who was Lord Grey's secretary and a friend of Sidney's better-known son Philip, belonged to that circle, and Sir Philip Sidney probably gave him the hint for his masterpiece. In *The Faerie Queene* he expands the Arthurian part of the Tudor myth, not only enlarging on the themes from Geoffrey of Monmouth, but drawing Malory's romance-world back into unison with them.

Spenser owed a debt to the romantic epics of the Italian poets Boiardo, Ariosto and Tasso. In late medieval Italy, the Matter of Britain had blended with the Matter of France. Boiardo wrote within the French story framework of paladins-versus-paynims, with Charlemagne, Roland and other French characters; but he shifted the

Ills. 10, 11

interest to the exploits of individual knights, and even credited Charlemagne with a round table. The amours, enchantments and interwoven episodes of the new Italian tales were closer in spirit to the Matter of Britain than to the real legend of Charlemagne. Tasso's epic *Jerusalem Delivered* had a more serious tone than Boiardo's or Ariosto's, and a more authentic setting. But the shape of the poem was the same: romantic rather than classical.

THE FAERIE
QVEENE.

Difpofed into twelue books,
Fashioning
XII. Morall vertues.

LONDON
Printed for William Ponfonbie.
1 5 9 0.

Ills. 10, above, and *11*, right. The title page and a woodcut from the first edition of Spenser's *The Faerie Queene*.

The Faerie Queene follows these Italian models, and can thus digest Malory as well as Geoffrey. However, there is a further increase in moral gravity. Spenser takes a lofty view of his responsibilities. He is called to serve his sovereign by inciting her people to virtuous actions. *The Faerie Queene* is dedicated to Elizabeth; every book opens with a prologue addressed to her; and the prefixed sonnets commend its message to her courtiers and ministers. In a letter to Raleigh which sketches some of his intentions, Spenser explains that he is holding up examples of virtue. The knights embodying various moral qualities are all attached to the court of Gloriana, the Fairy Queen, who stands (more or less) for Elizabeth. Moving through the whole series of episodes is the figure of the young Prince Arthur as hero, devoted to Gloriana and sharing the perils of her knights. The reader is witnessing his personal education before he was king. Spenser planned a sequel displaying his public greatness of soul as a ruler. But he never came near to writing it; *The Faerie Queene* itself is only half finished.

He expounds the Tudor myth at some length. Two passages aggregating seven hundred lines (in Book ɪɪ Canto *x* and Book ɪɪɪ Canto *iii*) versify the whole of Geoffrey's *History* except the Arthur chapters themselves, which would presumably have been retold in the sequel. The Tudor dynasty is declared (ɪɪɪ, *iii*, 48–50) to be the kingdom of the Britons restored. Elizabeth is given a genealogy in suitable terms. Events and people in the Arthurian age are made to foreshadow Tudor England. Spenser introduces Merlin and Tristram, and at least names other Malory characters. His failure to bring in more of Malory is simply the failure of his existing text to take Arthur's life far enough.

One notion hovers in the background. Arthur is not only a magnificent prince: he is occasionally symbolic of Christ. Spenser writes during the war with Spain, and pushes the Tudors' messianic pretensions farther than ever. Elizabeth, he implies, presides over a realm which is God's instrument for overthrowing the powers of evil and achieving the Apocalypse. The Arthurian monarchy has a tincture of the divine.

Ill. 8   Though the last Tudor died childless, the Tudor myth went on. James ɪ had become aware of it while he was still only king of Scotland. He read *The Faerie Queene* and apparently approved of its main drift. But he took offence at Spenser's portrayal of his mother, Mary Queen of Scots, as the wicked Duessa in Book v of the poem. He invited a certain William Quin to reply. Quin politely dedicated some sonnets to James, expressing his hope of the English throne in the anagram: *Charles Iames Stuart   Claimes Arthurs Seat*—Charles James Stuart being the king's full name. In fact, he possessed as good a title to the Arthurian succession as Elizabeth had, being descended himself from Henry vɪɪ. Even apart from Henry he had a British pedigree through the Welsh wife of his ancestor Fleance, from whom the Stuart line came down to him (the 'show of eight kings' in *Macbeth*). When he received the crown of England in 1603, he revived the name Great Britain for his double domain. Hitherto it had merely distinguished the island from Little Britain or Brittany. Now it had a sound of grandeur. Michael Drayton, a finer poet than Quin, saluted King James as carrying on the Arthurian resurrection.

The mystique, however, was failing. Under James it ceased to be patriotic and turned political. He clashed with Parliament, and his British claim became entangled with his concept of divine right, which was far more partisan than the broad heavenly blessing ascribed to the Tudors. Parliamentary lawyers countered him by invoking the Anglo-Saxons as the true fathers of the constitution, and deploying new resources of critical scholarship. Arthur's Britain fell into disrepute as a royalist fantasy. Geoffrey of Monmouth's credit crumbled at last.

When the historical presence faded, the literary spell seemed to fade with it. For a century after Spenser, an Arthurian epic was still trying to get written, and never succeeding, largely because the Matter of Britain was now so widely felt to be propaganda without roots in reality. Milton took it up and dropped it. As a Roundhead he could not invest Arthur with a meaning satisfactory to himself, and he shared the growing scepticism about the Briton's existence. Contrasting his preferred biblical theme in *Paradise Lost*, he wrote with lofty scorn of the poets who had been at such pains to 'dissect, with long and tedious havoc, fabled knights in battles feigned'. He recorded this rejection of chivalrous legend and romance during the reign of Charles 11, which brought a last glow of the embers. Arthur figured in the plans of the chief Restoration poet, John Dryden. Like Milton he thought of an epic, and like Milton he gave it up, though his motive in doing so was merely to write plays which would pay better. Finally he produced *King Arthur*, an opera with music by Purcell. His operatic king fights Saxons, loves a princess named Emmeline, contends with hostile magic and foresees British-Saxon unity in a happier day. The accession of William of Orange made parts of the opera sound seditious and Dryden had to revise it. In the 1690s, Arthur was not only suspect historically, but Tory—perhaps Jacobite —in implication.

The final twist in this phase of his fortunes was a grotesque attempt to revalue him. Politics caused the Arthur epic, which two major poets had turned away from, to be tackled and discredited by a third poet who was abysmal. Sir Richard Blackmore, a fashionable doctor and amateur versifier, not only wrote such an epic but went on to write another, borrowing brazenly from both Milton and Dryden, with special attention to the latter's translation of Virgil. Blackmore made Arthur a liberty-loving religious prince, his career an allegory of William III's. The topicality of the poems gave them more fame than they deserved. In the upshot, this association of Arthur with bad and pretentious writing did much to banish him into eclipse, as a Gothic ghost whom an age of rational good taste could not usefully evoke.

Nevertheless, in 1757, a poet as learned and fastidious as Thomas Gray still judged it proper to recall the Tudor myth in his ode *The Bard*. Here a medieval Welsh prophet equates the advent of Henry VII with the reinstatement by proxy of 'long-lost Arthur', and claims Shakespeare and even Milton as fruits of a renaissance under 'genuine kings, Britannia's issue'.

The Stuart cause perished. The Age of Reason waned. The Matter of Britain could revive undebased by irrelevant passions. But would it? Astonishingly, it did. Archaic as it looked, an unguessed-at inner vitality renewed its life.

The change came with the Romantic movement. William Blake uttered the most profound judgement of all: 'The stories of Arthur are the acts of the Giant Albion.' Blake was foreshadowing the insights of a generation unborn. To most of the writers whose lives overlapped his, the stories were still stories and nothing more. But as such, they deserved rediscovery. Southey, Scott, Peacock, Bulwer Lytton and Matthew Arnold all dabbled in British legend—the last two, indeed, with a copiousness and inventiveness that went beyond dabbling. William Morris began as a poet with *The Defence of Guenevere*, published in 1858. Through him several of the themes passed into Pre-Raphaelite art. But the rebirth of Arthur's Britain, as an imaginative whole, was due to Alfred Tennyson.

Ill. 12

No one could have been more appropriate. Poet Laureate, admirer of the Prince Consort, friend of Queen Victoria, Tennyson was a spokesman of his age and a best-seller unrivalled by any English poet before or since. For a vast public, poetry meant the sort of thing Tennyson wrote. The vastness of that public endowed his work with an influence which was more than literary. So, for a third time, the visionary kingdom shone through the real one, with visible effect on the minds of its inhabitants. As King Arthur had become involved with the Plantagenets, and again with the Tudors, so now he became involved with Victoria, Albert, Gladstone and Joseph Chamberlain.

Arthur lodged himself in Tennyson's mind through sheer chance: the poet's friendship with, and loss of, the adored Arthur Hallam of

Ill. 12. A page from William Morris's *The Defence of Guenevere and Other Poems.* Morris was one of a number of nineteenth-century writers who adapted the Matter of Britain to Victorian tastes and imagination.

In Memoriam. The namesakes, Hallam and the king, blended in his imagination and symbolised each other. Both were taken away by death, yet were really deathless and destined to return to those who longed for them. In the autobiographical *Merlin and the Gleam* it is hard to tell which of them Tennyson is talking about.

When he started *In Memoriam,* he was already pondering an epic on the other Arthur. He had notions of allegory: the Round Table was to stand for liberal institutions. However, the first solid result of his reflections was more encouraging. It was the fragment *Morte d'Arthur,* a blank-verse treatment of the king's passing, presented as the eleventh book of an epic in twelve. The choice of that part of the legend was no doubt related to Hallam's passing. Its famous opening lines plunge straight into the disaster of Camlann:

> So all day long the noise of battle roll'd
> Among the mountains by the winter sea,
> Until King Arthur's table, man by man,
> Had fallen in Lyonesse about their lord.

Not published immediately when written, the poem came out in 1842 with added prologue and epilogue. By then Prince Albert had arrived to marry Victoria. The epilogue included an odd dream-sequence with Arthur returning in a ship, 'like a modern gentleman', amid cheers. The composite hero, in fact, was beginning to absorb a third figure. Tennyson became Laureate in 1850 because of Albert's admiration of *In Memoriam*. Thus, King Arthur and the real monarchy and his own deepest experience were intertwined; and he himself was the royal bard.

His *Idylls of the King*, started in 1855, recreated Malory's world and brought it again into relationship with an actual England. They did not do so at once. Tennyson's intention was to explore moral issues—'Sense at war with Soul, ideal manhood closed in real man'—through Malory's characters. He disliked being tied down to definitions. However, he said: 'By Arthur I always meant the soul, and by the Round Table the passions and capacities of a man.' The first four Idylls which he composed dealt mainly with figures of Arthur's court. Merlin, Guinevere and Lancelot were more prominent than the king. But Prince Albert's death in December 1861, early and tragic like Arthur Hallam's, reoriented the project. Henceforth, it became virtually Laureate work, a command performance. The young Princess Alice expressed a wish that Tennyson should 'idealise' her late father in verse. He felt unable to do this literally, but did approach the assignment symbolically, making the Arthurian scheme, in his own words, sacred over Albert's grave. To a new edition of the Idylls already written, he prefixed a dedication:

Ill. 3

> These to His Memory—since he held them dear,
> Perchance as finding there unconsciously
> Some image of himself . . .

After a pause he proceeded with further Idylls in the same spirit, inevitably shifting the centre of gravity.

He met Victoria at Osborne in 1862. She praised *In Memoriam* and drew obvious parallels. Henceforth the relation of Laureate to Queen was romantic and chivalrous. The *Idylls of the King* grew round Princess Alice's hint. Arthur took substance as a sovereign, an Albertus Redivivus resembling the Consort even in looks.

The later-written Idylls, with the early ones suitably placed among them, formed a structure in which Arthur's own career was paramount and supplied the unity of the sequence. Tennyson had done careful research, and he exploited traditions which Malory had passed over. Some of them came from the eccentric Robert Hawker, vicar of Morwenstowe in Cornwall and a poet in his own right, best known as the author of what would today be called a protest song, *And shall Trelawny die?* As Tennyson developed his use of Celtic lore, he drew a little nearer to the authentic Britain of the dark ages; and the imagery of his fable became more social, more clearly centred on Arthur's realm and the king as its embodiment.

In the finished scheme, the evil in human nature is typified by Saxon heathendom and the beast-infested wasteland, which Arthur has to master. The ideal of Soul ordering Body, of the Eternal realising itself in the world of sense, is expressed in an institution: Christian marriage. King Arthur holds that his knights should have wives. A sanctified wedlock is part of the system of the Table. This motif breaks with the medieval tradition. There are hints toward it in Spenser, even in Malory. But only Tennyson, echoing the rectitude of Victoria's court, goes all the way.

While he was building up the *Idylls*, Victoria was in morose retirement, and English republicanism was a rising force. Tennyson wrote against the trend, opposing the radicals with his image of a religious monarchy. After his own fashion, he pursued Spenser's unfulfilled plan for a sequel to *The Faerie Queene* portraying Arthur's virtues as ruler. His message was not so much that religious monarchy would work as that it was the social order best worth trying to make work. In the complete cycle, tragedy prevails. Glory occurs, but slowly gives way to gloom. Chivalry is sapped from below by the sensual factor: Guinevere's adultery with Lancelot sets a deadly example and breeds cynicism. Chivalry is sapped from above also: the Holy Grail, though not an illusion, inspires spiritual strivings of the wrong kind, which unfit the knights for the duties of their station. Doubts about Arthur's birth undermine loyalty—Tennyson's point, perhaps, being that the basis of moral authority never seems sure enough. Finally the fabric collapses. Yet its fall contains the promise of the Return, of a fresh cycle. Arthur is immortal, like Hallam. His experiment is not a failure to be rejected, but a model for others who may repeat it more successfully.

During the Franco-Prussian War, Tennyson's work moved closer to public affairs. He was then composing the Idyll entitled *The Last Tournament*, portraying knighthood in decline. Newspapers reported the birth of the Third Republic, the siege of Paris, the Commune. Tennyson detested the 'red fool-fury of the Seine' and what he described as the frightful corruption of French literature, which, in his view, had done much to ruin French morale. *The Last Tournament* includes a curious episode about a Red Knight with a subversive and lawless rival court. Arthur overthrows him (or, to be more precise, he overthrows himself), yet there is no sense of victory. The Laureate was well aware that the dawn of another French republic had raised

English republicanism to an apex, under the leadership of Joseph Chamberlain, Charles Dilke, and fellow-campaigners who appeared no less formidable.

Then came a reversal. The Prince of Wales contracted typhoid and was expected to die. The surge of popular emotion when he recovered swept anti-royalism away. Soon after, in 1872, Tennyson published the whole series of Idylls in what was nearly its final form, with lines addressed to Victoria.

> O loyal to the royal in thyself,
> And loyal to thy land, as this to thee—
> Bear witness, that rememberable day,
> When, pale as yet, and fever-worn, the Prince . . .
> Past with thee thro' thy people and their love,
> And London roll'd one tide of joy thro' all
> Her trebled millions.

And so on. He put in a direct retort to the deflated radicals, speaking of England as already possessing a 'slowly-grown and crowned republic'. His colossal prestige and mass readership ensured that the coincidence of events would be fruitful. A nation receptive to royalism again was presented, just at the right moment, with its Laureate's unfolded daydream of Christian monarchy, firmly linked to the queen and her almost canonised husband.

The *Idylls of the King* were read—genuinely read and by millions, not merely praised. They were translated into other media. They inspired playwrights and painters, and even a photographer, who broke new ground by illustrating the stories with painstakingly posed stills. Arthur's Britain played an appreciable part in refurbishing that royal glamour which the four Georges, and Victoria's dismal widowhood, had almost effaced. It helped to foster that latter-day English state of mind in which medieval ritual and feudal titles could coexist with democracy. No continental monarchy found a Tennyson, and no continental monarchy managed to keep such a halo.

So, for some years, the visionary kingdom flourished again; and the results were to persist. One aspect of its revival was very much Tennyson's. By making the Round Table sexually respectable, he helped to associate royalty with a virtue which, after the Georges, it stood in need of. His Arthur was a 'blameless king'. The epithet, in its context, meant that he was proof against the temptress Vivien. Tennyson applied it also to the Hallam-Arthur of *Merlin and the Gleam* and to Prince Albert. Respectability had awkward artistic consequences. The love-stories with which the Matter of Britain had once been almost synonymous could no longer be dwelt upon. Guinevere's infidelity was the turning-point of Tennyson's own plot, yet he avoided giving any outright account of it. Nor could he trace Tristram's affairs in any detail. He circled round these topics, he alluded to them, but he never got near enough to provoke a blush. The logic of his scheme was relentless. By banishing courtly love in favour of propriety, the best-selling Laureate underlined his sovereign's public example and won the praise of Mr Gladstone. But he weakened the august theme and left it in a cul-de-sac. Not even Thomas Hardy, in his drama *The Queen of Cornwall*, could take it much further. As shaped by Tennyson, the legend could only decline into children's books, romantic little societies, the gift-shops and pastiche Hall of Chivalry at Tintagel.

The inner history of the *Idylls* was not fully disclosed until 1949, with the appearance of a biography of the poet by his grandson Sir Charles Tennyson. By then there were signs of yet another Arthurian revival (described in chapter 11). This is still with us. It is not a sequel to Tennyson's work but a fresh departure, or series of departures. The possibilities have changed with the setting. Monarchy is no longer a norm, facile idealisations of history are no longer welcome. Above all, the facts behind the fantasy are at last showing through. Even such a conservative as T. H. White, author of *The Once and Future King*, could not quite shrug off certain contemporaries who were delving into the dark ages for the reality of Arthur's Britain . . . and finding it. He scorned them as iconoclasts. He was wrong. The visionary kingdom stands, unshaken by time, with the power and immortality of the imagination. But the modern age has indeed brought a gift of its own.

That gift is enrichment, not destruction. We are beginning to see where the vision came from. We are glimpsing the outline of the historical fact which Geoffrey of Monmouth and the rest turned into mythology.

2   *The Arthurian Fact*

Geoffrey Ashe

FROM A STRANGE MEDLEY of clues, patiently pieced together in the last forty or fifty years, one certainty at least emerges. The Arthurian Legend, however wide-ranging its vagaries, is rooted in an Arthurian Fact. As the legend is unique, so the fact is unique. In essence, it is this. Britain, alone among the lands of the Roman Empire, achieved independence before the northern barbarians poured in, and put up a fight against them—a very long, and at one stage a successful, fight. Between Roman Britain and Anglo-Saxon England there is an inter-regnum, which is not a chaos as historians once imagined, but a creative epoch with a character of its own. This rally of a Celtic people in some degree Romanised and Christianised is the reality of Arthur's Britain. It occurs in a dark age, the mysterious gap in British history. The modern investigator's problem is to bring light into the darkness—where it may, possibly, reveal the features of Arthur himself.

The story begins farther back, in the middle of the fourth century AD. 'Britannia', divided into four provinces, stretched from the Channel up to Hadrian's Wall, with a debatable zone beyond. The people were Celts, related to the Gauls and the Irish. But at the higher social levels there was no longer a sharp distinction between ruling 'Romans' and subject 'Britons'. Only in Wales was Roman rule predominantly an affair of alien garrisons. Elsewhere, the civil servants and army officers came from various countries, and some were British by birth or adoption. All free men were citizens of the Empire, and the better-off intermarried, spoke Latin and gave their children a classical education. While Caesar's word was law, Britons enjoyed a growing autonomy in local government and defence; London was a fairly important trading centre. The landowners, merchants and magistrates assembled on regional councils. The peasants supplied recruits for the army.

For some decades, a quiet reassertion of Celtic life-patterns had been going on within the imperial scheme. Towns—the conquerors' special institution—were less important than they had been. Celtic preference for the country expressed itself in the adoption of the Roman villa. Especially in the south-east and in what is now Glou- cestershire, luxurious houses disposed round courts dotted the landscape. Here, with central heating and every comfort, lived many of the wealthier Britons as well as officials from other lands. Their households were large. Their dozens of slaves grew food and sup- plied basic needs. Britain was nearer to self-sufficiency than in previous centuries, though exporting as much: grain, iron, coal, hides, hunting- dogs (which were famous) and slave labour.

Ill. 16

Christianity, rescued from persecution by the protection of the Emperor Constantine, was now the ascendant faith of the Roman world. It had been practised in Britain for many years. Its strength came from the educated class and their dependants. The peasants in the villages remained pagan. Britain had given four martyrs to the calendar, the best-known being St Alban of Verulamium. In the fourth century, British bishops went overseas to the Church's coun- cils, and British pilgrims made the long trip to the Holy Land, where priests exclaimed at their energy.

The island, indeed, deserved a share of the credit for the Church's prosperity. The reason lay in a sequence of events which proved that Britain was no mere backwater, no inert subject territory, but a place where things could happen. Within the memory of the oldest in- habitants, Britain had been the centre of an imperial crisis. An admiral named Marcus Aurelius Carausius, equipped with a fleet to drive off Saxon pirates, had set himself up as ruler of Britain c. 286 and de- clared his independence. The Emperor Constantius at last recaptured Britain, striking a medallion portraying London at his feet, with the motto 'Restorer of the Eternal Light'. Constantius remained in the country for some time, rebuilding the economy and protecting the coast with a chain of forts. The greater Constantine was his son, and in 306, at York, the army of Britain proclaimed Constantine emperor. He overthrew all his rivals, made Christianity the state religion and gave the Empire a peace marked in London by coins imprinted *Beata Tranquillitas*. At mid-century, that phrase was still not wholly ironic.

Ills. 17

Ill. 19

Ills. 13, 14

For Britons, the imperial system began to dissolve in 367. The island was suddenly attacked by three barbaric nations together. From across

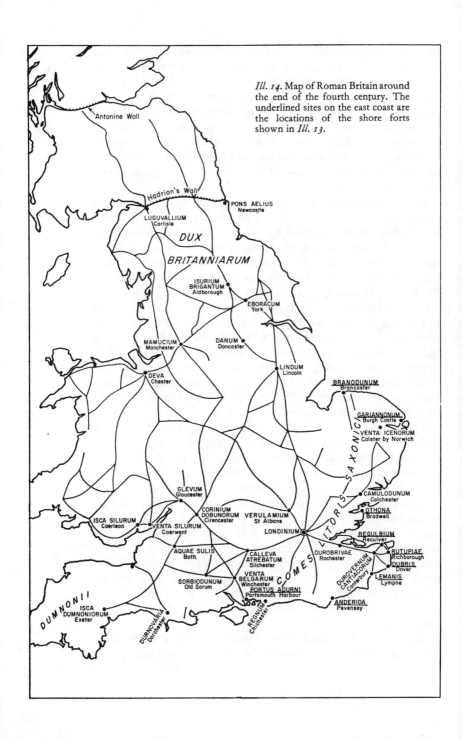

Ill. 14. Map of Roman Britain around the end of the fourth century. The underlined sites on the east coast are the locations of the shore forts shown in *Ill. 13.*

the North Sea, after a long lull, came Saxons—fierce, tricky Teutonic warriors in crazy boats, carrying short-swords, bows, lances and round wooden shields. Their ancestral home was in Schleswig-Holstein, but they had been advancing along the German coast. In the north, parties of Picts scrambled past the garrisons and over the Wall— bearded, tattooed and armed with slings. In the west, the shores were harassed by Irish tribes whom the Romans called Scots, after one of their chief groups which had not yet settled in Caledonia. They sailed in hide-covered curraghs and blew terrifying blasts on enormous curled war-horns. Ill. 15

Raids had occurred before, but never in such force and never in concert. The defences collapsed. For months the invaders controlled the countryside, strengthened by runaway slaves and peasant mal-contents. Towns were cut off. Roman authority was not fully re-stored till 369, and the social order did not recover even then. Too many villas had been wrecked, too many slaves had gone. Henceforth the Britons, in their exposed position far from the imperial centre, were more inclined to look to themselves. New temples were built to their old gods, in pursuance of a lead given about the time of the disaster, at Lydney in the Forest of Dean. Maiden Castle, the Dorset hill-fort, was the site of another such temple. Rustics camped in deserted villas and lit their cooking fires on the splendid mosaics. Ill. 16

But most of the Britons who had a voice in public affairs still saw themselves as members of the imperial world. They shared its civilisa-tion with the citizens of other provinces, all the way to Mesopotamia. They had no wish to give up this heritage and merge totally into outer darkness. The question was whether they could survive. During the next hundred years, by a strange, zigzag process, Britain was to achieve her unparalleled status as a Roman land detached from Rome, holding out against the barbarians.

Unluckily, our chief witness to this process, and almost our only native one, is an irritating monk named Gildas. Somewhere about 545, he wrote a diatribe against the rulers of Britain in his day. This includes a survey of recent history, and is described very frankly as a *liber querulus* or Complaining Book. It is rhetorical, cryptic and some-times plainly wrong. In retrospect Gildas exaggerates the Britons' tendency to be restless and unassimilable under Roman rule. But he gives us glimpses of the transition through the eyes of a literate cleric of Roman sympathies.

Gildas dates the essential break as far back as 383, when the army in Britain repeated the York coup of 306 by proclaiming its own

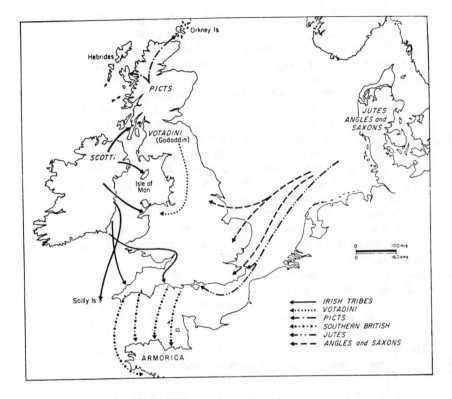

Ill. 15. Map showing the invasions and migrations into Britain in the fourth to sixth centuries and the routes taken by those Britons who fled from the Saxons into Armorica.

emperor. Maximus was Spanish; but he probably had a British wife, and the revolt was largely a movement of Britons in protest against the government's corruption and its weakness in the face of continuing barbarian threats. Maximus asserted his claim throughout Western Europe. He captured Rome with a force which included Britons, many of them, it would seem, rashly withdrawn from the Wall. Unlike Constantine, he failed to progress beyond Italy. In 388, he was defeated and killed by the Emperor of the East, Theodosius. But his impact on the country which had enthroned him was permanent. It is said that the British settlement in Armorica, the future

Ill. 15

Brittany, was begun under his auspices. He lives on in the traditions of later ages as Prince Macsen, a hero of Welsh and Cornish folklore. Because of his adventure, the British sense of identity grew stronger.

However, it was a deeply troubled identity. After Maximus, Roman power was never completely re-established. Administration devolved on the regional councils or *civitates*, which soon had to cope with fresh assaults from three sides. In 395, the High King of Ireland, Niall-of-the-Nine-Hostages*, led a pirate invasion that sacked Chester and Caerleon. Some of the Irish seized bits of territory in Wales and stayed on. Gildas—correct in his main drift, though sometimes wildly astray in his details—describes a series of British appeals for help. It may have been in response to the first of these that the imperial general Stilicho, himself partly German, came to Britain about 399 with reinforcements. He drove back the barbarians and tried to create an autonomous defensive system, entrusting the highlands and borderlands to native magnates under whom Celtic tribalism began to revive. Most of his troops left, but in 405 the Britons won a sea victory, killing Niall and much reducing the menace from Ireland.

Ill. 20

The following year a Teutonic inroad into Gaul cut Britain off. After several internal coups, the remnant of the army again proclaimed its own emperor, a soldier who assumed the title of Constantine III. This is the Constantine who figures in Geoffrey of Monmouth. He also figures in Welsh legend as Bendigeit Custennin, Blessed Constantine, perhaps because he had close ties with the Church. Hopes that he would stay in Britain were dashed. Afraid to wait in case the real Emperor Honorius organised his removal, Constantine took the last legionaries overseas in 407 and traversed Gaul. His second-in-command was a Briton, Gerontius or Geraint. Becoming disillusioned, Gerontius undermined his leader's authority in the rear. Whether the Briton had what would now be called nationalistic motives, it is impossible to tell. But after another Saxon attack on Britain in 410, the regional councils, in effect, declared British independence. They wrote to Honorius saying they were still in the Empire, but not as subjects. He replied with a vague message telling them to look to their own safety, and leaving the question of sovereignty in the air. Constantine and Gerontius both perished in the continental turmoil, and the island stood alone.

Ill. 22

*Niall's personal status and dates have been matters of dispute. But this, at least, was the beginning of the worst phase of Irish raiding.

The network of local dignitaries that now governed Britannia took measures for defence. Again there seemed to be a respite, again it did not last. The Picts, aided by Scottish settlers, continued to raid southward. Meanwhile, the Saxons were multiplying and spreading. They were planting themselves along the opposite coast, and they were overrunning Frisia, the modern Holland. Frisia could never satisfy them. The natives lived miserably on earth mounds, in constant fear of inundation, eating fish, drinking rain-water, burning peat and building up their mounds with rubbish and dung. The Saxons mingled with the mound-dwellers and found footholds in the silt. However, as their numbers increased, the prospect of colonisation in nearby Britain looked more and more alluring. A few perhaps were already living there, with or without official connivance, but not nearly enough to ease the pressure.

With the growth of danger, there may have been a British appeal to Rome to return. Gildas speaks of a second military rescue like Stilicho's. A strange source, the *Anglo-Saxon Chronicle*, records a Roman expedition to Britain in 418. Scanty clues suggest that these hints may be right, and that by some agreement with the regional councils, an imperial force did come back. If it did, the reoccupation was spectral. By 425 at latest, British independence was an accomplished fact. But the spiritual ties were not broken. Towards the middle of the fifth century, Prosper, a Gaulish chronicler, still contrasts the 'Roman' island of Britain with the 'barbarian' island of Ireland.

Over wide areas, the last of the urban and villa people remained in control for several decades. They kept up a shaky version of the old administrative system, and stayed in touch, through trade and otherwise, with the Mediterranean. They spoke a somewhat debased Latin, wrote the language in a fashion that aspired to be classical, and were mostly Catholic Christians, although a sense of established proprieties perhaps counted for more than conviction. The first Briton to affect the intellectual life of Europe was the heretic Pelagius, who taught in Rome and elsewhere from 405 onward. His writings are the earliest specimens of British literature. A waterer-down of Christian doctrine, he clashed with St Augustine and was condemned by the pope. But his ideas were brought back to his native country by a preacher named Agricola.

The peasants spoke only the Celtic British language, the ancestor of Welsh and Breton. They were still largely pagan, though Christianity was doubtless beginning to gain ground, as it had been gaining in Gaul since the missions of St Martin of Tours in the 370s. Apart from one or two technical innovations, their life was what it had been for centuries. But they were quietly rising in importance. The end of Roman rule had stopped the compulsory export of British grain, and the rural population was eating better and bringing new land under cultivation. In Verulamium the Roman theatre was a ruin, but not disused, because the traders in a neighbouring and flourishing vegetable market used it as a rubbish-dump.

Meanwhile, in the higher and wilder country, and especially in Wales, forces were astir which seemed likely to quicken the reversion to rural ways. Here tribalism was fast returning, and regional despots, who were already in effect tribal chiefs, had entrenched themselves. They claimed to be legitimate successors of Rome. The main basis of this claim was the frontier policy of which Stilicho had been the major exponent. British tribes had been planted north of the Wall to subdue the Picts, and dispositions of the same sort had been made in the west against the Irish. At some point, Cunedda, a northern chieftain, migrated to Wales, where he wiped out Irish buccaneer colonies and his sons founded local dynasties. But, besides deriving a title from such real or asserted measures of security, several British kinglets apparently claimed kinship with the pretender Maximus.

These new leaders appear in Welsh genealogies and legends with the title *gwledig*. The first *gwledig* is Maximus himself, Prince Macsen, the Briton-by-marriage. Those who come after him (with one exception to be noted) are manifestly men who stood for the Celtic way of life rather than the imperial. As their influence grew—promoted in lowland Britain, perhaps, by the exploitation of peasant grievances against Romanised landlords—the ancient Celtic culture revived further. After centuries of eclipse, craftsmen were again making delicately embellished bowls and experimenting with designs in linear tracery. These craftsmen were to be found not only in Wales but in the south-east also.

Ills. 137,

The old religion, though doomed as such, also acquired a brief vigour that enabled it to live on in another form. At Lydney, the god Nodens inhabited a temple which was still fairly new. As Britain drifted into her age of transition, kindred Celtic figures emerged from the shadows into mythology, if not worship. It was a strange, confused, haunting mythology which passed later into Welsh folklore and the Arthurian Legend itself. Arthur, in one of his weirder guises, is a Wild Huntsman who rides through the clouds snatching the spirits of the dead; and his companion is Gwyn-ap-Nudd, Gwyn the son of Nodens. Gwyn is King of the Fairies and the underworld. Another transmuted god was Maponus, who became the hero Mabon. Another was Belinus, who became Beli son of Manogan, king of Britain and brother-in-law of the Virgin Mary. Among his relations was Bran the Blessed, who made an enchanted voyage across the Atlantic, and whose head, buried on Tower Hill, protected Britain against invasion. Both Beli and Bran occur in the pedigrees of several Welsh families. British consciousness, in fact, was flung by independence into a kaleidoscope of motifs and images. One of the results was the slow formation of the legends of Glastonbury, where Christian hermits were possibly already living. Gwyn-ap-Nudd was eventually said to have an unseen palace on Glastonbury Tor, and Bran reappeared as Brons, a keeper of the Holy Grail.

It would be wrong to picture a sharp early conflict between Romanised citizens and Celtic masses reverting to tribalism. Indeed, the key to Arthur lies in the fact that some Britons occupied intermediate ground, and that these included the best and most creative figures the island produced. Such were St Ninian, who went northward to Galloway as a missionary among the Picts, and St Patrick, who was the true founder of the Church in Ireland, though not the first Christian who ministered there. Patrick came from a western coastal district and his Latin was rustic. But his name was Roman—Patricius—and he regarded his Irish converts as Romans, Christianity being, for him, the religion of the imperial civilisation.

When a real cleavage divided British society, it happened because there were too few Britons like Patrick to hold it together. This was clearly a time of questioning and heart-searching. With the rise of a chieftain known as Vortigern, the trend away from Rome seems to have reached a point where it would not be absurd to speak of Celtic nationalism. Vortigern's home was probably in central Wales. He began to extend his influence about 425. His party favoured the Pelagian heresy as a native version of Christianity. This policy brought an envoy from Rome: not political but ecclesiastical Rome. Pope Celestine I sent over Germanus, bishop of Auxerre, a versatile cleric who is said to have practised as a lawyer and served as governor and commander in Armorica. Germanus sailed from Boulogne in 429 and threw all his abilities into the problems of Britain. He toured the decaying towns, meeting civic dignitaries and opposing the heretics in public debate. Also he led a British force to repel a combined host of Pictish and Saxon raiders. The victory was bloodless. Coached by

Germanus, the British soldiers roared 'Alleluia!' and the invaders fled in panic. For the moment, his efforts were fruitful. The Pelagians were not yet politically strong enough to hinder the mission. There is reason to think that a British bishop named Faustus, who had a brilliant career in Gaul, was a son of Vortigern whom Germanus detached from his heretical father.

Then the Saxons returned and grew steadily more menacing. By the 440s, their unrefuted boasts that they had things all their own way in Britain created an impression abroad that they had conquered the island. This was not so. Whatever Saxon settlements existed were not yet extensive. The raids, however, were severe, and the Britons had little military capacity left. According to Gildas, the councils sent a last appeal for imperial help, addressing it to the great general Aëtius in or about 446. No help was forthcoming, and the discredited Romanised element succumbed to the nationalists. Vortigern rose to ascendancy over much of Britain. The bishops, fearing a Pelagian revival under his aegis, had already asked Germanus to come over again. But the preachers of heresy were not numerous. Germanus founded schools for the better training of priests, and secured sentences of banishment against the active Pelagians: sentences in which Vortigern seems to have been driven to acquiesce.

The theological faction was no longer of use to Vortigern. He was in a strong position, and a flash of economic recovery gave him confidence. His resources, however, were unequal to the double challenge of Pict and Teuton. Though a seceder from the Empire, he adopted an imperial strategy: allowing one set of barbarians to live in the country as auxiliaries *(foederati)* and paying them to fight another set of barbarians. Somewhere about the middle of the fifth century, heathen warriors from across the North Sea began entering Britain as permitted colonists instead of as raiders and squatters. Three types could be distinguished: Saxons, Angles and Jutes, though the old term 'Saxon' tended to be used to cover them all. They came from various parts of the continental littoral. The record of their first and subsequent settlement is confused. But, roughly speaking, the Saxons made their way into Britain via Hampshire, Sussex and Essex; the Angles, across the east coast; and the Jutes, chiefly (though not solely) through Kent.

Ill. 15

Their first authorised colonies did not stretch so far. The oldest accounts represent Vortigern and his council as inviting the Jutish brothers Hengist and Horsa to make their homes in Kent—the Isle of Thanet is mentioned—with three shiploads of mercenaries. More warriors and their families then arrived, and were stationed at various points on the east coast. Vortigern's plan succeeded in its immediate aim. His allies marched north and repulsed the Picts for good. But, lacking the Empire's treasury, he could not keep the policy up as the emperors had done. A dispute arose over the payments in kind which he had contracted to give. Negotiations broke down. The reinforced Jutes pushed forward to the Medway. The *Anglo-Saxon Chronicle* notes a battle at Aylesford in 455, and the English monk Bede, a much better historian than the chronicler or Gildas, says that about the same time the Angles joined forces with the Picts whom they had just defeated. Legends of this crisis, which were used but not invented by Geoffrey of Monmouth, describe a fresh treaty and a marriage of Vortigern to Hengist's daughter. But if any peace was patched up, it did not last. The *Anglo-Saxon Chronicle* claims that in 457 the Britons were overwhelmed at Crayford and fled to London, abandoning Kent.

For a while the collapse was total. Massacre and pillage spread to the western sea, and refugees streamed away to the mountains, across to Armorica, and even to Spain. These Teutons who invaded Britain were not like those who invaded Gaul and Italy. The latter were Christians, although of the Arian heresy, and open to civilisation. The bandit swarms that swept Vortigern's regime into ruin were neither. They were more terrible; but also, in the end, they inspired a stronger will to resist.

After their first onslaught subsided and they were back at their bases, the question was not whether Britain could recover its former condition, but how much could be saved at all. Most towns were deserted, the semblance of political unity was gone. The local rulers were squabbling despots who could no longer produce even a genuine coinage. The Church, which had still been in touch with Gaul before the rout, was almost cut off.

Yet the discreditable failure of Vortigern had a surprising result. Over an area large enough to matter, the remnant of the Romanised and Catholic party came to the fore again. Its leader was Ambrosius Aurelianus, who was destined to join Vortigern and the pretender Constantine III as a character in Geoffrey of Monmouth's *History*. Reasons exist for connecting him with Gloucestershire, where the villa society reached an apogee. In Welsh tradition, Ambrosius is the *gwledig* Emrys, a borderland chief like other borderland chiefs, established in a citadel in northern Wales bestowed on him by Vortigern. But even the legends portray him as leading a rival party, and he clearly stood for a different culture and conviction. According to Gildas, his family had 'worn the purple'. Whichever emperor or pretender that phrase points to, Ambrosius raised his own standard, and the people who still called themselves 'citizens'—subjects of the Empire—flocked to it.

By the late 460s, a shrunken but not negligible Britannia was moving toward re-entry into the imperial scheme. Ambrosius is said to have built a navy. Certainly Britons could cross the Channel in large organised bands, despite the Saxon fleets, and the departure of fighting men did not lead to new Saxon inroads at home. In 470, a seaborne British force joined the Armorican settlers to fight for the Emperor Anthemius, who was trying to restore Roman authority in Gaul. The campaign failed and the final crumbling of Rome in the West halted this initiative. But it did occur. Ambrosius's Britons were the last nation north of the Alps to show any active loyalty to a Western emperor.

Within Britain, the Roman revival can hardly have been spectacular. It gave a last spell of popularity to the custom of calling children by Roman names: for example, Tacitus (which became Tegid), Constantine (Custennin), Paternus (Padarn), and—curiously—Tribune (Triphun). A dragon emblem, borne by the later emperors, was perhaps adopted at this time, whence ultimately the Red Dragon of Wales. 'Dragon' became a royal title. Gildas applies it to Maelgwn, the most important Welsh king of the sixth century, and in Arthurian legend Uther is called Pendragon, the Head Dragon.

Besides these details, the British Church became confirmed in its Catholicity, in its communion with the see of Rome and the orthodoxy of its teachings, although it was bound to diverge in its practices and very soon did. The wealthier Britons of the west imported oil, wine and other luxuries from the Mediterranean. A biographer of Germanus, writing fairly soon after Ambrosius's rise, felt able to speak of Britain as prosperous. Yet none of these developments would have carried much weight if Britain had been passively waiting for the next Saxon offensive. What gave Ambrosius his place both in history and legend was the fact of his taking the offensive himself.

The fortunes of the British counter-attack are obscure. Gildas makes nothing plain, except that it went on through victories and defeats for many years—probably about forty—and culminated in a British triumph at the 'siege of Mons Badonicus'. This battle brought a generation of peace and relative order, marred only by British feuds, not by heathen harassment. An early Welsh source, the *Annales Cambriae*, dates the 'battle of Badon' with a slight ambiguity in 516 or 518. The *Anglo-Saxon Chronicle*, while it ignores the Anglo-Saxons' defeats, sheds a little light by the petering-out of their victories. We get a dim impression of Hengist's Kentish kingdom being driven back into consolidation; of fresh Saxon landings along the south coast, followed by containment; and of a near-cessation of advance in mainland Britain from 514 to 547. Archaeology is consistent with a major Saxon retreat early in the sixth century, after a disaster in the region between Reading and Gloucester.

Interest centres on Mount Badon. This victory undoubtedly happened, and such things do not happen without leadership. But it comes too late for Ambrosius Aurelianus. The obvious question is the identity of the general who completed the work Ambrosius began. Gildas, while stressing the battle and its results, does not name this general. His only allusion is doubtful and oblique. But Gildas has an annoying habit of seldom naming anybody, and in this case he may have had a personal motive. Welsh tradition gives the commander's name with complete unanimity. It was Arthur; and the phase of British ascendancy after Badon was what Geoffrey made out to be Arthur's reign.

In assessing the value of this tradition, the first query is whether 'Arthur', as the name of a Celt born somewhere about the 470s, is credible. The answer is that it fits very well. It belongs to the same class as Tegid and Custennin, being a Celticised Roman name, in this case Artorius. A third-century officer called Artorius Justus held a command in Britain and may have left descendants. But the history of the name gives a more positive support to tradition than mere credibility. Before the sixth century, none of the known Artorii are natives of Britain. After 550, we have records of several such, including a prince in Argyll. The inference is that all these Arthurs were named after a British hero of slightly earlier date.

Ills. 122, 123

Another theory—that Arthur was a Celtic god, the centre of a pagan patriotic revival—will not bear looking into. Admittedly, the Arthur of legend has mythical attributes. He rides through the sky, he slays giants, he takes the form of a raven. But a Celtic deity with a Roman name seems unlikely. The extant records of Celtic religion show no trace of him. Also, we have Gildas's testimony. He denounces the sixth-century Britons for every wickedness under the sun . . . except apostasy. Their nominal Christianity is never in question. If a pagan revival had occurred, the vitriolic monk would have mentioned it.

Arthur, then, was a human being if he was anything. His status as a leader with an intelligible career rests mainly on one chapter in a Welsh *History of the Britons*. This chaotic work was compiled early in the ninth century by Nennius, a Bangor cleric striving to reassert national dignity after a long eclipse. His most valuable matter dates from a time not too hopelessly remote from Arthur's. The strongest point in Nennius's favour is, paradoxically, his sheer badness as a writer and scholar. On his own showing, he has simply 'made a heap of all he has found' in rummaging among ancient parchments and translating Welsh stories into his clumsy Latin. The result is not a literary fraud like Geoffrey of Monmouth's book, because Nennius is plainly not equal to that. The ingredients of his heap are authentic, whatever weight we give to them.

Nennius (or rather the document he transcribes when writing of the British war effort around 500) introduces Arthur as a man without dynastic rank. There were 'many more noble than he'. Then comes a sketch of his campaigns.

Ills. 23, 2

Arthur fought against the Saxons alongside the kings of the Britons, but he himself was the leader in the battles [*dux bellorum*]. The first battle was at the mouth of the river which is called Glein. The next four were on the banks of another river, which is called Dubglas and is in the region Linnuis. The sixth was upon the river which is called Bassas. The seventh was in the wood of Celidon; that is, Cat Coit Celidon. The eighth was by Castle Guinnion, in which Arthur carried on his shoulders an image of St Mary Ever-Virgin, and there was a great slaughter of them, through the strength of Our Lord Jesus Christ and of the holy Mary his maiden-mother. The ninth was in the City of the Legion. The tenth was on the bank of the river which is called Tribruit. The eleventh was on the hill called Agned. The twelfth was on Mount Badon, in which—on that one day—there fell in one onslaught of Arthur's, nine hundred and sixty men; and none slew them but he alone, and in all his battles he remained victor.

In an appendix Nennius adds some bits of folklore. These connect 'Arthur the soldier' with places in Brecknockshire and Herefordshire, Ill. 118 and refer to a son, Anir, whom Arthur himself killed and buried. They do not look like history. The passage about the battles does. Precisely because the names are obscure, they are likely to be genuine. A literary contriver would have given us a comprehensible war fought on well-known sites. Arthur's lone exploit at Mount Badon has been invoked to dismiss the whole paragraph as fabulous. But the deeds of the great do get exaggerated. A similar tale is told of the Emperor Constantine. It is more to the point to ask where the places are, and whether Nennius is correct in ascribing so many victories to the same leader.

Ill. 24

To begin with, the battles seem to be widespread. Various attempts to locate them all in one area are unconvincing and tend to cancel each other.*

For three of the sites—Bassas, Guinnion and Agned—no cogent identification exists at all. The City of the Legion is Chester or Caerleon. The river Glein could be the Lincolnshire or the Northumberland Glen. Linnuis is probably the Lindsey district of Lincolnshire, bordered on the north by the Humber. The wood of Celidon figures in Welsh legend, and must be sought around the head-waters of the Tweed and Clyde, Celidon being Caledonia. Tribruit belongs to the same part of the Scottish Lowlands. This battle is mentioned in a Welsh poem which includes Bedwyr—the original Bedevere—among the warriors.

Glein and Linnuis could represent action against the Angles, encroaching up the Wash and the Humber. Celidon and Tribruit take Arthur to a turbulent region where the Picts were still strong, and where the British chieftains, to judge from a letter of St Patrick and other clues, were freebooters liable to strike out at anybody. Some foray into this lawless area might have produced a conflict that found its way into the list. The City of the Legion is frankly awkward. As for Badon, Gildas's Mons Badonicus, historical considerations confine

Ill. 25

it to the south. A good candidate (not the only one) is Liddington Castle, a hill-fort near Swindon, which has a village called Badbury at its foot. 'Badbury' is Saxon—Baddan-byrig—but the first part of this name could be derived from a Celtic 'Badon'. Britons of Arthur's time might have reoccupied the imposing earthworks.

This is probably the best that can be done with the map at present. How much further do we get with Arthur himself?

To Nennius, he is clearly a commander-in-chief rather than a king.

---

*A theory recently revived, which places the whole series of battles in central Scotland, comes to grief on the simple fact that there were no Angles or Saxons there. If we accept Nennius's list, we cannot at the same time reject his testimony that at least the more important battles were fought against the Teutonic invader.

in rub o igneo. secundo modo in monte q̄
dragint̄a dieb; & q̄dragint̄a noctib; iciuna
uit. tercio modo similes fuit etate centu ui
ginti annis. quarto modo sepulchru illi ne
mo scit. S; moc̄culto humat̄ nemine sci
ente. quindeci annis incaptiuitate. in iciesi
mo quinto anno ab amatheo sco episcopo
subrogat̄. octingentoru & quinq; annoru.
in hibernia p̄dicauit. Et erat exigebat
ampli loqui de sco patricio. sed tamen p
copendio sermonis uolui breuiare.

n illo tempore saxones inualescebant in
multitudine & crescebant in brittannia.
Mortuo aut henguito octha fili eu transi
uit de sinistrali parte brittanuie ad reg
nu cantoru. & de ipso orti sr reges canteor.

une arthur pugnabac contra illos.
in illis dieb; cu regib; briccoru. s; ipse dux erat
belloru. Primu bellu fuit in ostiu flumi
nis quod dicit glein. sedin. & t̄ciu & q̄r
tu & quintu. sup aliud flumen quod
dicit dubglas. q̄ in regione linnuis.
Sextu bellum sup flumen quod uoca
t̄ bassas. Septimu fuit bellu
in silua celidonis. id̄ cac coit celidon.
Octauum fuit bellu in castello guinni
on. In quo arthur portauit imagine
sc̄e marie ppetue uirginis sup humer
ros suos. & pagain uersi sr in fuga in
illo die. & cedes magna fuit sup illos
p̄uirtutem dni nri ihu xpi & p uirtutẽ
sc̄e marie uirginis genitricis eī. Nonu
bellu gestu̅ in urbe legionis. Decimu
gessit bellu in litore ~ Fluminis quod
uocat̄ tribruit. Vndecimu factu̅
belli in monte qui dicit agned. Duo
decimu fuit bellu in monte badonis
in quo corruet in uno die ñ genti sexa
ginta uiri de uno impetu arthur.

In the *Annales Cambriae* he is likewise uncrowned. Under the year 516, or 518, we find the following:

> The battle of Badon in which Arthur carried the cross of Our Lord Jesus Christ, for three days and three nights, on his shoulders, and the Britons were victorious.

And twenty-one years later:

Ill. 5   The battle of Camlaun in which Arthur and Medraut were slain; and there was death in England and Ireland.

Here are Medraut, otherwise Modred the traitor, and the 'last weird dim battle'. Camlaun could be Camboglanna, a fort on Hadrian's Wall, at Birdoswald in Cumberland. But the river Cam in Somerset, and the Camel in Cornwall, cannot be ruled out.

Records of a strictly historical kind yield no more. They disclose a British leader who almost certainly did command at Badon, because the immense credit of that triumph was never claimed for anyone else; and who fell at Camlaun. Even the two dates cannot be relied on, though the error is not likely to be great. To assess Nennius's grandiose picture, with its national captaincy, we must study Arthur as he appears in other contexts.

First, in Welsh poetry. This began with a school of bards in what is now Cumberland but was then the British kingdom of Rheged, toward the close of the sixth century. They and their successors know Arthur as a war-leader of proverbial glory, and take it for granted that their audiences do, never pausing to explain who he was. About the year 600, Aneirin composed a long poem, *Gododdin*, lamenting over a corps of nobles who died fighting the Angles at Catraeth (*i.e.*, Catterick). He says of one of them that, 'although he was no Arthur', his valour was great. That, unfortunately, is all. Arthur's presence in a poem about northerners does not imply that he was one of them. Aneirin knows southerners as well: a certain Gereint, for instance.

An early poem in a collection called the *Black Book of Carmarthen*

◄   *Ill. 23.* A page from a twelfth-century manuscript of Nennius's *History of the Britons* describing Arthur's twelve battles, culminating in his great victory at Mount Badon. The translation of this passage, from line 17 on, is given on page 40.

Ill. 24. Map showing a few populated centres which probably existed as such in the early sixth century either as towns of a sort (*e.g.*, London) or as important British monasteries (*e.g.*, Llantwit Major). It also shows the approximate areas of Teutonic settlement, and the whereabouts of a number of British kingdoms which were already formed or in the process of formation. The sites indicated for some of the battles which Nennius attributes to Arthur (*Ill. 23*) are those suggested by Professor Kenneth Jackson.

gives a list of Arthur's followers. Among them are Kei and Bedwyr, *i.e.*, Kay and Bedevere. The same volume contains poems alluding to Arthur's son Llacheu and to a West Country force apparently known as Arthur's Men. None of these poems refers to Arthur as a king, but the last refers to him as *amherawdyr*, the Latin *imperator* or emperor. That title recurs in a medieval Welsh tale, *The Dream of Rhonabwy*.

Further poems speak of Arthur's horse, his kinsfolk, his bards, but only briefly. The most interesting are *The Spoils of Annwn* and *The Song of the Graves*. The former is the one that describes a quest for a magic cauldron, and looks like a tenth-century version of the Grail legend. The latter is a list of renowned warriors and their alleged places of burial. Arthur is the exception. His grave is said to be a mystery. Perhaps the poet implies only that the Britons tried to conceal his death from the Saxons, or to protect his grave from desecration. But the line may be the germ of the prophecy about his return.

In Welsh legend, as distinct from poetry, the search leads to results equally tantalising. Most of the actual stories are lost. With a few precious exceptions, the best of them in the *Mabinogion*, all that has come down is a jumbled mass of 'triads'. These are mnemonics. Story-tellers grouped their favourite themes in linked sets of three: the *Three Great Treacheries*, the *Three Exalted Prisoners*, and so on. Each triad was a summary of three stories, located in a glorified 'Island of Britain' before the Anglo-Saxon conquest.

Most of the triads that mention Arthur or companions of his are medieval, influenced by French romance, and devoid of any historical interest. Some, however, give glimpses of him in more primitive and barbaric guises. He is one of the *Three Red Ravagers* and one of the *Three Frivolous Bards*. He is guilty of one of the *Three Wicked Uncoverings*: digging up the head of Bran, Britain's talisman against foreign invasion, on the ground that Britain should not rely on magic. Several triads introduce Medraut and Arthur's wife Gwenhwyvaer. Arthur is stated, most surprisingly, to have had three wives all so named. One of these ladies was assaulted by Medraut in a raid on Arthur's fortress at Kelliwic in Cornwall. Medraut made a treacherous treaty with the Saxons which caused the fatal battle of Camlaun, a sort of Bosworth where many combatants changed sides.

Meagre as the triads are, they convey at least one crucial fact: Arthur's uniqueness. No other hero is so frequently mentioned. He is the only person so important that triads are enlarged into tetrads to fit him in. An instance is the triad about the *Three Exalted Prisoners*. After saying who they were, it adds that there was another more famous even than they, and this was Arthur. His imprisonments, as sketched in the triad, have a mythical air. Yet the fact that he was thought of as a prisoner at all should not be overlooked. The oldest traditions do not make him a serene, triumphant monarch. He sounds more like an adventurer with a background of guerrilla war and plain feuding. The strangest of all the triads is the *Three Powerful Swineherds*. It ends:

> The third was Trystan son of Tallwch, who guarded the swine of March son of Meirchion while the swineherd had gone on a message to Essyllt to bid her appoint a meeting with Trystan. Now Arthur and Marchell and Cai and Bedwyr undertook to go and make an attempt on him, but they proved unable to get possession of as much as one porker either as a gift or as a purchase, whether by fraud, by force, or by theft.

These few sentences supply six familiar names—Tristram, Mark, Iseult, Arthur, Kay, Bedevere—and the Tristram-Iseult motif. Yet the whole assemblage is concerned with nothing grander than an inglorious attempt at pig-stealing.

Out of the shipwreck of Welsh legend, the *Mabinogion* has saved one Arthurian story intact from the pre-Geoffrey era. This is *Culhwch and Olwen*. It tells how the gallant youth Culhwch (pronounced Kil-hooch, with the *ch* as in 'loch') enlists Arthur's aid in performing a fantastic series of tasks, which he must do to win Olwen as his bride. The verve and savagery of the tale, its fierce humour, exuberant richness and occasional beauty, belong to a wholly pre-romantic world. It testifies, just as the triads do, to Arthur's special position in folk memory. The author makes Culhwch go to him for help because, in this way, a vast medley of ready-made Arthurian saga matter can be brought in. There is a list of over two hundred of Arthur's followers. Many take part in the adventures. Some are fairy-tale figures: men who can drink up seas, hear ants fifty miles away, and so forth. But among them are Bedwyr, Cei (another variant of the name which reaches the romances as Kay) and also Gwalchmei, who eventually becomes Gawain.

One further source, while extremely suspect, supplies hints that have a certain value; partly in themselves, partly because of the way they interlock with the other data. Medieval Wales and Brittany produced a mass of Saints' Lives. As the Celts bestowed the title of 'saint' most generously, hordes of dark-age priests from the West British regions are embalmed in this form. To anybody who cares for sound history the Lives are depressing, with their childish miracles, anachronisms and would-be edification. However, though few of them can be trusted singly, the effect of taking many together is more impressive. They shed light on each other; they give cross-references and a vague time-scheme; they reveal attitudes. And several bring in Arthur. The Welsh ones are associated with the abbey of Llancarfan. Their authors seem to be drawing on a body of tradition current in southern Wales.

The *Life of St Cadoc*, composed by Lifris about 1100, has a preface on the marriage of the saint's parents. Gwynnlyw, king of Glamorgan, eloped with a Brecknock princess named Gwladys and took her into his own domain with her father in pursuit. Fleeing over a hill, they found Arthur playing at dice with Cei and Bedwyr. Arthur took an unwelcome interest in Gwladys, but the two warriors (with a curious anticipation of the romances) reminded him that it was their custom to help those in distress. He confronted the pursuing father and made him go home. The lovers married at once—perhaps as a precautionary measure—and in due course Cadoc was born.

Long afterwards, we are told, when he was abbot of Llancarfan, Cadoc gave sanctuary for seven years to a man who had killed three of Arthur's soldiers. This length of time was doubtfully legal. The ageing chieftain finally ran the fugitive to earth, and came to the Usk to argue with Cadoc and the monks. They stayed on the other bank. An arbitrator awarded Arthur a herd of cattle as compensation. He demanded that all the cattle should be part red, part white. The monks got them, with divine aid, and drove them across a ford. But when Arthur's soldiers took charge, the cows changed into bundles of fern. Arthur was understandably daunted and recognised Cadoc's right to give sanctuary for seven years, seven months and seven days.

However baseless these incidents may be, at least two points of interest emerge. First, the Welsh monastic tradition would seem to have been unfriendly to Arthur. Even when he is well-established as a national hero, Lifris portrays him in a way that presupposes this minority view. Secondly, though Arthur pays homage to Christian duty, he appears as a hard-bargaining warrior chief out for what he can get. Does the second fact explain the first? Did the monks dislike him because he harassed them and tried to extort goods from them?

The plausibility of such an idea is strengthened by the portrayal of Arthur in other Saints' Lives. That of St Carannog describes the holy man as launching a floating altar on the Bristol Channel, and vowing to preach wherever it landed. He traced it to the neighbourhood of Dindraethou—Dunster, in Somerset—where Arthur reigned as junior colleague of a prince named Cadwy. When Carannog reached the spot, the altar was nowhere to be seen. Arthur, however, was near by, looking for a huge serpent which was annoying the people of Carrum (Carhampton). Carannog asked where the altar was. Arthur promised to tell him if he would help in disposing of the serpent. Carannog banished it in the same manner as St Patrick, and then Arthur produced the altar. He had commandeered it himself and used it as a table, but everything he put on it fell off. In gratitude he allowed Carannog to settle at Carrum.

The *Life of St Padarn* was written in the twelfth century, when a respectful tone toward the hero could be expected unless the monks' adverse tradition was very stubborn. Yet it speaks contemptuously of 'a certain *tyrannus* by the name of Arthur'. *Tyrannus* is the word used by Gildas for Vortigern, implying power without legitimacy. Arthur, it seems, burst into Padarn's cell and demanded that he hand over a tunic given him by the patriarch of Jerusalem. When the saint refused, Arthur persisted. Thereupon the earth opened and he sank in up to his neck. He had to apologise before he escaped.

Both these legends give the same impression as *Cadoc*. Arthur is a military despot who tries to plunder the monks. Historically it is a fair deduction that he requisitioned church property to maintain his troops. A parallel case is Charles Martel, who did this in the eighth century to finance his defence of France against the Arabs. Although he saved western Christendom, ecclesiastical authors treat him as a villain.

We may, indeed, have an explanation here for Gildas's curious unwillingness to discuss the Badon campaign in detail, or to name its leader: clerical rancour. Arthur was unmentionable, a deliverer whom he could not attack yet would not praise. The Welsh *Life of St Gildas*, by Caradoc of Llancarfan, at least hints at strained relations. According to this, Gildas was a northern Briton, one of the many sons of Caw, who lived near the Clyde. Most of them were driven by Pictish raids to migrate to Wales. The eldest, however, named Hueil, stayed in the north. The brothers fought against Arthur—described as a *tyrannus* and a *rex rebellus* claiming to rule all Britain—until Hueil was captured and put to death. Gildas was the family spokesman in demanding compensation, and Arthur had to pay. Later they met again. Gildas was now at Glastonbury. Melwas, the king of Somerset, kidnapped Arthur's wife 'Guennuvar' and kept her in Glastonbury, which was protected by the river and marshes. Arthur arrived with levies from Devon and Cornwall. Battle was imminent, but Gildas and the abbot negotiated a treaty by which the lady was restored.

The abduction of Guennuvar, or Guinevere, is an episode that turns up again in the romances. As to the indications of Arthur's power in the West Country, and Glastonbury's role as a stronghold, their value depends on corroboration (if any) from other sources. But the story of Caw's sons has a feature of genuine interest. It brings Arthur into conflict with lawless elements in Pictland and northern Wales. The war with Caw's sons could account for the battles of Celidon and Tribruit, even for the City of the Legion, if this is Chester. We may not be getting facts, but we may be getting glimpses of whatever saga has gone into Nennius. There are more hints in *Culhwch and Olwen*, where Arthur's fight with Hueil is mentioned, and he and the other sons of Caw, presumably subdued, are at Arthur's court.

Outside Wales there is one very strange Saint's Life, that of the Breton Goeznovius. Its preface recalls the flight of Britons to Armorica during the Saxon invasion. The tide was stemmed, it continues, by Arthur, 'the great king of the Britons', who won victories in Britain and Gaul. After he was 'summoned from human activity', the Saxons advanced again and the flight to Armorica was resumed. Here we have Arthur crowned, making war overseas, and not dying. The monastic writer has drawn on a tradition quite unlike the Welsh. To judge from this, it was chiefly in Brittany that imagination began transforming the soldier into the immortal King Arthur, whose myth the French priests collided with at Bodmin in 1113. From there, as well as from western Britain, Geoffrey of Monmouth and the romancers must have drawn the themes which they worked up into literature.

Historically speaking, the Arthurian Fact is far clearer than Arthur himself. Some time before 500, the Britons rallied against the invader. Their leaders clung to the Roman and Christian heritage, and their struggle had a staunch conviction that was not found in other imperial provinces. As the years passed, Celtic resurgence doubtless reduced *Romanitas* to a hazy mystique with little meaning outside religion. But the rally went on, and the triumph at Badon brought a spell of peace and good order which even Gildas admits. Not until the middle of the sixth century did the heathen begin to bite again into mainland Britain.

Arthur became the symbol of the rally and, in tradition, the winner of all the victories after Ambrosius's death or retirement. Some such person existed. Or at any rate, it is much easier to suppose that he did than that he did not. To deny his reality would solve no problems. It would merely mean postulating another British leader to fill the same role—or, at all events, to win the decisive battle of Badon—and then explaining why he was totally forgotten. Arthur, however, was not king of Britain, or even a local king, except in the petty Irish sense. We may picture him as a rustic noble, born in the 470s or thereabouts, of still dimly-Romanised stock. Hence his name, Artorius. His youth was spent in raiding and feuding. By an unusual flair for leadership he attracted a following. His personal corps—the 'knights', if we care to use the word—aided British kings against Anglo-Saxon encroachments. He made himself indispensable over the whole zone of his operations, becoming Ambrosius's successor and, in a crude way, a statesman. But, despite victory, his standing was never quite secure. Quarrels with the monks, probably over levies in kind, deprived him of proper recognition in the writings of the only people who wrote. He met his end fighting an enemy to whom there is no reason not to give the name Modred.

As far as it goes, this is a credible career. No one need assume that the later growth of mythology casts any doubt on it. Even in recent times, tall stories have gathered round American folk-heroes such as Davy Crockett (a man perhaps not unlike Arthur). Yet some at least of those folk-heroes were real people. With the faintly outlined Briton, for whom we cannot hope to find so much evidence, the amount of filling-in that can ever be done is open to debate. However, there are three questions which can be asked with some prospect of getting answers.

First: Where was Arthur's home territory? Here, all tradition con- Ill. 118 verges. The problem is whether tradition can be trusted. It makes him a West-Countryman. Even such nebulous clues as place-names and local legends point that way. They cover, indeed, a vast stretch of Britain (nobody else is commemorated so widely, except the Devil); and, as Tennyson said, Arthur's name streams over the land like a cloud. But the cloud has shape as well as extent. In all its length, from the Isles of Scilly to Perth, only the West Country supplies Arthur with dwelling-places. His Cornish home is Kelliwic, probably a hill-fort in the parish of Egloshayle near Padstow. Cadbury Castle in Somerset, which is close to Queen Camel (formerly plain Camel), has been identified with Camelot from time immemorial. The oldest triads locate Arthur in Cornwall. The *Life of St Carannog* connects him with Dunster. The *Life of St Gildas* portrays him summoning the troops of Cornwall and Devon. If Kelliwic, Dunster and Cadbury are all authentic, he must have moved as his power increased. But the vital point is that no comparable places exist outside the West Country. The courts at Caerleon and Winchester are found only in medieval literature. Geoffrey of Monmouth himself gives the same testimony. His story of the birth at Tintagel is not evidence as to history, but it shows that Arthur was supposed, even in Wales, to have come from that quarter. Likewise, even the Welsh bard who spoke to Henry II indicated that Somerset, not Wales, was thought of as the right place for his burial.

Many investigators today are disposed to accept the area in general if not the legends in detail. Those who disagree point out that Arthur looms large in the north also, and very early. Aneirin's *Gododdin* proves that he was already proverbial there before the close of the sixth century, and Prince Arthur of Argyll was the first and most notable of the men named after him. Nor are these the only considerations.

Whatever inference we shall draw from this aspect of his fame is bound up with a second question. Was he a local resistance leader afterwards inflated by legend and credited with exploits in places he never saw; or could he have been mobile—a national figure, so far as the term had meaning then, who really did leave his home territory and go everywhere?

The former view of him looks more likely, yet it leads to trouble. We cannot confine him either to the south-western or to the northern zone without perplexity over his status in the other. Not only the shape of the tradition, but historical and archaeological arguments, point to the south-west. Yet on purely literary grounds the case for the north may well be stronger. If we look at the saga alone, or what little is left of this, it is far easier to believe that it began in the north and was carried southward rather than the reverse. A north-south movement can be documented in other cases, a south-north one cannot. The more romantic alternative view turns out, in fact, to cover the data somewhat better. A wide-ranging Arthur could have lived where tradition says, and gone out to fight where Nennius says: Glein and Linnuis representing a Lincolnshire campaign against Angles, Celidon and Tribruit taking him to quell Picts or dissident Britons, and Badon bringing him south again, with a reputation left behind everywhere, but exploited first in poetry by the northern bards.

The case against this tempting idea is that it may suggest more

Ill. 24

cohesion among the Britons, and better communications, than they would actually have had. That objection leads in turn to a third question. What sort of leader was Arthur? What were his official rank and his mode of warfare?

Two epithets in Welsh literature look like titles: the *imperator* of the poem, and the *dux bellorum* of Nennius. *Imperator* may have its primary Latin meaning of commander-in-chief. Or it may echo some last tremor of imperial politics, such as an attempt by the British soldiers to proclaim Arthur emperor, as their predecessors proclaimed Constantine and Maximus. Both interpretations are guesswork. Yet however we take the word, if it implies anything at all, it implies a big rather than a small leader.

Dux bellorum raises more serious issues. Though not a recognised title, it certainly seems to hint at some military office. In 1891, Sir John Rhys ventured the theory that Arthur held, or revived, a specific Roman command set up toward the end of the Western Empire. Generals in charge of provincial defence had the ranks of *dux* and *comes*, the original forms of the words 'duke' and 'count'. Britain, early in the fifth century, was allotted a *Comes Britanniarum*—Count of the British Provinces—with a roving commission from the Channel to Caledonia. His command was never effectively organised. But Rhys thought Arthur might have restored it in his own person, or been appointed to it by an alliance of British kings.

Rhys's conjecture was pursued further by R. G. Collingwood in the first volume of the *Oxford History of England*. He fastened on the likelihood that the tide of warfare was turned by a change in methods. This raised the topic of cavalry. The Anglo-Saxons fought on foot and had very little horsemanship for even civilian purposes. Procopius, the Emperor Justinian's court historian, notes that when some Anglian envoys came to Constantinople, they were laughed at for their failure to ride properly in a parade. Before the fifth century, on the other hand, Rome had developed mailed horsemen called *cataphractarii* and *clibanarii*. The latter—whose arms and tactics were imitated from Persia—wore helmets and carried spears, and horse as well as rider was protected by mail. While the frontiers were manned by peasant militia, mounted forces could move swiftly behind them to threatened areas. The technique came too late to save the West, and was probably less effective than some historians have assumed, but it was a factor in the long endurance of Constantinople.*

The *Comes Britanniarum* was assigned six cavalry units. Perhaps they only existed on paper. However, the Britons may have seen mounted

Ill. 28

soldiers in 418. Although Gildas does not mention any as taking part in the first rescue of Britain by Stilicho, he does mention 'unexpected bands of cavalry' in the second rescue, which happened about 418 if it happened at all. Collingwood argued that Arthur, as *Comes*, recreated a mounted force to which the enemy had no answer.

This theory, as stated by Collingwood, is open to grave criticism. It implies a fuller survival of Roman Britain than the rest of the evidence attests. By Arthur's time, even the Romanising effect of Ambrosius must have largely worn off. But he might have adopted a remembered title and organised cavalry of a sort: do-it-yourself *clibanarii*, so to speak. Aneirin's poetry shows that British nobles were riding to battle quite soon after Arthur's time. Whether they, or for that matter the horsemen of the Empire, charged and fought in the saddle like medieval knights is an unresolved question. It is uncertain whether the stirrup, or any comparable device, was known in Europe so early, and how much a man on horseback could do without it. But even 'mounted commandos' (the phrase is suggested by Robert Graves) would have given Arthur's Britons two advantages: moral effect and mobility. As to the first, mounted men undoubtedly could strike panic into superstitious barbarian mobs. Constantine the Great is said to have routed an army with only twelve, a feat hardly less amazing than Arthur's alleged onslaught at Mount Badon. Tactical mobility, the capacity for swift movement and surprise, might also have made a decisive difference under a bold leader.

If Arthur had cavalry, whatever meaning we attach to that term, the view of him as ubiquitous rather than local acquires further plausibility. Long marches can, of course, be made on foot, even in rough country. But the only account we actually have of sixth-century British warriors traversing a great distance is in Aneirin's *Gododdin*, and they do go on horseback.

Assertions are sometimes made about Arthur's cavalry as if there were direct proof of it. There is none. Nennius and the poets leave us in the dark about his methods of war. Still, the theory remains an attractive way of fitting the evidence together. And archaeological support is not beyond hoping for.

*Earlier discussions are largely superseded by John W. Eadie's article 'The Development of Roman Mailed Cavalry', in the *Journal of Roman Studies* for 1967.

Ill. 28. A graffito (early third century AD) of a Roman *clibanarius* from Dura Europus. A *clibanarius* was a helmeted horseman armed with a spear. Both rider and horse were protected by mail. The Anglo-Saxons were not horsemen and one theory has it that Arthur owed his successes against the Saxons to his revival of Roman cavalry techniques.

Just as the Arthurian Fact—the British rally which Arthur stands for —is better outlined than the hero himself, so its ramifications are easier to feel sure of than his human associates. Which of the famous characters are, in fact, real people? A defensible answer would be: Kay, Bedevere, Modred, Tristram. Probably, Guinevere. Possibly, Mark, Gawain and Iseult. They are the medieval guises of British Celts who appear earlier as Cei, Bedwyr, Medraut, Trystan, Gwenhwyvaer, March, Gwalchmei and Essyllt. The first two are always Arthur's lieutenants, and continue so in Geoffrey and Wace, though they yield the limelight afterwards to undocumented knights, such as Lancelot. Medraut is normally hostile and never friendly. Trystan is a puzzling nobleman connected with Cornwall, whose name was originally spelt Drustans and looks Pictish. Of Arthur's wife we can say very little. Gwalchmei is scarcely more than mentioned, but at least he is mentioned before Geoffrey of Monmouth wrote.

A further word is needed about Merlin. Although he was invented by Geoffrey, the invention was not quite devoid of factual basis. There was a northern British bard named Myrddin, whose name Geoffrey used, changing it a little to avoid an unfortunate French pun. Myrddin flourished around the year 573, when he was involved in a battle near Carlisle. If he met Arthur at all, he can only have done so as a boy in the commander's advanced years. Even apart from magic, his legendary role is impossible.

All these variously shadowy figures have a feature in common. They would never have been immortalised for their own sake. It was the British rally that gave their names an imperishable setting. Yet since the rally finally failed, why did it leave so deep a mark?

Partly because of poetry, and the stubborn pride of Wales and Cornwall. But the poetry and the pride had unique matter to feed upon. For fully thirty years the rally preserved what was, in effect, the last remnant of the Western Empire. Throughout the imperial world, moreover, Arthur was the only fighter against Teutonic invaders who drove any substantial number out again after conquest. Once in Gaul, the barbarians stayed. In Britain, most of them stayed likewise, but some did not. Some became discouraged and looked elsewhere. For this retreat we have two witnesses. Neither is conclusive alone, together they confirm each other.

Procopius, writing in Constantinople toward the middle of the sixth century, describes Britain as inhabited by Britons, Angles and Frisians, the last being evidently Saxons named from their previous home. All three races multiply fast, he says, and the surplus population goes over to the continent, where the Frankish rulers permit settlement. Procopius's information seems to have come from some northern Angles who were at Constantinople with a Frankish embassy between 534 and 548. His British emigration is the movement out of the West Country that was now turning Armorica into Brittany. But the Angles and Saxons never took to the sea without solid reasons. They must have gone out of Britain because the way to further land-seizure was barred.

A ninth-century chronicler at the German monastery of Fulda gives another aspect of the same story. Speaking of 'Saxons' living north of the Unstrut, he explains that they are descended from Angles forced out of Britain by the need for new land. They joined the Frankish king Theuderich in a war fought in 531 and he gave them a conquered area to live in. The area which the monk has in mind is still known as Engilin.

Faintly, but satisfactorily, a picture emerges. The Teutonic advance in Britain was disputed by Ambrosius and turned back by Arthur. A rough demarcation line wandered southward from Yorkshire. West of it, Britain could take breath and recover. In one respect at least, this Indian summer of the Celts brought a renaissance which, like the rest of their achievement, had no counterpart abroad. Behind the barrier raised by the soldiers, the Church burst into flower. St Patrick's lonely eminence ended, and he began to have successors.

The reborn Christianity of the Celts was now cut off from the Church on the European continent, and different in system and atmosphere, though not in doctrine. Its centres were rural monasteries instead of city sees, and its heads were abbots instead of bishops. Celtic community life was less binding on the individual than the Rule of St Benedict. Each monk had his separate cell. All ate together and assembled for worship in a chapel, but they enjoyed some freedom of movement. They were not only priests and missionaries but teachers, doctors, farmers and builders. Britain's religious renewal was primarily an upsurge of energy in Wales, and the work of one remarkable man, St Illtud.

Illtud may have attended one of the schools set up by Germanus, and it is said, though on no very safe authority, that he served as a soldier under Arthur. After some years as a hermit, he founded the monastery of Llantwit Major in Glamorgan. His monks reclaimed land and pioneered an improved method of ploughing. Illtud became, in the words of Gildas (who, however, does not name him, any more than he names Arthur), 'the polished teacher of almost the whole of Britain'. His disciples—Gildas himself, St Sampson, St Paul Aurelian, Prince Maelgwn who became king of Gwynedd—made their mark outside Wales. Sampson and his own disciples virtually created the Breton Church. Meanwhile, independently of Illtud, St Cadoc founded Llancarfan, and travelled north to Pictland and south to Cornwall.

The success of these tireless clerics was a direct result of military triumph and British security. Thence also came the preservation of the work of St Patrick. Going westward across the sea, and welcoming Irish pupils in their own schools, the monks of Britain regenerated the faltering Church of Ireland. The blaze of Celtic genius which made the smaller island a beacon to dark-age Europe was possible because Arthur had kept the heathen at arm's length.

The effects of the Arthurian Fact were profound; and they were lasting. When the conquest finally came, it was slow and piecemeal. Devon held out till 710, Cornwall till 825. Wales and parts of north-west England never succumbed to the Anglo-Saxons at all. Moreover, the Anglo-Saxons who did eventually conquer were no longer the savages of the fifth century. Christian missions from Rome in the

Ill. 145 south, and from Celtic Iona in the north, had opened up their little states to civilising influences. The England which took shape under Alfred, and the United Kingdom which grew round that, were fusions of many elements—the Celtic included.

When Geoffrey of Monmouth took up that Celtic element, and evoked Arthur's Britain in medieval guise, how far was he falsifying? Of course, he depicted a better organised realm than can possibly have existed, with an unreal monarch, a glamourised Christian knighthood, an absurd empire. Yet he did not desert the truth altogether. Arthur led warriors, who may well have been mounted; he beat the Saxons; he and his men were Christian, at least in name. Arthur's Britain, however divided and ruinous, did stand for such civilisation as it remembered, and gave this, through the Church, a fresh vigour in all the part of the British Isles which its victories protected.

In the modern search for that buried reality, there are limits to what the historian can hope to accomplish. Too little was written down. Too much even of that has perished. But the twentieth century offers searchers another technique: archaeology. Can the spade fill the gaps which the pen has left? Let us see what it has achieved so far.

3   *Romance and Reality in Cornwall*

C. A. Ralegh Radford

Tintagel

TINTAGEL IS ASSOCIATED with the birth of Arthur. The legend goes back to the twelfth century, but is perhaps more conveniently related in the thirteenth-century version of *Percival li Gallois*, as translated by Sebastian Evans in the *High History of the Holy Grail*:

> [Arthur, Lancelot and Gawain] rode right busily on their journeys until they came into a very different land, scarce inhabited of any folk, and found a little castle in a combe. They came thitherwards and saw that the enclosure of the castle was fallen down into an abysm, so that none might approach it on that side, but it had a right fair gateway and a door tall and wide whereby one entered. They beheld a chapel that was right fair and rich, and below was a great ancient hall. They saw a priest appear in the midst of the castle, bald and old, that had come forth of the chapel. They are come hither and alighted, and asked the priest what the castle was, and he told them that it was the great Tintagel. 'And how is this ground all caved in about the castle?' 'Sir', saith the priest, 'I will tell you. Sir', saith he, 'King Uther Pendragon, that was father of King Arthur, held a great court and summoned all his barons. The king of this castle that then was here was named Gorlois. He went to the court and took his wife with him, that was named Ygerne, and she was the fairest dame in any kingdom. King Uther sought acquaintance of her for her great beauty, and regarded her and honoured her more than all others of his court. King Gorlois departed thence and made the Queen come back to this castle for the dread that he had of King Uther Pendragon. King Uther was

Ill. 6

very wroth with him, and commanded him to send back the Queen his wife. King Gorlois said that he would not. Thereupon King Uther Pendragon defied him, and then laid siege about this castle where the Queen was. King Gorlois was gone to seek for succour. King Uther Pendragon had Merlin with him of whom you have heard tell, he was so crafty. He made him be changed into the semblance of King Gorlois, so that he entered there within by Merlin's art and lay that night with the Queen, and so begat King Arthur in a great hall that was next to the enclosure where this abysm is. And for this sin hath the ground sunken in on this wise.' He cometh with them toward the chapel that was right fair, and had a right rich sepulchre therein. 'Lords, in this sepulchre was placed the body of Merlin, but never mought it be set inside the chapel, wherefore perforce it remained outside. And know of a very truth that the body lieth not within the sepulchre, for, so soon as it was set therein, it was taken out and snatched away, either on God's behalf or the Enemy's, but which we know not.' 'Sir', saith King Arthur, 'And what became of King Gorlois?' 'Sir', saith he, 'the King slew him on the morrow of the night he lay with his wife, and so forthwith espoused Queen Ygerne, and in such manner as I tell you was King Arthur conceived in sin that is now the best King in the world.'

All the essential features of the priest's tale appear a century earlier in the *History of the Kings of Britain* of Geoffrey of Monmouth. He adds some topographical detail that makes it clear that he had in mind the site of Tintagel. As Uther prepares to attack the castle, one of his followers, Ulfin of Ricaradoc, counsels him as follows:

And who shall give thee any counsel that may avail, seeing that there is no force that may prevail whereby to come into her in the castle of Tintagel? For it is situate on the sea and is on every side encompassed thereby. Nor none other entrance is there save a narrow rock doth furnish, the which three armed knights could hold against thee, though thou wast standing there with the whole might of Britain beside thee.

There follows the tale of Merlin's art and Uther's entry: 'And upon this same night was the most renowned Arthur conceived.'

This classic version of the birth of Arthur cannot be traced further back than Geoffrey of Monmouth, though there are slight indications that before this date he was known as the son of Uthyr and Eigr (Ygerne). But normally Welsh tradition, as represented in the *Triads of the Island of Britain,* names him without a patronymic. By the late thirteenth century, Arthur has become the son of Uthyr, the son of Constantine of Dumnonia, a ruler denounced by Gildas, who was reigning in the middle of the sixth century. This would place Arthur's reign at the end of the sixth century, a chronology at variance with the better sources, including the old Welsh Annals, in which the fatal battle of Camlann is placed shortly before 540. This pedigree and later elaborations may be dismissed as products of the imagination stimulated by the increasing popularity of the romances.

The Tintagel known to the writers of the twelfth and thirteenth centuries was the medieval castle on the headland within the manor of Bossinney. In 1086, *Domesday Book* records that the manor belonged to the monks of St Petrock of Bodmin, but that it was held by Count Robert of Mortain, a half brother of William the Conqueror and the greatest landowner in Cornwall. There is no mention of a castle. But a typical Norman motte and bailey, that can still be traced in the village, must have been erected about this date. In 1141, at the beginning of the civil war between King Stephen and the Empress Matilda, Reginald, an illegitimate son of King Henry I, was created earl of Cornwall. He then became the effective holder of the manor of Bossinney, including the site of Tintagel castle. It is to this period that the first erection of the castle on the headland must be attributed. A massive bank, originally crowned with a palisade, bars the approach to the headland. In front is a wide v-shaped ditch. The bank now carries a later stone curtain.

Excavation has proved that the bank was of two periods, the second dating from the twelfth century, and that the ditch had been recut at the same date. Bank and ditch run from the edge of the sharp fall to the valley on the east side to within ten feet of a prominent boss of rock, which has been artificially scarped. Bank and ditch, but on a slighter scale, are returned along the top of the steep slope falling to the eastern valley. Within these defences the whole headland is enclosed; it is surrounded on other sides by cliffs falling steeply to the sea. The only entry to the castle is along the narrow passage left between the end of the ditch and the scarped side of the boss of rock. The approach runs along the side of the valley, though another track can be traced running west towards the parish church, the earliest part of which is contemporary with the twelfth-century castle.

Within the enclosure, the plateau then ran out to the headland without interruption, offering an ample space for the buildings required. The chapel lay on the plateau itself above a low cliff facing

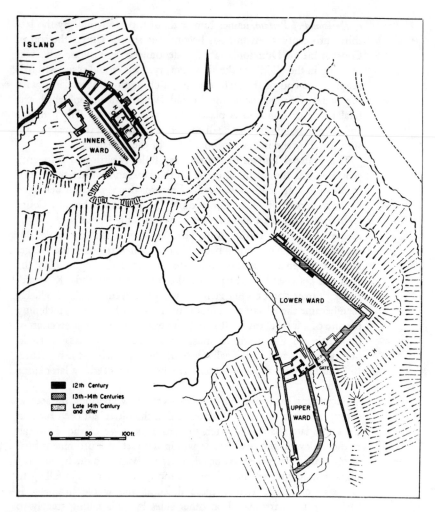

Ill. 40. Plan of Tintagel Castle.

east; it was a small building consisting of a nave and chancel. Sculptured stones found during the nineteenth-century clearance indicate a date in the middle of the twelfth century. On a shelf on the eastern cliffs lay the great hall of stone, also of mid-twelfth-century date. There were doubtless other buildings of wood or half-timbered, but of these no trace is now visible.

Such was the castle erected by Reginald shortly after he was created earl of Cornwall in 1141. Geoffrey's *History of the Kings of Britain* appeared in the form which has come down to us about 1145; this was the second edition. The first edition is known to have been in existence in 1139 and probably dated from 1136–38. There is no certainty that it contained the episode of Arthur's conception or, if it did, that the scene was placed at Tintagel. Geoffrey's patron, Earl Robert of Gloucester, was another illegitimate son of Henry 1 and therefore a half-brother of Earl Reginald, the builder of Tintagel. It seems likely that the introduction of this site was a localisation due to Geoffrey himself.

The second great building period at Tintagel Castle dates from the middle of the thirteenth century. The manor had been alienated after the death of Earl Reginald in 1175. In 1236, Richard, the younger brother of King Henry 111, who had been created earl of Cornwall a few years earlier, recovered possession of the castle, the defences of which he proceeded to modernise. A stone curtain and gateway replaced the outer ramparts of earth and timber which were already

Ill. 32 100 years old and obsolete as a defensive system. The inner ward with the old twelfth-century hall was also surrounded with a stone curtain.

Ill. 33 On the eastern cliffs a new stone curtain with an iron gate was placed, blocking the path up from a small cove, where rock-cut steps show

Ills. 30, 42 that a landing place once existed. The chapel was enlarged and a walled garden and a rabbit warren formed on the plateau, in a fold sheltered from the prevailing westerly winds. There is no trace of alterations to the hall and the residential block in the inner ward, but alterations and additions may have been made to the timber buildings, which must have existed from the earliest days of the castle.

Earl Richard's castle passed to his son Edmund of Cornwall and on his death in 1300 reverted to the Crown. After short tenures by Piers Gaveston, the favourite of Edward 11, and by John of Eltham, the king's second son, Tintagel was granted to Edward the Black Prince, as part of the duchy of Cornwall, when this was created in 1337. A survey carried out at this time shows that the gulf between the mainland and the 'island' had already developed and that the gap was spanned by a bridge. The layout of the curtain erected by Earl Richard about 1240 shows that the ridge was still intact at that date; the encroachment of the sea can therefore be dated to between 1250 and 1330. The old hall was unroofed during the tenure of John of Eltham (1328–36) and was later replaced by a smaller building on the same site. The later development of the castle and its decay during the fifteenth century are not pertinent to the present theme. Enough has been said to show that the writers of the romances in the twelfth and thirteenth centuries were thinking in terms of the then existing castle of Tintagel, which was one of the stronger fortresses of the earls of Cornwall.

Repairs to the castle were last recorded about 1500, and by 1540 it was a ruin. So it remained till the nineteenth century. Once the bridge had fallen, the end of the headland—the 'island' of modern days—was accessible only with difficulty and served as a pasture for sheep and a refuge for rabbits. In the mid-nineteenth century, the growing numbers of tourists and the revived interest in the Arthurian cycle fostered by the poems of Tennyson, brought Tintagel back into the public eye. The romantic vision of the coast seemed a fit setting for the weird story of Arthur's birth. A rough rock-cut stair was *Ill.* 31 formed leading up to the inner ward on the island. This ward was again enclosed with a battlemented curtain, partly built on the old foundations, partly designed as an enclosure pierced by a door with the date 1852. Forty years ago, the Duchy of Cornwall placed the castle under the guardianship of the Commissioners of Works, now the Ministry of Public Building and Works. Concurrently with the consolidation and clearance of the ruins, excavations were undertaken and the earlier history of the site revealed.

These excavations showed that the headland of Tintagel had been the *Ills.* 33, 4 site of an extensive Celtic monastery. Four different phases identified in one of the buildings indicated a long period of occupation. Imported pottery from the east Mediterranean established an initial date *Ills.* 34, 3 in the fifth or early sixth century. A silver penny of King Alfred (871–99)—the latest artifact antedating the castle—may represent no more than the loss by a pilgrim to a deserted oratory which was no longer the centre of a living community. Pottery of the twelfth century and later, though relatively common on the site, was never found in the layers associated with the monastery.

Roman settlement in the neighbourhood of Tintagel—or, to use the older Cornish name, Bossinney—is attested by two imperial milestones. One, discovered near the parish church, about half a mile inland from the castle, bears an inscription to the Emperor Licinius (308–24). The other found at Trethevy, 1½ miles east of the village, was set up in honour of Gallus and Volusianus, and dates between 251 and 253. No Roman road has yet been identified in this area, nor are objects of provincial Romano-British type recorded from this

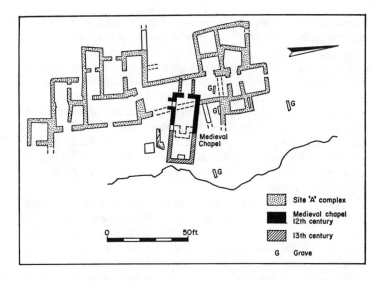

Ill. 41. Plan of Site A (*cf. Ill. 42*). The stippled walls show the Celtic monastery. The white square to the left of the medieval chapel is the *leacht*, a tomb shrine characteristic of Celtic monasteries which housed the relics of saints or founders. The small square room at the far left was probably the porter's lodge.

part of the north Cornish coast. It can only be concluded that sites, probably native in character and inconspicuous in appearance, await discovery. The point is not without importance. A Celtic monastery implies a certain concentration of population within a reasonable distance; only a hermitage would be established in the 'desert'. The character of the site now to be discussed is monastic, not eremitical.

The Celtic monastery of Tintagel was bounded on the landward side by an earthen bank, now crowned by the thirteenth-century curtain, and by a broad, flat-bottomed ditch. The upper part of the existing bank is a twelfth-century heightening, but the base, some 30 feet across and 8 feet high, dates from the fifth or sixth century. Like its medieval successor, the monastic bank ran from the edge of the scarp overlooking the eastern valley to within a short distance of the protruding boss of rock, leaving the same narrow entry. Early texts often speak of the monastic vallum, a term indicating the enclosure which fenced in the cashel or settlement occupied by the community. It seems always to have been a physical barrier, an earthen bank, a rampart of turf or a hedge. But it also had a spiritual meaning, separating the city of God from the world outside.

Within the bank, the headland stretched out seaward in an irregular mass with extreme measurements of half a mile from the gate to the furthest point and a quarter of a mile across. The effective space was very much smaller, with an area of the plateau somewhat larger than it now appears and as much space again provided by folds in the surrounding cliffs, wherever the natural or artificial terraces afforded a space for buildings or an enclosure for cultivation. Even so, the total area can hardly have exceeded ten acres, with perhaps as much more rough pasture for animals.

Within the enclosure the monastery consisted of groups of buildings, each with its special function. Eight such groups were located, of which six were explored and planned; the other two had been too far destroyed by the medieval castle. Two further sites were noted in folds of the cliff, and others probably await identification.

The first and largest site examined lay on the eastern edge of the plateau; it was centred on the twelfth-century chapel. The Celtic site consisted of a long range of buildings facing east on to a court which was bounded on the far side by the cliff, here forming the edge of the plateau. The range was approached from the south by a path running along the edge of the plateau; this is now reached by a modern zigzag approach rising up from the inner ward of the castle. The original way is likely to have been along the plateau, which has here been destroyed by the encroachment of the sea. At the south end of the range of buildings, a small square room thrust forward from the general line, together with the stub of a wall, suggest a gate with a lodge providing access to the court. Within the court, a much-ruined stretch of walling immediately south of the later chapel is probably part of an older oratory. Beside it is the base of a square block of masonry, a tomb shrine or *leacht*. These tomb shrines are a normal feature in Celtic cemeteries; they housed the relics of saints or founders.

On the far side of the chapel a number of graves have been discovered. The oratory with the tomb of the saint would be the primary objective of visiting pilgrims. In its immediate vicinity one would expect to find the various buildings catering for their needs. There would be a treasury containing other relics, perhaps possessions of the saint. There would also be the sacristy, where the vessels needed for the service of the oratory would be stored. A guesthouse for the refreshment of pilgrims might also be found in this area, together

Ills. 41, 42
Site A

Ill. 41

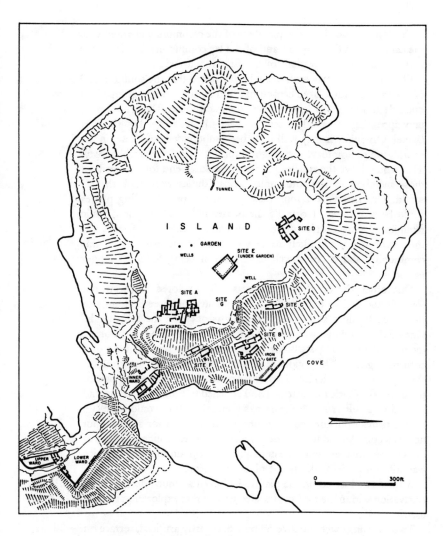

ISLAND

TUNNEL

SITE D

GARDEN

WELLS

SITE E
(UNDER GARDEN)

WELL

SITE A

SITE G

SITE C

CHAPEL

SITE B

IRON
GATE

COVE

SITE F

INNER
WARD

UPPER
WARD

LOWER
WARD

0   300 ft.

Ill. 42. Plan of Tintagel showing the
castle and the excavations at earlier
Celtic sites.

with rooms needed by those members of the community charged with the care both of the pilgrims and of the lay community, of which the pastoral care was the responsibility of the monastery.

On this basis, it may tentatively be suggested that the southern end of the range, with a large central hall and smaller rooms grouped on one side and to the back, represents the guesthouse. The central part, now appearing as a single room, has been much damaged by the later chapel. Originally it may well have been subdivided, and here, in the vicinity of the oratory, one might expect the treasury and sacristy. This would leave the smaller rooms at the north end for the needs of those members of the community whose duties were with the lay world. This range had a long history. Four distinct building phases could be recognised. Normally the phases indicated adaption, while retaining the main structure of older date. Even so, a life of some three centuries is not likely to be too long for the existence of this community, and it could well have been in being for a far longer period.

One other site on the plateau was fully explored. This lay out towards the end of the headland. It consisted of three buildings or ranges enclosing a small court which was open on the fourth side. One of the buildings was subdivided by slabs set on edge, a normal method of providing stalls for cattle. In another was the base of a corn-drying kiln. This evidence is sufficient to identify the group as the centre of the agricultural activities which formed a normal part of the life of the Celtic monastery. Land attached to the monastery would normally be cultivated by the monks themselves and would have lain on the plateau outside the enclosure. Corn required for storage, but not seed corn, would have to be parched to prevent mildew. This was the custom in the wetter western parts of Britain and the practice was still normal in Wales in the nineteenth century.

Ill. 42
Site D

A third site located on the plateau had been so much destroyed by cultivation within the medieval walled garden that exploration seemed useless.

Ill. 42
Site E

Two buildings were uncovered on a flat, partly artificial, terrace on the eastern cliff, just outside the inner ward of the castle. The lower of these buildings has one large room with a porch at the south end. On the upper side of the main room is a stone base with a series of slots formed along the forward edge, in order to carry a heavy wooden structure. On the lower side were two annexes, open at the far end and originally entered from the main room. The arrangement suggests that here lay the library and scriptorium, with a heavy

Ill. 42
Site F

wooden cupboard or presses to contain the books or rolls possessed by the community, and smaller huts with an open end for writing: a formalised version of the writing hut mentioned more than once in the life of St Columba. The purpose of the upper building, consisting of a single large room, could not be determined. The position suggests that it may have been a school.

Ill. 42 *Sites B and C*

Beyond these a path, closed by a gate at the upper end, led down to three groups of buildings which formed cells or dwelling quarters. They were ranged on either side of a fold in the cliffs, down which water from a spring on the plateau had been led in a channel with basins, from which it could be dipped. The main group of buildings lay at the foot of the path. A range of rooms of varying sizes was backed against a cliff face; one at least was of two stories. The range faced on to a small court. On the other side, on the edge of the slope down to the sea, were two or three isolated buildings, one of which had been a sweat bath. Also on this side was a much larger room which must have served some communal purpose and was, perhaps, a refectory. Beyond the fold, a range of three rooms almost filled a

Ill. 42 *Site C*

terrace, which had been artificially built up; above this range a smaller terrace disclosed no sign of buildings, but produced evidence of intensive cultivation. From the main group a terraced path, with steps, led up towards the plateau. The upper part of the path could not be recovered, but it must have reached the plateau a short distance north of the oratory. Immediately under the oratory was a further group of cells, a range of small rooms opening out of a corridor. These groups of buildings must have formed the main dwelling quarter of the monks. They would probably have accommodated a community of about forty or fifty. But the texts suggest that a large monastery would often have more than one dwelling quarter, and there is no reason to argue that this was the only group of cells at Tintagel. Others may await discovery on the cliffs or have been destroyed by the encroachment of the sea. Buildings of monastic date, located when underpinning the walls of the twelfth-century hall, may represent another group of cells, but these could not be explored.

The most important objects found in the course of the excavation were fragments of imported pottery from the eastern Mediterranean. There were two main varieties, now known as Tintagel A and B. A fine red ware, not unlike the Samian of Roman Britain, was found

Ill. 34, 35
Ill. 36

mainly in the form of hemispherical and wide shallow bowls. In several cases, crosses of various types were impressed in the centre of the base. It is difficult to decide what use, other than liturgical, an ascetic community could have found for these vessels. Normally in Britain or Ireland this type of pottery is confined to secular, aristocratic dwellings. The second variety, consisting of broken pieces of large amphorae or containers for oil and wine, is more easily explicable. There are, in fact, references to wine being brought to Irish monasteries. The exact provenance within the east Mediterranean area of these wares has not yet been determined. Different varieties are known to have been widely used in the later fifth, sixth and seventh centuries. The discovery of fragments of pottery in the native Romano-British tradition suggests a date in the fifth century for the origin of the monastery at Tintagel, and the life of the community probably continued at least until the interruption of trade with the east Mediterranean caused by the Muslim conquests of the later seventh century.

Castle Dore

The story of King Mark and of the tragic love of Tristram and Iseult held a high place in the repertory of the Middle Ages. In the later period it became connected with the Arthurian cycle and the legend of the Holy Grail, but in origin it was separate. The oldest surviving versions date from the twelfth century, but scattered references in Welsh and Breton sources show that it was known to the Celtic world at a far earlier date.

There are two recensions of the story as told in the romances. The more primitive form appears first in an incomplete twelfth-century poem composed by the Anglo-Norman Beroul. In this poem Mark is king of Cornwall and his residence is situated at Lancien. The neighbouring church, to which the court repairs, is described as the monastery of St Sampson. These places can be identified with the modern farm of Lantyne (or Lantian) in the parish of St Sampson in Golant, the present parish church representing the former monastery. Ill. 38

The poem tells us little enough about Lancien. Tristram and his companions 'have come to Lancien, to the city, so far have they journeyed. They dismount and enter the city. The watchmen loudly sound the horn. They pass through the ditch and come straightway to the hall.' It is a conventional picture and implies no knowledge of Lancien by either the poet or his source. More revealing is the episode of the visit to the neighbouring church.

By the paved road they go up to the monastery of St Samson. The queen and all the barons, a great number are met together. . . . The great baron, Dinas the brave, carried thither a garment of rich silk embroidered with gold; it was worth fully one hundred marks of silver and the like was never possessed by count or king. And the Queen Iseut took it and laid it on the altar as an offering. It was made into a chasuble, which was kept in the Treasury and used only once a year on the great anniversary feast. It is still kept in the church of St Samson as those who have seen it bear witness.

Such particularity argues a knowledge of the actual church either by the poet or, more probably, by his source.

In the thirteenth century, Lantyne was the administrative centre of a feudal honour with lands scattered throughout the greater part of Cornwall. In 1086, it was held under the great count of Mortain (the half-brother of William the Conqueror) by Osfers, a Saxon landowner of some standing, who had held Lantyne, together with other manors, before the Conquest. Within the manor, and in the parish of St Sampson in Golant, lies the earthwork known as Castle Dore, which forms the subject of this note.

The early seventh-century life of St Sampson records that a monastery was founded in Cornwall by the saint. This life was written about half a century after his death; among those cited as authorities for the information included in it is Henoc, a cousin of the saint and a deacon, who had lived nearly eighty years in the monastery. The account of the foundation speaks of the site as alongside a river, near a cave, in which the saint had subdued a dragon. The location and the general account of his activities in Cornwall, fits Golant, but not Southill, the only other Cornish church under the patronage of St Sampson. The evidence is sufficient to prove that a monastery named in honour of the saint existed in Cornwall in the seventh century and that it was probably at Golant.

Shortly after the Norman Conquest, Richard Fitz Turold, the lord of Cardinham, founded the Benedictine priory of St Andrew of Tywardraeth, a dependency of the great abbey of St Sergius and Bacchus at Angers. Among the possessions granted to the new priory were the church of Tywardraeth, with the chapelry of St Sampson in Golant. This remained the position till the early sixteenth century, when the parishioners of St Sampson rebuilt their church and freed themselves from their dependence on Tywardraeth. No one acquainted with this area and writing after the foundation of the priory of St Andrew would place a ceremony such as that described by Beroul in any church except that of the priory. It is therefore clear that Beroul was relying on a source which dated before the Norman Conquest, *i.e.*, not later than the early eleventh century, and that the story of Tristram and Iseult had been localised in Cornwall as early as this date. A reversal of the relative positions of Tywardraeth and St Sampson could well have taken place, either as a result of the disturbance to church holdings which is clearly recorded in *Domesday Book* (1086), or at an early date in the ninth century when the Saxon conquest of Cornwall disturbed the Celtic ecclesiastical organisation.

One other monument in the area is relevant to the association with the romance and the understanding of Castle Dore. A mile north-west of Fowey and about two miles south of the earthwork, a reset monolith, some seven feet high, stands in the centre of the road, opposite the lodge gates of Menabilly. It was first recorded lying by the roadside about two hundred yards further north. On one face is an inscription in two lines running vertically downwards:

Ill. 37

DRUSTANUS HIC IACIT
FILIUS CUNOMORI

(Tristram lies here, the son of Cynvawr.)* Epigraphically, a date in the middle of the sixth century may be accepted; it is the gravestone of a chieftain or of a scion of the royal house.

Though the manuscript sources for the royal house of Dumnonia —the British kingdom of which Cornwall was part—are not older than the twelfth century, there is no reason to doubt that they are based on a good tradition. The kings in the sixth century are Cynvawr, Constantine (the ruler denounced by Gildas, who wrote about 545), Erbin and Gereint, who was a contemporary of a number of heroes of the late sixth century and whose name is mentioned in connection with the battle of Catraeth in *c.* 600. The death of Cynvawr would fall in the second quarter of the sixth century, and that of a son might be expected about the middle of the century or a little later. It is therefore possible that the individual commemorated on the monolith was a son of the Cynvawr who was king of Dumnonia, and a brother of Constantine, Cynvawr's successor.

The name Tristram is Pictish in origin, and Welsh tradition makes him a son of Tallwch—also a Pictish name. Drust son of Talorcan is a Pictish king of the late eighth century. The name in its older

---

*'Drustanus' is the sixth-century form of the name which becomes 'Tristram' or 'Tristan' in the romances.

Ill. 43. Tristram playing the harp for
King Mark on a tile from Chertsey
Abbey.

forms had been taken over by the British as early as the sixth
century, and is known in south-west Scotland as well as in Cornwall.
Mark is also known to Welsh tradition. He is associated with Tristram

Ill. 43   and is March son of Meirchyawn (Mark, son of Marcianus). These are
British names and the same tradition regarded him as a ruler in Wales.
Breton tradition, recorded in the life of St Pol written by Wrmonoc,
a monk of Landevennec, at the end of the ninth century, mentions a
famous king Mark, whom by another name they call Cynvawr. This
Cynvawr or Commorius is a well-known figure in Breton hagio-
graphy and folklore; he is a wicked opponent of the saints. There is
no reason to doubt that he was a real ruler in sixth-century Brittany
and his power, like that of earlier rulers, may well have extended to

both sides of the Channel. That the Commorius of Breton tradition was the same as the Cynvawr recorded in the royal house of Dumnonia is a reasonable conjecture, but no other source suggests that he was also named Mark, still less that he is to be identified with the King Mark of the romances.

The transfer of stories from one part to another of the Celtic world is a well-known feature of the earlier Middle Ages. Heroes of these tales were localised in various places to suit the convenience of the bards or of their patrons. So many of the links have been lost that it is impossible to be sure of the original identity of any of these persons. But the combination of so many indications around Lantyne creates the possibility—it is no more—that the historical characters that lie behind the most moving of the medieval romances were associated with this district. It was these considerations that led the Cornwall Excavation Committee to undertake excavations at Castle Dore in 1935 and 1936.

Castle Dore lies on the east side of an ancient trackway running from Bodmin down the spine of the peninsula to the sea at Pridmouth. The trackway had been used, though on a rather different alignment, as a transpeninsular road as early as the Early Bronze Age at the beginning of the second millennium B C. In its later form (now B.3269) it is marked by a series of crosses, dating from the ninth to the eleventh century. Castle Dore, three miles inland from Fowey, or from the older landing place at Pridmouth, is the principal earthwork in the district. It lies in the parish of St Sampson in Golant and on the manor of Lantyne.

The excavations proved that the earthwork had a long history. It was first thrown up in the pre-Roman Iron Age, as early as the third or even the fourth century B C. This settlement lasted down to the beginning of the Christian era; there was no trace of occupation during the Roman period, which began in Cornwall in the last quarter of the first century A D and lasted for some 350 years. There was a substantial reoccupation in the sub-Roman age, covering the fifth, sixth and seventh centuries. A slight occupation in the twelfth or thirteenth century was attested by pottery, but could not be associated with structural remains.

The earthwork has two defences, each consisting of a bank about eight feet high with a deep outer ditch. These two ramparts are adjacent on the upper side where they reach the summit of the ridge

III. 39

and give an outlook to the further side. The enclosure lay entirely on the eastern slope, where the ramparts gradually diverge, forming an outer defence or barbican, which covers and strengthens the entrance lying at the lowest point of the circuit. The plan dates entirely from the pre-Roman age. Below the earthwork is a larger enclosure with a very slight bank. It can have been no more than a corral or a hayfield; its date is unknown.

The deserted pre-Roman site, which had lain derelict for about 400 years, was reoccupied and perhaps refortified in the fifth or sixth century. The evidence for refortification is of the slightest. North of the gate a stretch of the inner rampart was uncovered, showing a rough revetment of dry stone added to the old bank at a point about half way down the inner slope. The revetment was cut into the core of old bank at a date when this had already spread; it was undated, but unlikely to belong to any other period than the fifth or sixth century. No trace of a similar refortification was found in any of the other trenches cut across the rampart. This is hardly surprising when the much denuded and overgrown state of the banks is considered. The tracing of such revetments now standing only a few inches in height, or of the post-holes which might be expected to accompany them,* is seldom possible. The slight revetment found north of the gate may be tentatively interpreted as the rearward toe of a bank with an internal slope leading up to a level fighting platform retained by a more substantial facing of timber and dry-stone, of which all trace has disappeared. Such is what might be expected round the dwelling of a Celtic chieftain of the sub-Roman age.

Through the gateway a roughly cobbled road had been formed on top of some two feet of fallen rubbish from the pre-Roman gate. Within and overlooking the inner end of the road on the south side was a small oval platform, measuring 24 feet by 18 and revetted in dry walling. This again lay over the spread debris of the earlier rampart. It may be explained as the base of a look-out, perhaps the site from which the watchmen blew their horns.

---

*Post-holes are important archaeological clues. They are places in the ground where wooden posts were originally set up, to support a structure of some kind. The wood of the posts has rotted away, yet the remains of decayed timber and packing material are visible as dark patches when the turf and topsoil have been taken off. An archaeologist once said: 'There are few things more difficult to destroy than a hole in the ground.' By plotting post-holes on a chart we can sometimes make out the plan of a vanished wall or building.

The interior was circular, some 220 feet across; about one third of the area, mainly on the south side, was uncovered. Two wooden buildings were located and almost completely explored. A third was found on the north side but could not be fully stripped.

The principal building was a large hall, measuring over-all 90 feet by 40. The floor had been completely destroyed by medieval and later ploughing, leaving a series of stone-lined post-holes as the only structural indications. These holes were arranged in irregular lines running both longitudinally and transversely. The plan indicated an aisled hall of three bays with the aisle returned along one end. Posts on the central line indicated direct supports for the ridge. The aisles were narrow, less than half the width of the main space. On the north side, a porch was set in front of the central bay facing the space into which the entrance roadway led. At the back, a small rectangular annexe projected from one corner. The only internal feature that could be recovered was a hearth set near one end of the central space and off-centre to avoid the posts supporting the ridge. The irregularity of the setting of the uprights and the crooked lines suggest the use of ill-formed local timber for the horizontal members. The size of the posts, the majority squared and measuring between 10 and 14 inches, is evidence of a building of some size and distinction. While the complete destruction of the floor levels precludes any real possibility of reconstruction, it may be noted that the plan is consonant with what is known from literary sources in the Celtic world and with the remains still visible of the far greater hall at Tara.

A second hall was found. It measured over-all 65 feet by 35 and ran transversely across one end of the first, from which it was separated by a passage some 12 feet across. It lay nearer the summit of the enclosure and ploughing had proved more destructive. While the building was of the same type as the first, it was not possible to say more about it. A third building of the same character on the north side of the enclosure was uncovered only in a small trial trench. It was rather better preserved, with traces of a cobbled floor.

Two small settings of post-holes of the same character were rectangular, one measuring 7 feet by 5. By analogy with earlier structures, they should probably be interpreted as granaries for seed corn, which would be stored in large containers set on raised platforms. The corn for use was probably parched.

The dating of the structures was established not only by the fact that they arose when the pre-Roman site, which became disused in the first century, had long been deserted, but also by scanty finds of

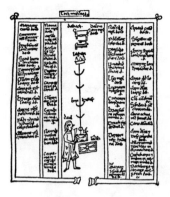

Ill. 44. Plan of the Banqueting Hall at Tara, the palace of the early high kings of Ireland. Each of the compartments in the five aisles is marked to show the profession and grade of society appropriate to it, as well as the joint of meat allotted to the occupant at a banquet. The figure is a table attendant. The plan is given in the twelfth-century *Book of Leinster*. Irish kings, one of the most famous of whom was Niall-of-the-Nine-Hostages, frequently raided Britain in the later fourth century. The boy Patrick, the future apostle of Ireland, was captured in one of these raids. It was at Tara that Patrick later confronted Laoghaire, the high king, and his druids, when accused of lighting the Easter fire in defiance of the royal commands. The smaller hall at Castle Dore was a building of the same character as the hall of Tara.

pottery of the period ranging from the fifth to seventh century. The evidence that Castle Dore was occupied as a chieftain's residence at this date is conclusive and the identification as the court (*llys*) of Cynvawr can hardly be avoided. Whether we may go further, and claim that it was the dwelling of King Mark and the original Lancien of Beroul and other poets of the full Middle Ages, cannot be conclusively proved on the evidence available.

4 Wales in the Arthurian Age

Leslie Alcock

THE PHASE OF BRITISH HISTORY that includes Arthur was above all an era of formation. During well over a century, from about AD 370 onward, the complex group of nations which now inhabits the British Isles was coming into being. Anglo-Saxons and kindred Germanic migrants were laying the foundations of England. The Scotti, or northern Irish, were moving into the nearer part of what is now Scotland, and establishing the kingdom which ultimately absorbed the Picts. Other Irishmen were settling—either by force or as an act of Roman military policy—in south-west Wales. Meanwhile, the Britons of the west were becoming Welsh or Cornish, or were migrating to the land that came to be called Brittany after them.

All this was accompanied by the decline and eventual collapse of Roman authority. But the decline in the material power of Rome was balanced by a new spiritual influence; for this was also the period when the British Isles were effectively Christianised by men like Patrick and David, Columba and Augustine of Canterbury.

Creative and fascinating as the whole epoch is, its detailed history is extremely obscure. That is one reason why we sometimes speak of the 'dark ages'. Nowhere has the darkness of the fifth and sixth centuries been deeper than in Wales. Only the scantiest of contemporary records have come down to us. In default of adequate literary evidence, it might have been hoped that archaeology would help to fill out the picture. But, until the middle 1950s, even our archaeological data were severely limited. We had a good knowledge of the Christian memorial stones scattered through the Welsh counties, which bear witness to the Christianity of the time. Yet the relevance even of these for social history had not been worked out. Besides the stones, we had a few very fragmentary ecclesiastical remains. But of secular sites, of the settlements of the people, we had no certain knowledge. The few alleged facts were grounded on

Ill. 46

79

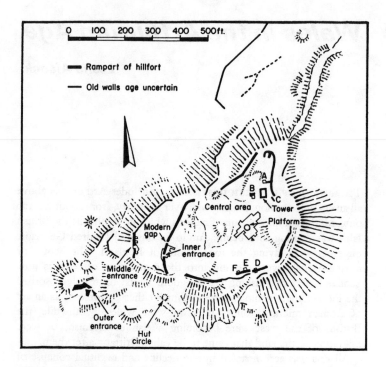

Ill. 45. Plan of the hill-top fortifications of Dinas Emrys. It shows the defensive wall surrounding the summit of a craggy hill with two lower outworks protecting the approach from the west. The main dark-age occupation was concentrated around the platform which was built in a swampy hollow. The tower is a small twelfth-century keep. The letters 'A' to 'F' show excavated areas.

dubious arguments. Thus, there was a tendency to assign a dark-age date to anything anomalous or degenerate, whether pottery or fortifications, merely because it was anomalous or degenerate.

Since the mid-1950s, however, new information has dramatically changed the state of affairs; and one of the first steps forward was the direct result of testing a tradition connected with Arthur—or, at least, with the train of events which is said to have led up to him. In 1954–56, Dr H. N. Savory of the National Museum of Wales undertook, on behalf of the Caernarvonshire Historical Society, to excavate the hill-top fortifications of Dinas Emrys in Snowdonia. The Welsh personal name Emrys is derived from Ambrosius. Welsh authors give it to Ambrosius Aurelianus himself, and since at least the ninth century Dinas Emrys has been associated with this precursor of Arthur in British leadership. While Dr Savory's work did not prove that Ambrosius lived there, it did prove that a British chief, whether he or another, was in possession toward the close of the fifth century, enjoying a measure of luxury and wealth.

Other probings of dark-age topographic lore were equally fruitful. During 1954, Mr A. H. A. Hogg, the Secretary of the Royal Commission on Ancient Monuments in Wales and Monmouthshire, excavated Garn Boduan. This is a hill-fort in Caernarvonshire with a name recalling or commemorating the sixth-century chieftain Buan. Here too traces were found of occupation at about the right time, though on a small scale. Within decayed Iron Age ramparts enclosing twenty-eight acres, there was a post-Roman stone-walled fort of rather less than half an acre.

Another Welshman belonging to roughly the same period as Buan, and of greater fame, is King Maelgwn of Gwynedd, or north-western Wales. He is the most notable of the five British rulers denounced by Gildas. His life probably overlapped Arthur's, and he is stated to have died of plague about AD 547. When various legendary frills (such as his holding the first Eisteddfod) are stripped from Maelgwn's history, there remains a hard core suggesting that an alleged fortress of his, Degannwy Castle, actually was a centre of power in the sixth century. As at Dinas Emrys and Garn Boduan, archaeology has supported tradition.

At Degannwy the research was sponsored by the Board of Celtic Studies of the University of Wales, in association with the Caernarvonshire Historical Society, and was directed by myself. Degannwy stands on the east bank of the Conway. This river is a major dividing line, both geographic and cultural. Eastward is country now highly Anglicised, penetrated anciently by Saxon and Norman. On the west, one enters *Pura Wallia*, the heart and citadel of the land of the Welsh princes. The river frontier, an impressive barrier in itself, is overlooked at its northern end by two craggy hills of great natural strength. They form the site of *arx Decantorum, castrum de Gannoc*, Degannwy Castle.

My attention was first drawn to the rich potentialities of the site by Mr Hogg. Excavations were carried out for a total of fourteen weeks over the years 1961–66. The main feature is the castle of Henry III,

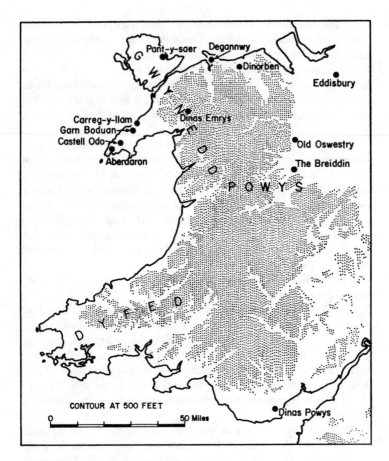

Ill. 46. Map of Wales showing the dark-age kingdoms of Gwynedd, Powys and Dyfed and the sites mentioned in the text.

savagely pulled to pieces in 1263 by Llywelyn ap Gruffydd. But underlying Henry's castle are traces of previous inhabitants, going back to some sort of Roman occupation in the third century and perhaps beyond.

Ill. 47

The remains of the age of Maelgwn include about a dozen sherds of east Mediterranean amphorae of Tintagel class B, datable to the late fifth or sixth century. To judge from its inscribed memorial stones, Maelgwn's dynasty, the Venedotian, was the most cultured and

Romanised in Wales. The apparent importation of Mediterranean wine confirms this view. Yet if Degannwy was a principal seat of the dynasty, as tradition asserts, the paucity of the imported pottery calls for comment. Much larger amounts of the same ware have been found at comparatively insignificant places. Clearly, the quantity of ceramic refuse found by the archaeologist is no safe index of the social status of a site. Indeed, a tempting interpretation offers itself which suggests an inverse relationship: the more sophisticated the status, the greater the cleanliness observed, and the less the archaeologically interesting filth that is littered around.

Did Degannwy's post-Roman occupation grow, without a break, out of its use as a stronghold in Roman times? Continuity cannot be proved, because in western Britain there is as yet no known material basis for dating anything between the last Romano-British coins and the beginning of the Tintagel imports. However, the Roman presence

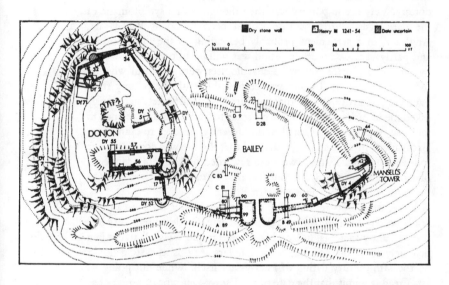

Ill. 47. Plan of Degannwy Castle, Caernarvonshire, showing the excavations carried out in 1961–66. It is probable that the citadel of King Maelgwn of Gwynedd occupied the higher of the two hills on which the castle is built and which was later used as the donjon of the medieval castle. Apart from the natural protection provided by precipitous crags the higher hill was also defended by a drystone wall of which traces were found on the eastern flanks in cuts DY-1 and 31. It is possible that the low ground between the two hills— the bailey of the medieval castle— was used for a settlement of serfs or bondmen in the dark age.

at Degannwy is attested by a coin series running from Gallienus (260–68) to Valens (364–78). It is natural to think that this late Roman use of a hill-top fortification—paralleled elsewhere in Wales—reflects unsettled conditions caused by Irish raiding. But a dry-stone wall which may be no later than the second century implies that even the occupation marked by the coins was not the first. The 'Arthurian' kings at Degannwy rooted themselves in a long British and Roman past.

Despite these successes, it should not be supposed that all research directed toward the dark ages has actually led there, or, conversely, that all dark-age discovery was planned as such. Before asking in detail what the three sites disclose, we must consider several others where the facts emerged more deviously.

One that used to be assigned to this period was the small hill-top settlement of Castell Odo, near the tip of the Lleyn peninsula. A bad excavation in the early 1930s produced a single sherd of very crude pottery. Very crude pottery was then thought to be symptomatic of the dark ages—partly because it had been found at Pant-y-saer, Anglesey, in a settlement probably belonging to the fifth century, and partly because no other period was willing to own it. However, by the middle 1950s, several archaeologists were doubtful whether the Castell Odo sherd really was comparable with the pottery from Pant-y-saer. In 1958, the Caernarvonshire Historical Society generously asked me to pick a site of my own choice for excavation. It seemed to me that the date of Castell Odo urgently needed re-examining. Excavations in 1958 and 1959 showed that the site was not a dark-age foundation at all. Instead, we were rewarded with an abundant haul of Iron Age pottery of the fourth century BC, probably referable to the earliest migrations into western Britain.

The Castell Odo results have cast serious doubt on the value of crude pottery as diagnostic of a dark-age date. Crude pottery very like that of Pant-y-saer has, in fact, been found in the Welsh Marches in a definitely Iron Age context. Some scholars see this as casting doubt on the fifth-century dating of Pant-y-saer itself. While not going so far, I readily admit that the date of the Pant-y-saer type of pottery has become an open question.

Castell Odo was a case where a clue pointing to the dark ages (though, to be fair, not a clue based on tradition) turned out to be false. On the other hand, the richest of all Welsh harvests from this period was gathered accidentally, and before some of those already mentioned, at a site explored with a wholly different object: Dinas

uuc tout eftour merueuloufe

lac qui puib lefpee le roy artu

vant g*les voit que

Ills. 3–5. According to Geoffrey of Monmouth, Arthur reigned over the wealthiest and most civilised kingdom in Christendom. The legendary Roman emperor Lucius demanded that Arthur pay tribute to Rome and Arthur took an army to Gaul where he defeated Lucius (*Ill. 3,*). It seems certain that Geoffrey was interweaving the history of Maximus, who in 383 was proclaimed emperor by the army in Britain and who proceeded to hold western Europe and even captured Rome. It has been suggested that 'Lucius' is the Latinised version of a Welsh 'Llwch' and that Geoffrey's ultimate source was a Welsh tradition of a battle between Arthur and a Welsh champion. In Geoffrey's history, after Arthur defeated Lucius he advanced towards Rome but was recalled to Britain by the rebellion of his nephew Modred whom he met and killed at the battle of Camlann. The illustration of this battle (*Ill. 5,* overleaf) is from the fifteenth-century *St Albans Chronicle.* In other versions, including Malory's, Modred's rebellion follows a long period of peace during which Arthur and his knights have brought prosperity and a high order of chivalry to the realm. In these versions, the collapse of the Round Table and all it symbolises is directly connected with the love between Guinevere and Sir Lancelot. At the battle of Camlann Modred is killed and Arthur is mortally wounded. He commands Sir Bedevere to cast away his fabulous sword, Excalibur, which was made for him by the Lady of the Lake. Bedevere, captivated by the sword's beauty, twice hesitates to obey but eventually complies with the king's order and the sword is caught by the Lady of the Lake (*Ill. 4,*). Arthur is

then borne away to Avalon, which tradition associates with Glastonbury, to be healed. In this fourteenth-century illustration from the manuscript of *Le Roman de Lancelot du Lac et de la Mort du Roi Artu*, the wounded king is depicted hunched in the foreground.

Ill. 8. The Round Table in the hall of Winchester Castle (*cf. Ill. 7*). This oaken table, eighteen feet in diameter, is first mentioned by the chronicler Hardyng (about 1450) who believed it to have been Arthur's. The table may have been made as early as the thirteenth century—most probably for one of the medieval festivities known as a Round Table which were held in imitation of the feasts of Arthur and his knights. Another theory is that it was made as a 'wheel of fortune' for Henry III. It would seem that it was first decorated in Henry VII's reign and it is possible that it was the presence of this table that led Henry to ordain that his son be born at Winchester and christened Arthur in 1486. Henry VIII is known to have displayed it to the emperor Charles V in 1522. The Tudor rose in the centre and the twenty-four alternating spokes in white and green—the Tudor colours—demonstrate the Tudor claim to descent from Arthur.

Ill. 9. A distinctive feature of the Matter of Britain was its religious aspect: the Holy Grail and the quest for the mysterious vessel. The concept of the Grail is a bewildering one. It seems to contain elements from Irish sagas of mortal heroes who are feasted from a horn of plenty at palaces of gods, and of Welsh versions of a waste land which can be delivered only through the healing of the wounded king. Other symbols are often associated with the Grail: frequently a bleeding lance and sword. These symbols, as well as the stories of a wounded king of a stricken kingdom, reveal the presence in the Grail concept of pagan fertility beliefs that the reproductive forces of nature are intimately connected with the potency of the ruler. Christian elements were early introduced into the Grail legends, such as the identification of the Grail with the cup used by Christ at the Last Supper, and of Joseph of Arimathea – the custodian of Christ's body – with the wounded king. In the early thirteenth-century *Queste del Saint Graal*, in which the Grail is a symbol of divine grace, specific correspondences can be seen between the story and the mystical doctrines of St Bernard of Clairvaux concerning the problems of the role of grace, of transubstantiation and the part of human freedom in salvation. In some versions of the quest for the Grail it is Perceval who achieves it, but in the best known and most influential, including Malory's, it is Galahad.

Galahad is the son of Lancelot and Elaine, the daughter of Pelles, keeper of the Grail Castle and a descendant of Joseph of Arimathea. Galahad is born after Lancelot has been magically deceived, by Pelles and a sorceress, into believing Elaine is Guinevere. It was necessary that Elaine have a child by the greatest knight in the world because it had been foretold that only such a child could deliver the land from its troubles and achieve the Grail. On the 454th Pentecost, Galahad was presented to Arthur's court by an old man. The old man led Galahad to the Siege Perilous on which appeared the words: 'This is the siege of Galahad, the haut prince.' Galahad then passed a further test by removing a sword from a stone which had appeared floating above a river. At the feast at the Round Table that evening, the Holy Grail appeared, covered with white samite and passed through the hall 'and every knight had such meats and drinks as he best loved in all the world'. As the Grail had been covered, none of the knights had seen the vessel itself and after it had departed they each took a vow to search for it in order to see it 'more openly than it has been seen here'. Arthur, however, was displeased because he realised that the quest for the Grail would mean the breakup of the Round Table and the dispersal forever of 'the truest of knighthood that ever were seen together in any realm of the world'.

telle maniere que nulz deulz, nauoit pou
oir de parler anne se regardoient auffi
comme ceulz fuffent tous beftes, muees·
Lors entre leans le fainc graal couuert
dun blanc famie, mais il ny ot oncques
cellui qui peuft veoir qui le portoit Si vint
par my le urant huye du palaie·

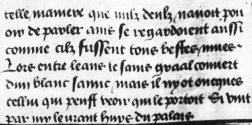

T maintenant quil yfut entrez
fu le palaie rempliz de fi bonne
odeure que fi toutes lee efpices
du monde y feuffent entrees et efpandue
et il afa tout entour le palaie dune part
et dautre et tout ainfi comme il paffort p
deuant lee tablee eftoient tout mainte n
rempliee endroit chun fieye de telle viande
comme chun defiroit Et filz furent feruiz

Ill. 16. A fourth-century floor mosaic from a Roman villa at Hinton St Mary, Dorset, *in situ*. The male head, with the Chi-Rho monogram, the Christian symbol, behind it is undoubtedly meant to be a representation of Christ. It is not only probably the earliest known representation of Christ made in Britain but is also the only known picture of Christ in a mosaic floor in the Roman Empire. The mosaic indicates the degree of luxury reached by Roman civilisation in Britain. It is the collapse of this civilisation which Gildas laments, and its 'barbarian' successors whom he excoriates. Arthur probably defended what remained of the Roman tradition against the heathen Saxons.

Ill. 16. A fourth-century floor mosaic from a Roman villa at Hinton St Mary, Dorset, *in situ*. The male head, with the Chi-Rho monogram, the Christian symbol, behind it is undoubtedly meant to be a representation of Christ. It is not only probably the earliest known representation of Christ made in Britain but is also the only known picture of Christ in a mosaic floor in the Roman Empire. The mosaic indicates the degree of luxury reached by Roman civilisation in Britain. It is the collapse of this civilisation which Gildas laments, and its 'barbarian' successors whom he excoriates. Arthur probably defended what remained of the Roman tradition against the heathen Saxons.

Ills. 17–22, previous page. Towards the end of the third century, Britain was the centre of an imperial crisis. An admiral, Marcus Aurelius Carausius, set himself up as 'Emperor of Western Rome' *c.* 286 and minted coins in London (*Ill. 17*, upper left corner). Equipped with a fleet he drove off Saxon pirates from the British shores. He died in 293 and was replaced by another usurper, Allectus (*Ill. 18*).

The emperor Constantius Chlorus finally defeated Allectus and recaptured Britain, striking a commemorative medallion (*Ill. 19*, centre right, bottom right), with the motto REDDITOR LUCIS AETERNAE (Restorer of the Eternal Light) and depicting London at his feet. He restored the economy and protected the coast with a series of forts. His son, Constantine the Great, was proclaimed emperor by the army of Britain at York in 306. By 367 the imperial system, under the pressure of forays and invasions by Saxons, Picts and Scots, had suffered such setbacks that it never entirely recovered. Gildas dates the crucial break with the system to 383 when the army named Magnus Maximus (*Ill. 21*, top centre), a Spaniard, emperor in protest against the weakness and corruption of the Roman administration. Maximus asserted his claim throughout western Europe and captured Rome. He was eventually defeated in Italy, in 388, by Theodosius, the emperor of the east. Maximus's impact upon Britain, however, was permanent. It is said that the British settlement of Armorica, the future Brittany, began under his auspices. He survives in Welsh and Cornish folklore as Prince Macsen. After his death imperial rule was never completely restored in Britain. Invasions from Ireland continued and Gildas speaks of British appeals for help. The imperial general Stilicho (*Ill. 20*, panel, bottom left) was sent, *c.* 399, in response to one of these appeals and he temporarily drove back the barbarians. After his departure and many internal coups, the army in 406 proclaimed its own emperor, Constantine III (*Ill. 22*, top right) who figures in Geoffrey of Monmouth and in Welsh legend as 'Bendigeit Custennin'.

Ill. 25. Liddington Castle, an Iron
Age hill-fort near Swindon, which
was possibly Mount Badon, the
site of Arthur's decisive victory over
the Saxons.

Ill. 26. In the middle of the fifth century, the most powerful British chieftain was Vortigern. He adopted a policy of permitting colonies of barbarians to settle in Britain and used them as military auxiliaries. The policy proved disastrous as the colonists fell out with the ruler and Vortigern's regime was destroyed by mercenaries and new invaders. Giraldus Cambrensis speaks of a Merlin, 'called Ambrosius, who prophesied in the time of King Vortigern'. The illustration from Peter Langtoft's *Chronicle of England* shows a royal consultation with Merlin.

Ill. 27. Lancelot rescues Guinevere in an illustration from a French manuscript dated 1274. The manuscript, which contains the third part of the *Lancelot*, the *Queste* and the *Mort Artu*, is the earliest dated Arthurian manuscript now known. It contains ninety-five miniatures.

The illustrator was guided in part by rubrics above the panel space but he did not always fulfil the written requirements. Thus, although the flames which were to burn the adulterous queen are roughly suggested at the right of the picture, Guinevere herself is omitted.

Ill. 29. Tintagel Castle from the mainland looking toward the 'island'. The lower ward, on the mainland, is on the distant cliff at upper left. A modern path drops from the ward, crosses the narrow ridge of land which joins mainland and 'island', and rises to the inner ward, the ruins of which are outlined against the sky.

Ills. 30–32. The aerial view of Tintagel reveals how the sea has all but eroded the headland or 'island' away from the mainland, leaving only a slender ridge between them. To the left on the upper plateau the narrow white rectangle marks the site of the medieval chapel (*Ill. 41*) which partly overlay the Celtic monastery (Site A on plan, *Ill. 42*). The larger white rectangle in the centre is the site of the medieval walled garden (Site E). To the right is the complex of agricultural buildings (Site D). The Iron Gate (*Ill. 33*) is in the lower foreground and the locations of other monastic buildings can be seen on the terraces (Sites B, C and F). Parts of the upper and lower wards (plan, *Ill. 40*) have collapsed into the sea. The white escarpment in *31*, top right, shows where they have fallen away with the cliff. The precipitous path leads from the lower ward to the inner ward on the 'island' itself. The archway at the rear of the inner ward (lower left foreground) is also visible in *30* as a small white triangle in the rear wall of the inner ward from which a path leads to the excavations along the terraces. The remains of the interior of the inner ward are shown in *Ill. 32*, right, with the mainland in the background and the archway at left. The right-angled foundations at the far right are those of the walls of the Great Hall, a twelfth-century building which stood within the inner ward. The southern end has fallen over the cliff but what is preserved is nevertheless eighty-eight feet long. The roof of the hall was dismantled early in the fourteenth century and a series of buildings were erected upon the site.

Ill. 33, above. The Iron Gate guarded a cleft in the rocks on the north-western shore of the 'island' which served as an ancient landing place (see also *Ills. 30, 42*). The spot is sheltered from the prevailing westerly winds. A path ran from the sea about fifty feet up the cliff where further access was controlled by a curtain wall. The path led through an archway which was formerly closed by an iron gate from which the wall is named. There was a wall-walk behind the curtain, protected by a battlemented parapet with slits for arrows. The whole dates from the middle of the thirteenth century. Above the wall is Site B, and to the left Site F.

Ills. 34–36, right. *Ills. 34* and *35* show reconstructed bowls of Tintagel class A-I and A-II; *Ill. 36* shows sherds of Tintagel class A-I pottery with a decoration of impressed crosses. Pottery which is classified by the Tintagel system is known to have originated in the eastern Mediterranean. It demonstrates the existence of trade with the Mediterranean in the period following the severance of the political links between Rome and Britain in the early fifth century. This trade continued until it was interrupted by the Muslim conquest of North Africa in the seventh century. Tintagel ware, now one of the most important factors in the dating of British sites of this period, is also found at Dinas Powys, Cadbury and Glastonbury Tor among other sites (*Ills. 53, 54, 62, 86–89, 105*). Tintagel A ware is a fine red pottery and was probably used as tableware or for liturgical purposes as the presence of impressed symbols suggests (*Ills. 36, 53, 62*). Tintagel B ware is coarser and was used for large vessels containing wine, oil and possibly other imports.

Ill. 37, left. Tristram's stone. This monolith, some seven feet high, now stands opposite the lodge gates of Menabilly, near Fowey, Cornwall, about two miles from the earthwork known as Castle Dore (*Ill. 39*). The monument was originally discovered lying by the roadside about two hundred yards to the north of its present location. On one face of the stone is an inscription reading: DRUSTANUS HIC IACIT FILIUS CUNOMORI (Tristram lies here, the son of Cynvawr). The stone unquestionably marked the grave of a chieftain, or the scion of the royal family. On epigraphical evidence it may be dated to the middle of the sixth century. One of the sixth-century kings of Dumnonia – the kingdom of which Cornwall was a part – was Cynvawr (*c.* 540). Drustanus is the sixth-century form of the name which becomes 'Tristram' or 'Tristan' in the romances.

Ill. 38. The sixteenth-century church of St Sampson in Golant, Cornwall, which is built near the site of an earlier monastery. A monastery of St Sampson is associated with King Mark, Tristram and Iseult in the versions of the story by the twelfth-century Anglo-Norman poet Beroul. Mark resides at Lancien, the name of which is preserved in the modern farm of Lantyne in the parish of St Sampson. The farm is the successor of the medieval manor of that name on which is located the earthwork of Castle Dore (*Ill. 39*). Beroul describes a ceremony, in which Iseult takes part, at the monastery of St Sampson. The oldest surviving versions of the Tristram and Iseult tales date from the twelfth century, but Welsh and Breton references show that the stories were known to the Celts far earlier. Sampson was a sixth-century saint and it is known that a monastery founded by him and named in his honour existed in Cornwall in the seventh century. The monastery was probably at Golant.

Ill. 39. The Castle Dore earthwork on the ridge three miles north of Fowey, Cornwall, was erected at least as early as the third century BC. It was occupied until the last quarter of the first century AD, then abandoned until the fifth century from which time it was reoccupied for several generations.

Ills. 50-52, opposite. Early Christian memorial stones from Wales. *Ill. 50,* left, shows two sides of a stone on Penmachno in Caernarvonshire which reads: 'Cantiorix lies here. He was a citizen of Gwynedd [and] cousin of Maglos the Magistrate.' Gwynedd was the kingdom of Maelgwn, whose seat was at Degannwy Castle and was the most Romanised of the Welsh kingdoms. Maelgwn was one of five contemporary princes whom Gildas denounced and he came in for the most scathing criticism. Gildas refers to him as 'Insularis draco' (the dragon of the island) and says that he was foremost in evil as well as in military strength. *Ill. 51,* below, shows the stone in memory of Cadman, an early seventh-century king of Gwynedd of Maelgwn's dynasty. The inscription reads: 'Catamanus rex sapientisimus opinatisimus omnium regum'. 'Sapiens', in this context, means, even more than 'wise', 'learned' and learned in the classical Latin. A king of this period could have had access to classical writings as the Celtic monasteries were storehouses of classical manuscripts. *Ill. 52,* right , shows the memorial stone set up to Voteporix, prince of Dyfed and reads: 'Memoria Voteporigis Protictoris'. His name also appears on the stone in the Ogam script in its Goidelic form 'Votecorigas'. Although Voteporix is here called 'protector', Gildas describes him as a deceitful, foolish king, a murderer and an adulterer.

53

54

Ills. 53, 54. Sherds of pottery found at Dinas Powys. The fragments of only one ornamented bowl were found at this site, but the bowl is unique in the British Isles for its pattern of running leopards (*Ill. 53*, top, and reconstruction *Ill. 62*).
The bowl is of Tintagel class A, late Roman stamped ware from the eastern Mediterranean. This and other bowls were presumably used for serving food and drink. Other pottery vessels were imported simply as containers, or amphorae, for wine and oil. These were decorated with parallel grooves and ridges, as in the sherd in *Ill. 54*, which is of Tintagel class B.

Ill. 55. Sherds of scrap glass (top row, right) were also found at Dinas Powys. The nature of these sherds shows that no glass vessels were ever brought to the stronghold. What was imported, from Teutonic sources, was scrap glass, intended for melting down to make beads and vitreous inlays for bronze brooches. Three glass beads (bottom row, top right) are shown beneath the sherds. The bead at the left is coated in gold leaf and was probably made in Coptic Egypt.

Ills. 56, 57. Fragments of scrap metal from Dinas Powys (*Ill. 56*, right). At the bottom right is a piece from a lead die used for forming the moulds for making brooches. *Ill. 57*, below, is a reconstruction of a Celtic pen-annular brooch of bronze with enamelled terminals made after the design of the die. The other pieces in *Ill. 56* are of bronze ripped from Anglo-Saxon or Teutonic brooches, belts and buckets. These were intended for melting down and re-casting.

57

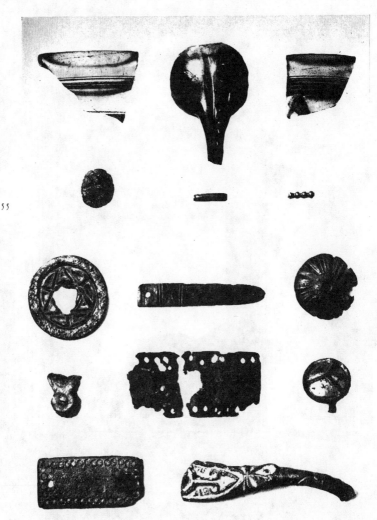

55

56

Ill. 64, left. Glastonbury Abbey. The view is west from the quire showing the crossing of the transept and the west end of the nave. The doorway led from the Galilee. The Lady Chapel is just visible beyond to the west. The Galilee was a porch on the west end of an abbey church and was named after the anthem 'When Christ Went Before Them Into Galilee'. This was sung on great festivals at the end of a circuit of the abbey buildings when the procession was remarshalled prior to the solemn re-entry into the church. The sign in the foreground of the photograph marks the site of the marble tomb in which the reputed remains of King Arthur and Queen Guinevere were reinterred in 1278. The abbey quire was erected between 1189 and 1214 and the nave was built during the next thirty years. The Lady Chapel was the first building erected after the fire of 1184 which destroyed the old abbey.

Ill. 65. South view of the late twelfth-century Lady Chapel and of the early fourteenth-century Galilee, linking the chapel and the great church, the west door of which is on the extreme right (*Ill. 65*).

Ills. 66–69. The grave in which Arthur's remains were found in 1190 lay fifty feet south of the third bay of the Lady Chapel. The grave lay between two 'pyramids', or tomb shrines, lying respectively forty and sixty feet south of the chapel. A modern trench revealed a major disturbance in the soil. This disturbance represents the hole made by the excavators of 1190 and refilled with the earth which had been dug up. The Hedda Stone (*Ill. 68,* top opposite page), an eighth-century shrine in Peterborough Cathedral, is the best preserved example in the country of a 'pyramid'. The Glastonbury 'pyramids' seem to have consisted of low partly underground chambers large enough to contain a coffin and marked by lofty standing crosses, like the shaft still in position in the churchyard in Bewcastle, Cumberland (*Ill. 69,* right opposite), which dates from the late seventh

century. *Ill. 67,* below right, opposite, shows a section of the early cemetery with graves like those in which the reputed bodies of Arthur and Guinevere were found. *Ill. 66,* top right, shows in the foreground the post-hole which held one of the main uprights of a wattled chapel. Further to the left are the paving slabs of a tenth-century building belonging to Dunstan's monastery (*c.* 940). A similar slab which lay over the post-hole has been removed.

Ill. 70, left, opposite. The site of Arthur's final tomb was discovered in 1931. All that remained was the base of the cavity, lined with fine ashlar. This has since been refilled and grassed over. The tomb itself was destroyed during the Reformation and the bones dispersed. The date of 1190 is now preferred for the original discovery of Arthur's body.

Ill. 71. Plan of Glastonbury Abbey (*Ill. 72*, page 99). Aerial view of Glastonbury Abbey. The view is from the south with the 'vale of Avalon' in the background. The walls and buildings in black on the plan are those which are still standing. From left to right on the photograph are the Lady Chapel and the Galilee; three bays of the south wall of the nave; the eastern piers of the crossing, and the remains of the quire. In the foreground are the remains of the cloister and of the refectory on its south side and some of the buildings of the east range.

Ill. 76. 'St Joseph's Well' now forms part of the late twelfth-century Lady Chapel. It was probably used for domestic and liturgical purposes from the earliest days of the monastery. The present name is not earlier than the late fifteenth century when Abbot Beere formed a new crypt under the Lady Chapel and the Galilee and dedicated it to Joseph of Arimathea.

Ill. 77. The Chalice Well, below, lies close to the Tor. It was fed by the most copious spring on the 'island'. The well-house dates from about 1200 when the spring was tapped to provide a better water supply for the abbey. The lining of the original shaft, some fifteen feet deep, is formed of huge blocks of blue lias which had originally served as quoins in the abbey church which was burned in 1184.

Ill. 78. Glastonbury Tor, dominated by the tower which is all that remains of the medieval church of St Michael. The usual explanation of the terraces on the slopes of the Tor is that they are either natural or the result of agriculture, *i.e.,* strip-lynchets. A recent theory, however, is that they are the remains of a three-dimensional maze constructed for religious purposes.

Ills. 83, 84. Excavations on Glastonbury Tor. *Ill. 83,* top, shows the
dark-age levels seen from the east
and reveals the weathering of the
natural bedrock. *Ill.* 84 shows the
pit and grave complex on the north
side of the summit seen from the
west. Part of the foundations of the
earliest church can be seen above and
to the right of the pit.

Ill. 85, above, shows the dark-age levels at the east-end complex seen from the north. Weathered ammonites and bones are scattered around the site.

Ill. 86, below. The cairn (*cf. Ill. 81*) found in the dark-age layer in the east-end complex. The purpose of the cairn is unknown. It has been suggested that it may have been a cenotaph, a bench, the foundation of some structure or an 'altar'.

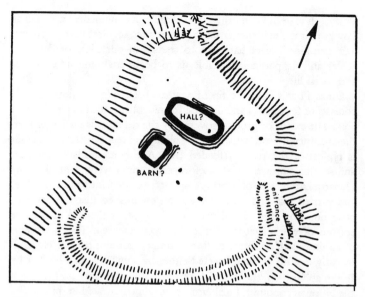

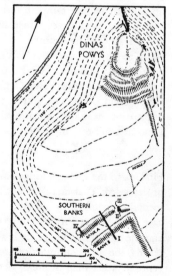

Ills. 48, 49. Plan of the site of Dinas Powys (Ill. 49, right). This hill-top stronghold was the seat of a Welsh prince or chief, a lesser contemporary of Arthur. Finds made here in the course of archaeological excavations are richer than those made at any other dark-age site in Wales. Traces of two buildings have been found (Ill. 48, above), the bigger of which is the largest dark-age dwelling so far discovered in Wales. It was probably the chief's hall. The smaller building was probably a barn or storehouse and perhaps slaves slept in it as well. The walls of the buildings have been conjecturally restored from the outline provided by the rock-cut drainage ditches which were dug around the buildings. The black spots represent hearths. Those by the barn were most likely used for domestic cooking. Those to the right of the hall were probably used for industrial purposes as iron slag and fragments of crucibles were found near them. The chief, his family and most important warriors presumably gathered around the hearth within the hall while his lesser retainers used the other end.

Powys, in eastern Glamorgan. It is largely in conjunction with Dinas Powys that the evidence from the other sites acquires its full weight. The combined effect has been to transform our ideas of dark-age Wales and, in particular, enable us to begin analysing its economy and social life.

Dinas Powys is at the tip of a whale-back ridge of limestone. It consists of four banks and ditches, formidably protecting a residential area. The extent of ground covered by the defences is far larger than the area they defend, which is only about 150 feet across. This layout is typical of the small defended Iron Age homesteads of the first and second centuries BC. Therefore, excavations were planned by my Department as part of a programme of research into the Iron Age, and carried out in 1954–58. We soon established that the defences were not Iron Age. But it was only in 1958, at the end of the five seasons of work, that their true character emerged. They were part of an unusually elaborate earth and timber castle of the late eleventh or early twelfth century, erected either by some Norman lord or by Iestyn ap Gorgan, the last Welsh prince of Glamorgan, on the eve of the Norman conquest. Furthermore, they incorporated in their make-up a much feebler rampart and ditch of the fifth century, together with a large quantity of refuse and debris from an occupation in that and the succeeding century.

So, to sum up, the known Welsh secular sites of the dark ages are now seven in number. We have Dinas Powys in Glamorgan; Dinas Emrys, Garn Boduan and Degannwy, all in Caernarvonshire; and Pant-y-saer in Anglesey. Besides these we can be fairly sure of dark-age occupation at Carreg-y-llam, also in Caernarvonshire, and at the Dinorben hill-fort in Denbighshire.

First, as to the external aspects. All the sites are more or less fortified or defended. That fact does not necessarily mean that dark-age settlement was confined to defended sites. More probably it reflects the ease with which fortifications can be recognised by archaeologists, and the attention which they have received from excavators. In other words, the list is an index of archaeological activity in the twentieth century rather than of life in the fifth and sixth centuries. Hence the prominence of Caernarvonshire, where the Royal Commission on Ancient Monuments has concentrated its work for some decades, and where the county's active Historical Society has sponsored research. The geographic imbalance of the list cannot yet be redressed.

Ills. 48, 49

Dark-age occupation has been claimed for a few hill-forts in the Marches, notably Eddisbury in Cheshire, Old Oswestry in Shropshire, and the Breiddin in Montgomery. But the case depends at present on the unsafe clue of crude pottery. Again, analogy with Ireland would suggest that the small circular earthworks of Dyfed, called 'raths', ought to belong to the period. But several 'raths' have been excavated without yielding sound evidence as to date.

Of the firmly acceptable sites, Dinorben is a normal Iron Age hill-fort which was later reused; there are traces of a circular house. The others contrast strongly with such forts, both in size and in scale. Iron Age defensive lines were often multiplied, with four or even five massive ramparts towering one above another. Often, also, they enclosed a large area: three acres or more in nearly half the instances, and occasionally twenty, thirty, even fifty. None of the dark-age enclosures covers more than two and a half acres, and the usual size is about half an acre. At Garn Boduan, with its tiny fort inside an enormous Iron Age rampart, the contrast is striking. The difference in size plainly reflects a difference in the social unit to be protected. The larger Iron Age forts contained numerous dwellings, housing a population at a relatively low level of wealth. They were the strongholds of tribes or clans. The small dark-age forts normally contain only one or two dwellings. In effect, they are fortified homesteads. At Dinas Powys and Dinas Emrys, the finds supply evidence of a certain wealth and luxury. Hence we may feel confident that these places are the dwellings of princes or lords, and maintain that interpretation of at least two of the other sites, Degannwy and Garn Boduan.

The actual defences are feeble by comparison with those of the Iron Age, and also with those of the earthen castles of the Normans and their Welsh imitators. It appears likely that fortified positions were not key points in the warfare of the time, and that attacks on them were not a major feature of strategy, the consequence being that no great pains were taken to strengthen them. This view is in harmony with the literary matter. Welsh chronicles record almost no attacks on castles or fortified places before 1093. The heroic poems of Taliesin and Aneirin give a picture of open, mobile warfare with mounted troops playing a large part. Of the battles listed by Nennius—three associated with a son of Vortigern, and twelve with Arthur—no less than nine are fought at river-crossings, and only two (the 'City of the Legion' and 'Castle Guinnion') are definitely in or near fortified places.

Thus, although these Welsh chieftains walled themselves in as a precautionary measure, they did it rather half-heartedly. Their homes were not strongholds in the same sense as a medieval castle.

To reconstruct their mode of life, archaeological and literary data must be brought together so as to shed light on each other. Some information can also be gleaned from the early Christian memorial stones. These are memorials of the upper classes, both lay and ecclesiastical. They carry brief inscriptions, not in British or Old Welsh, but in Latin written in Roman script, or Old Irish written in the curious Ogam script, or both. Irish influence also appears in the form of the monuments themselves, which are usually rough monoliths of undressed stone. At some point, Irishmen must have held an important position in society, especially in the kingdom of Dyfed or south-west Wales.

Ills. 50, 52

A hint at the way they may have achieved such eminence is supplied by a bilingual memorial from the border of Carmarthenshire and Pembrokeshire. It commemorates Voteporix, a king of Irish descent. As 'Vortiporius' he appears, like Maelgwn, in the diatribes of Gildas. A ring-cross emblem on the stone shows that he was at least nominally a Christian. Also he is given the Latin title 'Protector'. A 'protector' was an officer-cadet serving in the personal bodyguard of a Roman emperor, or on his staff. Voteporix himself can hardly have served in this manner, but one of his ancestors may have done so. Very likely the Irish founder of the dynasty in Dyfed was allowed to settle with his war-band by imperial authority in the late fourth century, to defend that part of Wales against other Irishmen. One of the sons of the dynasty might well have been taken into the emperor's bodyguard, partly for education in Roman ways, partly as a surety for the good conduct of his family. He would thus have acquired the title Protector, which his descendants then treated as hereditary. If this explanation is right, it implies that the Irish in Dyfed were not usurpers. They were planted there with Roman authorisation when the Roman writ still ran throughout southern Britain.

Ill. 52

Nevertheless, the stones show that Dyfed was not the most Romanised of the Welsh kingdoms. That distinction belongs to north-western Wales: Maelgwn's realm of Gwynedd, where Degannwy is. There, Irish Ogam inscriptions are rare. The formulae on the stones are closer than those of Dyfed to the Christian memorials of Gaul and

the Mediterranean. Gwynedd's Romanisation is well illustrated by
the stone of Cadman, a king of the house of Maelgwn. It was set up
by his grandson Cadwaladr at the church of Llangadwaladr in
Anglesey around the middle of the seventh century. Inscribed in
what was then an up-to-date continental script, the stone calls
Cadman *sapientis(s)imus, opinatis(s)imus omnium regum*: the wisest and
most renowned of all kings.

With every allowance made for eulogistic inflation, the term 'most
renowned' may quite well refer to a real claim of supremacy over
other kings and princes in Wales. However, it is the expression
'*sapientisimus*' which now concerns us. *Sapiens* in this context is an
almost technical term meaning not just 'wise' but 'learned'; and
learned not in the vernacular oral traditions of the Celtic peoples, but
in classical Latin book-learning. Cadman's descendants were claiming
that he was educated in the Roman fashion. When we bear in mind
that the Celtic monasteries were storehouses of classical manuscripts
during the centuries when Europe was in travail and Rome itself in
barbarian hands, it is possible to believe that Cadman's learning was
indeed of a high standard.

There are other stones in Gwynedd besides Cadman's that bear
witness to a Romanised sophistication. On one, a man is described
as a 'citizen' of Gwynedd. It is not easy to decide what the term can
mean in an area lacking the essential requirement of Roman citizenship, namely, a town. But the same stone refers to a magistrate,
suggesting the survival of a Romanised structure of local government. In Gwynedd, also, we come across a doctor, 'Melus son of
Martin' in Llangian churchyard. Further stones reveal a little about
Gwynedd's ecclesiastical establishment. Inscriptions mention priests
and probably bishops. Some of the memorials give the names of
saints known from documents. A stone at Aberdaron, near the end
of the Lleyn peninsula, records the burial of a priest 'with a host of
brethren'. The phrase implies burial in the cemetery of a monastery,
and is thus valuable, because early monastic remains like those of
Ireland are rare in Wales.

Ill. 58. An inscription from a stone
found in north-western Wales to the
memory of a doctor named Melus.

With the memorial stones in mind, as well as the various literary sources, we can go forward to draw tentative conclusions from archaeology about the Welsh life of the period—or, at any rate, the life led by the princes and chiefs whose homes are known to us.

Under Rome their ancestors had dwelt in extensive villas regularly laid out, with mortared masonry, heated bath suites, decorated walls and mosaic floors. They themselves did not live so. Their houses were made of unmortared stone and were usually circular, in a traditional native style going back to the Bronze Age. Two such were excavated at Pant-y-saer. At Dinas Powys, there are traces of a couple of fair-sized buildings of roughly rectangular shape, outlined by drainage gullies cut to lead away the drip from the eaves. The absence of internal post-holes for roof supports suggests that the roof was laid on a fairly civilised arrangement of timber trusses, resting on the wall-tops. But the walls themselves were of dry-stone and clumsy, several feet thick at the base, and not perfectly straight but bowed outward.

The bigger of these buildings at Dinas Powys is the largest post-Roman dwelling so far found in Wales. It was probably the prince's hall, since it has a stone hearth toward one end. We may imagine his family and perhaps his war-band gathered around the hearth, while inferior retainers occupied the fireless portion. However, we must not think in terms of the spacious halls portrayed in early poetry. The inside dimensions were only about 40 feet by 15. As for the second building, it was nearly as wide, but not much over half the length. Doubtless it was a barn or storehouse, though slaves may have slept in it. Animals are unlikely, since there was no internal drainage system. The two buildings stood at right angles to each other, framing two sides of a yard which was open to the sun but partly protected from the wind. In the yard were three stone-built hearths. To judge from the scatter of occupation refuse, many domestic tasks were performed out of doors.

At the north-east corner of the surrounding enclosure were several other hearths, arranged to take advantage of the draught supplied by the prevailing winds. Iron slag and fragments of crucibles point to industrial rather than domestic use. Here archaeology confirms literature by showing that the princes patronised craftsmen. At Dinas Powys, the local Glamorgan iron ores were smelted and worked up into weapons, knives and other tools by a blacksmith who may have been resident. Dinas Emrys, also, gives evidence of iron-working. Furthermore, both sites disclose the casting of bronze and even gold

Ill. 59. Restored view and section of a lidded clay crucible of a type found at Dinas Powys. The lid was intended to keep pieces of charcoal from falling into the crucible, to prevent the oxidation of the molten bronze and to conserve heat when the crucible was taken from the fire. The maximum diameter of the bowl is one and a half inches. These lidded clay crucibles were characteristic of the Irish Sea culture province in the fifth to seventh centuries. Numerous fragments of crucibles were found around the north-east corner of the Dinas Powys site which suggests that the hearths in that area were used for industrial purposes. The hearths would have been open to the natural draughts of the prevailing wind.

Ill. 60
Ill. 59

Ills. 56, 57

Ill. 55

Ill. 140

Ill. 133

to make brooches and other jewellery. At Dinas Powys, scrap bronze was brought in, ripped off belts, brooches and buckets of Teutonic provenance. The metalworker folded the pieces up to fit them into his crucibles. The crucibles themselves were of an advanced type, with a lid attached to conserve the heat and keep the contents pure.

Dinas Powys yielded a fragment of a lead die or stamp, used in forming the moulds for brooches. Also an exotic glass bead was discovered. This had a coating of gold leaf and was probably made in Egypt. Additional beads were from Teutonic sources and perhaps from other parts of the British Isles. Besides the beads, there were more than 250 sherds of fine glass: scrap from broken Teutonic drinking vessels, for melting and reuse in ornaments of various kinds.

The lead die proves that the Dinas Powys brooches were of a penannular Celtic pattern. Pant-y-saer produced a similar brooch made of silver-plated bronze. The pattern is found in contemporary Ireland, and the crucibles too can be paralleled in that country. There is good reason to think that the jewellers who worked with such materials wandered from court to court and over the sea, like the missionaries and bards of that age. The tale *Culhwch and Olwen* witnesses to the respect enjoyed by such travelling artificers.

91

Surprisingly, the Welsh princes did not employ native potters. The east-Mediterranean ware discovered in Wales, as in south-western England and Ireland, was apparently imported to fill the gap left by a major collapse in the Romano-British pottery industry, which survived at best only in the crude workmanship of Pant-y-saer. Two main types can be distinguished. We come across pieces of fine imported red bowls with a glossy surface. Sometimes the interior of the bowl is decorated with stamped designs, including Christian symbols, such as the cross. A Dinas Powys sherd has a pattern of running leopards. Other imported vessels came from the Mediterranean as containers for wine and oil. These are the well-known amphorae: large jars with two thick handles, decorated with grooves in parallels or spirals. The wine and oil were used by the Church, but not solely by the Church. Among the aristocracy, a Romanised taste for wine survived, and olive oil may have been used for cooking. The persistence of Roman cooking methods, unknown among the pre-Roman Celts, is evinced by the discovery of grey spouted bowls with grits on the inner surface. These are *mortaria*, employed for mashing vegetables and soft fruit to make purées. They too were imported, probably from Gaul, as were a miscellany of coarse cooking-pots and pitchers.

Ills. 53, 62
Ill. 36

Ill. 54

Ill. 61

All this imported pottery is an interesting proof of trade and of the continuance of some Roman habits. But the total quantity of such types, at Dinas Powys, Degannwy and other sites, is far too small to meet all the requirements of princely households. Unless a great deal disappeared into unlocated rubbish dumps, it must have been supplemented with vessels of perishable substances, such as wood or leather, which archaeology can recover only under very favourable conditions.

What was the nature of the economy that paid for the imports and for the craftsmen's services? It was not a money economy. So far as we know, dark-age Wales had no coinage. Industry of a kind existed, and the lord of Dinas Powys doubtless exploited his local iron ore.

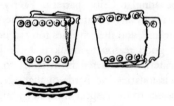

Ill. 60. Views of a strip of bronze, ornamented with repoussé bosses, which had been ripped from an Anglo-Saxon bucket. It was then folded to fit inside a crucible to be melted down. Scrap bronze was brought to Dinas Powys for recasting into Celtic-style brooches.

Ill. 61. Restoration of a *mortarium*, a spouted bowl in grey ware with blue-black wash, found at Dinas Powys. The interior surface of a *mortarium* was studded with grits, apparently for mashing vegetables and fruits to make purées. This was a purely Roman method of preparing food, unknown to the pre-Roman Celts, and the continued use of *mortaria* in the post-Roman centuries demonstrates the survival of Roman culinary techniques.

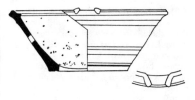

Ill. 62. Restoration of the leopard bowl found at Dinas Powys (*Ill. 53*). The diameter of the rim is nine inches.

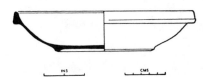

But the emphasis clearly lay on farming and stock-raising, precisely as tradition implies. Excavations turn up vast amounts of animal bones. Nearly all come from domestic animals: cattle, pigs and sheep, rather than stags, boars, wild-fowl or fish. The animals provided not only meat, milk, butter and cheese, but raw materials for the various crafts: leather for vessels, shoes and garments; wool; horn, sinew and gut; and bone for making combs and pins. The processing of cattle hides is demonstrated by skinning-knives, stone rubbers for finishing the hides, iron awls for piercing leather, and heavy iron needles for sewing it. Spindle-whorls and loom-weights show that wool was spun and woven into garments.

Ill. 63

Direct evidence of arable farming is lacking. A Romano-British field system at Pant-y-saer survived after AD 400, and may or may not have lasted for some time longer. An iron ploughshare from Dinorben stands alone, and is probably not a dark-age product; but continental sites where arable farming was certainly practised have yielded few plough parts, so the negative argument from their absence carries little weight. Some accounts of early Wales portray the people as not eating much bread. On the other hand, the *Laws of Hywel Dda*—compiled in the tenth century, but partly out of much older matter—

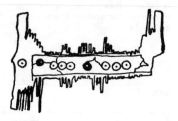

Ill. 63. Composite bone combs found at Dinas Powys. It seems unlikely that these unwieldy combs were worn decoratively as well as used for dressing hair. The Celts and other people, however, attached considerable importance to hair-dressing and combs and toilet articles assumed a highly personal nature. In *Culhwch and Olwen*, the most primitive of the Mabinogion tales, several of the tasks given to Arthur's cousin Culhwch and his comrades have to do with providing instruments for shaving and dressing the hair of the chief giant. The most costly task for Arthur's followers was obtaining the comb and shears and when Culhwch first entered Arthur's hall the boon he asked was to have his hair trimmed and 'Arthur took a golden comb and shears with loops of silver and he combed his hair'. This seems to be an echo of a pagan ritual connected with the first dressing of a young man's hair.

contain many allusions to ploughs, tillage, cereal crops, and bread specifically. Archaeology bears out the *Laws* on the last item and therefore, indirectly, the rest, because the four richest dark-age sites have all produced hand-mills for grinding corn. One of the examples from Dinas Powys is of an advanced type, a legacy of Roman Britain. Dinas Powys also yielded some discs of sandstone which probably served as griddles or bakestones. The medieval writer Giraldus Cambrensis mentions, as characteristically Welsh, thin cakes of bread which were baked daily.

Gradually a picture of Welsh dark-age society is taking shape, with archaeology and literary scholarship illuminating each other. *Culhwch and Olwen* has a fine phrase about Arthur's court: 'Knife has gone into meat, and drink into horn, and a thronging in the hall.' The archaeologist can show the knife and the bones of the animals that supplied the meat. He can speculate on the Mediterranean source of the wine. At Dinas Powys he can reveal the hall, not indeed of Arthur himself, but of a lesser contemporary.

Ills. 137, 139

The dark-age chieftain who emerges from this reconstruction is not a polished imperial citizen. But he is not an atavistic barbarian either. Though definitely Celtic, he retains some Roman tastes and techniques, with possibly an imperial title and a smattering of classical

94

education. He sponsors craftsmanship on a modest scale. He has his own beasts and farmlands, and tenants paying rent in kind. He imports luxuries as well as kitchen utensils from distant lands, and, in return, exports surplus hides and kindred agricultural by-products—perhaps also metal goods. His life is a curious mixture of grace and squalor, in a crude hall scarcely justifying the flights of bardic poetry. Yet, although the age is warlike, the household is peaceful. Our chieftain may prefer a defensible place, but he feels no need to add massive ramparts. When he rides to battle, the fighting is far off on open ground and does not involve the women, children, slaves and craftsmen going about their business in his own homestead and others.

Until lately, we might have guessed that this description would be valid outside Wales and apply equally to Arthur. As will appear, however, the step from Welsh contemporaries to the *dux bellorum* himself raises fresh issues.

5 *Glastonbury Abbey*

C. A. Ralegh Radford

As TINTAGEL is associated with the birth of Arthur, so Glastonbury is associated with his passing. An ancient tradition maintained that the king had never died and that he would return again. But Glastonbury claimed to possess his grave and his relics. These beliefs are well summed up in the early fifteenth-century vernacular poem in the *Red Book of Bath*:

> But for he skaped that batell y-wys
> Bretons and Cornysh sayeth thus
> That he levyth yet, pardi,
> And schall come and be a kyng aye.
>
> At Glastonbury on the queer
> They made Artourez toumbe there,
> And wrote with latyn verse thus
> Hic jacet Arthurus, rex quondam, rex futurus.

Arthur, the past and future king: this was the belief of the Bretons and Cornish, attested as early as the beginning of the twelfth century and certainly far older than that. It is implicit in the final words of Geoffrey of Monmouth, whose account of the fatal battle ends thus:

> Even the renowned King Arthur himself was wounded deadly and was borne thence unto the island of Avalon for the healing of his wounds, where he gave up the crown unto his kinsman, Constantine, son of Cador, in AD 542.

Geoffrey, it will be noted, does not attempt to localise the island of Avalon, either at Glastonbury or elsewhere. In the same way, his contemporary, William of Malmesbury, states that the 'tomb of Arthur is nowhere beheld, whence the ancient ditties fable that he is yet to come'.

97

William of Malmesbury first published his *Deeds of the Kings of the English* in 1125, and brought out a revised version before 1140. Between these dates, he spent a considerable time at Glastonbury, and drew up a treatise on the *Antiquity of the Church of Glastonbury*. This has survived only in a form much interpolated by later writers and dating from the thirteenth century. But the original text of the earlier part can be reconstituted from the later edition of his *Deeds of the Kings*, which incorporates large sections from the work on Glastonbury. William was a competent and scholarly historian. He made a detailed examination of the archives of Glastonbury and his analysis of the records of the old church is as thorough as any medieval historical investigation. Arthur nowhere occurs in connection with Glastonbury in the genuine works of William of Malmesbury; the passages in which he is brought into connection with the abbey are all in the interpolations in the surviving text of the *Antiquity of the Church of Glastonbury*. William does indeed mention Arthur in his general work, but in his proper context along with Vortigern and Ambrosius. He adds: 'This is that Arthur of whom the trifling of the Britons talks such nonsense even today; a man clearly worthy not to be dreamed of in fallacious fables, but to be proclaimed in veracious histories.' We would perhaps have been grateful for a record of some of those fallacious fables.

Arthur's connection with Glastonbury is first recorded in the *Life of St Gildas* written by Caradoc of Llancarfan about 1150 and preserved in a Durham manuscript of slightly later date. Melwas, king of the Summer Region (Somerset), had abducted Guinevere, the wife of Arthur, and held her captive at Glastonbury. Arthur, after a long search, gathered the forces of Devon and Cornwall and came up prepared for battle. Peace was made by the interposition of the saint, together with the abbot and clergy of Glastonbury. Guinevere was returned to Arthur. 'After this the two kings bestowed on the abbot many lands and they came to visit and pray at the church of St Mary.'

Both William of Malmesbury and Caradoc of Llancarfan knew the British name for Glastonbury: Ynyswitrin. Neither suggests any knowledge of the equation between Glastonbury and Avalon, which is recorded only at the end of the century. This equation first appears with the discovery in 1190 of the reputed relics of Arthur and Guinevere in the ancient cemetery of the abbey. These were exhumed and translated into the abbey church. The oldest account is that of Gerald of Wales, a contemporary. But the record of Adam of

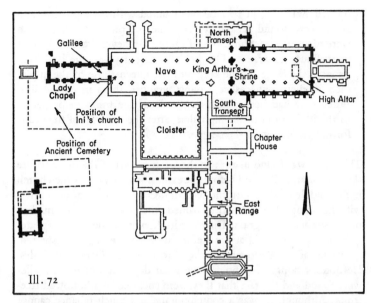

Ill. 72

Domerham, a monk of Glastonbury writing a century later, is based on the tradition of the abbey and probably more trustworthy:

Ill. 65

> The King [Richard I] . . . elevated as Abbot, Henry de Sully, Prior of Bermondsey, a man born of royal stock, ... He, frequently urged to dispose more fittingly of the famous king Arthur (for he had lain for 648 years near the old Church [*i.e.*, the Lady Chapel], between two pyramids, once magnificently carved), one day surrounded the place with curtains and ordered that digging should be carried out. . . . The Abbot and convent, raising up the remains, joyfully translated them into the great church, placing them in a double tomb, magnificently carved. The King's body was set by itself at the head of the tomb, that of the queen at the foot or the eastern part, and there they remain to the present day.

Ills. 67, 68

The position of this tomb is not specified. It was opened in 1278 in the presence of Edward I. A contemporary account in the *Annals of Waverley* states that the bones were extracted and placed in the treasury of the abbey until they could be more fittingly located. Adam of Domerham, who was probably present, gives fuller details:

> The lord Edward . . . with his consort, the lady Eleanor, came to Glastonbury . . . to celebrate Easter . . . The following Tuesday . . . at dusk, the lord king had the tomb of the famous King Arthur

opened. Wherein, in two caskets painted with their pictures and arms, were found separately the bones of the said king, which were of great size, and those of Queen Guinevere, which were of marvellous beauty. . . . On the following day . . . the lord king replaced the bones of the king and the queen those of the queen, each in their own casket, having wrapped them in costly silks. When they had been sealed they ordered the tomb to be placed forthwith in front of the high altar, after the removal of the skulls for the veneration of the people.

This tomb was found in 1931 in the western part of the quire before the high altar, as it stood before the extension eastward of the church in the middle of the fourteenth century. Only the base of the cavity, with its lining of fine ashlar remained; the position is now marked on the surface of the grass. The tomb itself, which is described by later writers, was destroyed at the Reformation and the bones dispersed.

Ills. 71, 72

Ill. 70

Details of the discovery in 1190 are given by Gerald of Wales. He notes, among other points, the great depth at which the bodies were found and the fact that they were enclosed in a hollowed tree-trunk. Although he was a contemporary, too much reliance cannot be placed on these details. According to his statement, a leaden cross was found fixed on the underside of a stone, with the inscribed face inwards. There can be little doubt that this was the cross later preserved at Glastonbury and engraved in the 1607 edition of Camden. The Latin inscription may be translated: Here lies Arthur, the famous king, in the island of Avalon. There is no indication that it included a mention of his wife, Guinevere, as stated by Gerald, who claimed to have handled the cross.

This is the first recorded instance of the identification of Glastonbury with Avalon, an identification which became a part of the accepted tradition of the abbey. The authenticity of the leaden cross has long been a matter of doubt, and many have favoured the solution that it was made by the monks in 1190. Epigraphically this is difficult to accept. There is no reason to doubt the basic accuracy of the letter forms as engraved by Camden, though the arrangement of the words and the form of the cross are not necessarily correct. The letters are debased and straggling Roman capitals. The square C (two instances) and the N with a horizontal cross bar (three instances) are consistently used. These forms are proper to the eleventh century or earlier, rather than to the twelfth. If the cross was really a fabrication of the late twelfth century, the maker was unusually consistent. It seems more

Ill. 73. Seventeenth-century engraving of a cross, since lost, said to have been found in Arthur's grave. From Camden's *Britannia*.

likely that it was a genuine relic of pre-Conquest date. This date may be more properly considered when the evidence of the recent excavations has been set out.

The excavations at Glastonbury, carried out in successive campaigns since 1908, have thrown some light on the Arthurian connection with the site of the abbey. Before turning to these results, it is desirable to examine the position of the 'island'.

Ill. 74   Glastonbury today is a group of hills almost entirely surrounded by the rich flat meadows of mid-Somerset. These flats were formerly marshland and swamp; the limits of this area are approximately marked by the present twenty-foot contour. Only on the south-east does a

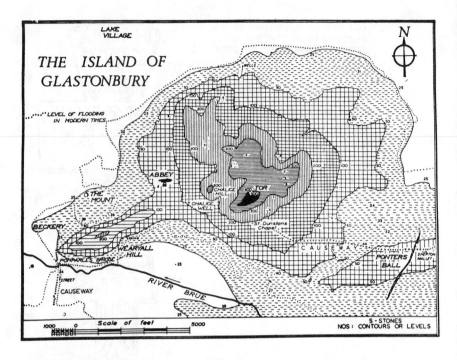

Ill. 74. The Island of Glastonbury. Geographically the 'island' is a group of hills, the highest of which is the Tor, rising prominently above flat surrounding meadows which were formerly marshes and swamps.

The 'island' is linked to the mainland by a low narrow causeway now followed by the main Shepton Mallet road. The hatching on the map represents contours.

narrow ridge link the 'island' to the hills of east Somerset. At its lowest point this ridge, now followed by the road to Shepton Mallet (A.361), is little more than a quarter of a mile across and rises barely 30 feet above the former level of the marsh. On the far edge of this isthmus lies Ponter's Ball, an eastward-facing bank and ditch running from marsh edge to marsh edge and interrupted only by the road, which follows the line of its medieval precursor. Where undisturbed, the bank (though doubtless much spread) still measures about 30 feet across and twelve feet high; the ditch on the east side is on a comparable scale, though considerably silted. Excavations carried out by the late Arthur Bulleid about 1900 showed pre-Roman pottery of the second or third century BC lying on the old land surface or incorporated in the lower make up of the bank. The ditch yielded sherds of the twelfth and thirteenth centuries in the upper silt.

A great barrier like Ponter's Ball makes little military sense; it could too easily be outflanked, either by working round the ends in a dry season or by landings on the long indented shore of the 'island'. As a boundary it must have been safeguarded by less material defences. It can best be explained as the *temenos* or enclosure of a great pagan Celtic sanctuary. The site at Glastonbury is well fitted to have been such. It possesses ample water to provide the sacred pools and springs recorded in classical writers, and the prominent natural hill of the Tor is a feature that would fit in with the concept of a sanctuary. A sanctuary of this kind would consist of an extent of land with sacred groves, possibly even a little wooden temple, like that found on the airport at Heathrow. So far no trace of such a sanctuary has been found at Glastonbury, but indications would necessarily be slight and the evidence is most likely to come to light by chance as the great Celtic treasure at Llyn Cerrig bach in Anglesey was found during the Second World War. Romano-British occupation within the 'island' is known both in the vicinity of the abbey church and on the western slope of Wearyall Hill, the latter probably a landing place.

The existence of a great pagan sanctuary would explain the foundation of an early Christian settlement at Glastonbury. It would not be the only instance where the Church took over heathen sacred sites and Christianised them: a policy recommended by certain early writers. Apart from this sanctuary, Glastonbury is unlikely to have been a centre of dense settlement in the Roman period, and the quantity of late Romano-British pottery, dating from the later third and fourth centuries, is inconsiderable compared with that of the earlier phase in the first and second centuries. So far, excavations on the site of the abbey have failed to discover either the existence of Roman remains in position or any trace of the sub-Roman imports that distinguished this period at Tintagel. It is not that imported pottery of this date is unknown in Somerset; it is recorded at Ilchester and at two places to be discussed hereafter: Glastonbury

Ills. 86–89, 105
Tor (chapter 6) and South Cadbury (chapter 7).

But the absence of these wares is not conclusive; there is other evidence for an early Christian foundation at Glastonbury. In the old church of St Mary, as it existed before the fire of 1184, the altar was flanked by two pyramids or shrines, containing the relics of St Indracht and St Patrick. These shrines were called pyramids from their house-like form with a cover shaped like the hipped gable of a
Ill. 68
roof. The Hedda stone of the eighth century, now in Peterborough

Cathedral, is an example of the type carved of a monolithic block of freestone measuring $3\frac{1}{2}$ by $1\frac{1}{2}$ feet and standing $2\frac{1}{2}$ feet high. A rather later example, formed of a number of interlocked pieces of stone, was found at St Andrews and now stands in the site museum in the undercroft of the priory.

St Indracht and St Patrick are Celtic saints, and it is difficult to believe that their cult was introduced at Glastonbury after the Saxon conquest of Somerset in the middle of the seventh century. St Indracht, in particular, is a saint whose cult has left but sparse traces in the south-west, and whose later connections were reputed to be Irish. St Patrick was, in the later tradition of Glastonbury, identified with the Apostle of Ireland, but this is probably an attempt to provide a Celtic saint, whose cult was traditional, with a more acceptable life and background. Another early cult with Irish connections was that of St Bridget in the chapel at Beckery. It was not claimed that her body lay there but that she had visited the site and left her wallet and distaff, which were preserved as relics. The existence of these cults is evidence of Christian worship at a date before the Saxon conquest. The evidence for their survival is largely due to William of Malmesbury, who, early in the twelfth century, records the devotion of Irish pilgrims coming to Glastonbury to venerate the relics of their saints. It is also William of Malmesbury who records the existence among the archives of the abbey of a charter granted by an unnamed king of Dumnonia. There is no reason to question the existence of this charter. The date to which it is attributed—AD 601—can rest only on a conjecture of the writer and may well be wrong.

Archaeologically, the literary evidence summarised in the foregoing paragraph is confirmed by the character of the ancient cemetery, with its stone-lined graves, its mausolea and its traces of post-holes indicating the former existence of wattled oratories corresponding to the traditional account of the beginnings of Glastonbury. The ancient cemetery, which remained the centre of the monastic traditions, lay on the south side of the Lady Chapel. The east wall ran just outside the late extension of the pre-Conquest church, through the south door of the thirteenth-century nave. The south wall, now indicated by a slope in the reformed grass levels, was some hundred feet south of the Lady Chapel. The entrance, which coincided with St Dunstan's Chapel, west of the Lady Chapel, was in the west wall. The position of the north side is unknown. Within this cemetery lay the old church of St Mary, traditionally said to have been built by actual disciples of Christ. This was a wattled building in a primitive

Ill. 66

Ill. 67

Ill. 65

technique attested both by the remains found on the site and by early Irish records of similar structures on the monastic sites of that island. When the Saxon conquest was effective, King Ini of Wessex (688–726) built a new church of mortared masonry further to the east; its remains were uncovered in 1924–26 under six feet of dumped clay on which the thirteenth-century pavement of the nave was set. The building of King Ini is in the continental style introduced into Kent by the Augustinian mission and thereafter used for all important churches in Saxon England.

The oldest monastic settlement at Glastonbury lay west of the crossing of the great church of the later Middle Ages. It was bounded on the east by a great bank and ditch, which were located in the crossing of the great church and in the chapter house to the south. This ditch was 25 feet across and about 10 feet deep. The bank which lay on the west side had been largely levelled by subsequent building. Though the much spread base, originally about 30 feet wide, remained in position, it had been pared down to a height of barely 18 inches. No direct dating evidence for this bank was found. The clay of which it was formed was clean and the natural silting of the ditch contained no artifacts. At a period when the bank was much spread, glass furnaces dating from the ninth century were dug into the inward slope. The time required for denudation to have reached the stage at which the glass furnaces were dug must be measured in centuries rather than decades. A date for the original bank is likely to be before rather than after the Saxon conquest of the middle of the seventh century.

The oldest remains within this enclosing bank were those found in the ancient cemetery. Post-holes were found belonging to at least four oratories of the wattled type already mentioned. In every case, the area was so disturbed by graves and by later structures that no full plan could be recovered. The best preserved was a small building 13 feet wide and over 17 feet long. The west end was destroyed by the foundation of a thirteenth-century wall. The oratory did not appear on the far side of this foundation, giving a maximum possible length of 24 feet. Little oratories or churches scattered about in the great cemetery of a Celtic monastery are characteristic. They may still be seen on sites like Clonmacnois in Ireland and Maughold in the Isle of Man. There were also two mausolea within the ancient cemetery. These tomb-shrines were rectangular structures, large enough to take one or two bodies. They were quite low and probably marked by a standing cross. They were designed to hold the bodies of saints or

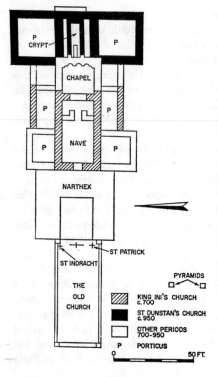

Ill. 75. Plan of King Ini's church.
King Ini of Wessex reorganised the western territories of his kingdom which had been conquered from the Britons in the preceding fifty years. These included modern Somerset and Dorset and parts of Devon. His ecclesiastical reorganisation included the establishment of a second bishop's see at Sherborne for the country west of Selwood (a boundary between the modern counties of Wiltshire and Somerset). The first bishop was St Aldhelm, a member of the royal house, who opened negotiations with the British church of Dumnonia in west Devon and Cornwall. Ini is the first king of Wessex whose laws have survived. They show his concern for reorganising the western territories and incorporating them into the Saxon kingdom. Ini was a great benefactor of the church at Glastonbury, confirming its possessions and making fresh grants. The rebuilt church was a visible sign of this interest.

revered founders of the community. Burial alongside them was a privilege much sought after, as such proximity was popularly supposed to ensure entry into Paradise. One of the Glastonbury mausolea lay outside the east end of Ini's church. It was subsequently incorporated into the eastward extension of this church added by St Dunstan, who became abbot of Glastonbury some years before the middle of the tenth century. The other mausoleum was found 50 feet south of the Lady Chapel and was probably marked by the southern of the two crosses shortly to be described. Mausolea of this type are rare in Britain. They are rather more common in Gaul and belong to a very early class of burial. A well-known example at Poitiers dates from the seventh century. At Glastonbury, they may be ascribed with some confidence to the period before the Saxon conquest, and it may be tentatively suggested that they formed the original burial places of St Indracht and St Patrick, whose translation into the old church of

St Mary is unlikely to date before the tenth century. The ordinary graves within the cemetery were rough chests formed of slabs of stone set on edge and covered with a flat stone or stones laid flush with the surface of the cemetery.

Two pyramids are recorded in the ancient cemetery south of the Lady Chapel. This term, though originally used to describe a special form of shrine, probably meant in the twelfth century no more than a venerated tomb or shrine or even, as other accounts of the Glastonbury cemetery suggest, the cross that marked it. According to William of Malmesbury, the monument nearer the chapel was of five stages and stood to a height of 28 feet. The second was of four stages standing to a height of 26 feet. Both were inscribed with names that could scarcely be read, though the imperfect transcription includes Saxon notables and two abbots with British names.

A trench was dug south from the bay of the Lady Chapel lying east of the doorway—the second bay from the east end of the late twelfth-century building. Forty feet south of the chapel, a hole 3 to 4 feet across was found. The damaged edges showed that a large object, probably a monolith, had been carelessly dragged from the hole. The shaft of a great cross, like that still standing in the cemetery at

Ill. 69 Bewcastle, Cumberland, would have left such an impression if it had been violently pulled down. In the filling of the hole was a scrap of pottery dating from *c.* 1500. Fifteen feet further south was the mausoleum already discussed. It measured over-all 8 feet by 7 and must have been marked on the surface by a cross, of which no trace was found.

These two pyramids or crosses form an essential link in the Arthurian connection with Glastonbury. Both the contemporary writer, Gerald of Wales, and the earliest account in the Glastonbury tradition agree that the bodies of Arthur and Guinevere were found in 1190 between the two pyramids in the ancient cemetery. In this position the excavation disclosed a large irregular hole, which had been dug and filled in after standing open for a very short time. At the bottom

Ill. 67 this hole had destroyed two, or perhaps three, of the slab-lined graves belonging to the earliest stratum. One of these destroyed graves was set against the wall of the mausoleum: a position likely to have been granted only to a person of importance.

At a date before the twelfth century, mausoleum and graves were covered by a bank of clay which still remains to a depth of three feet six inches. On the outer, south side, this bank was delimited by a stone wall of which the foundation trench was found. On the other side, it sloped down towards the Lady Chapel, which stood on the same level as the mausoleum and graves. It is recorded of St Dunstan that, while he was abbot, in the middle of the tenth century, he 'enclosed the cemetery of the monks on the south side of the church with a wall of masonry. The area within was raised to form a pleasant meadow, removed from the noise of the passers by, so that it might truly be said of the bodies of the saints lying within that they repose in peace.' A raising of the level of this whole area would have left the old church of St Mary half-buried; the formation of an enclosing terrace, as discovered in 1954, is practicable and conforms to the words of the saint's biographer.

The hole between the pyramids was dug through this bank and was immediately refilled with soil containing many masons' chippings of Doulting stone. Into this filling was dug a later series of graves, one of which contained an early fourteenth-century token. Doulting stone was first used at Glastonbury after the fire of 1184; the facing of the Lady Chapel is of this material with dressings of local blue lias. It was therefore in use in this area during the period 1184–89, while the chapel was being built, and it is unlikely that mason's chippings in this quantity would have been lying about the ancient cemetery at any other period. It is therefore certain that the large hole discovered in 1962 represents the excavation for the bodies of Arthur and Guinevere.

It is time to recapitulate. The foundation of a Christian sanctuary at Glastonbury can be traced back into the period of British rule before the Saxon conquest of Somerset in the middle of the seventh century. Christian inscriptions in Wales show that for laymen, mainly chieftains, burial within the monastic cemeteries gradually replaced the older use of small family burial grounds in the course of the sixth century. A man such as Arthur, if resident in mid-Somerset in the sixth century, would probably have been buried at Glastonbury, and a warrior of his fame might be expected to be found buried alongside the mausoleum of the saint. By analogy with custom in other British lands, one would expect his tomb to have been marked by a monolith recording in Latin his name and patronymic and possibly with a simple epitaph. The raising of the level in the tenth century would have buried this monolith even if it were not removed. It is at this stage that the replacement of the monolith by the leaden cross would be appropriate, and the lettering on the cross as engraved by Camden is more likely to be of the tenth than of the late twelfth century. Further than this the evidence will not take us.

Sceptics will object—and correctly—that the last paragraph is a chain of unproved hypotheses. Their positive case is based on two premises: that nothing recorded by Geoffrey of Monmouth should be believed; and that William of Malmesbury is silent on Arthur's connection with Glastonbury. The first is a dangerous argument but its discussion would require far more space than is here available. The second requires consideration. That William of Malmesbury knew more than he chose to set down is clear from his own words; he dismissed much information about Arthur as fables unworthy of the historian. It is clear that, if the hypotheses outlined above are accepted, then the grave of Arthur would have had no distinguishing mark in the early twelfth century. It is equally clear that it was not marked as such in 1190. Before Geoffrey's work appeared there was no reason to pay particular attention to Arthur; the ecclesiastical tradition, in so far as it mentioned him, regarded him with disfavour. An unmarked grave in the cemetery vaguely noted in the old traditions may well have seemed to William yet another meaningless tale; it may even have escaped his notice altogether. Once Geoffrey of Monmouth's history had become a best-seller, the position was changed. A later generation of monks realised that they had an additional attraction for the pilgrims who came to the abbey in growing numbers. In 1187, Constance of Brittany, the heiress of the native house, gave birth to a posthumous son by her husband, Geoffrey of Anjou, son of King Henry II. Arthur, the desired of the people, as he is called in a Breton register, was in 1190 recognised by Richard I as heir, to the exclusion of John. It may be this that finally stimulated the translation of the relics of the common antecessor of the English and Celtic throne.

The later vicissitudes of the relics identified as those of Arthur and Guinevere may be quickly summarised. It has already been suggested that through most of the thirteenth century they lay in the treasury in the east range of the abbey. This can hardly have been completed before about 1230; before that date there is no record of their location in the forty years immediately following the exhumation. The translation to the tomb in the quire of the great church took place in or shortly after 1278 on the express orders of the king. The tomb found in 1931 occupies the position normally chosen for a founder's tomb. Edward I had, in 1278, just completed his first successful offensive against Llywelyn ap Gruffydd of north Wales. The translation should probably be seen as a deliberate act of policy. Twenty-four years later, Edward I based his claim to the Scottish overlordship on the rights of King Arthur to the whole island as recorded in the pages of Geoffrey of Monmouth. In 1278, he was using the same weapon against the Welsh. Arthur, the champion of the British people against the heathen English invaders, had been received into the Valhalla of his enemies and was henceforth an English worthy.

6   *Glastonbury Tor*

Philip Rahtz

THE ASSOCIATIONS OF GLASTONBURY with Arthur have already
been discussed. Dr C. A. Ralegh Radford in the previous chapter has
examined the case for Arthur's having been buried in the abbey, and
has described the relocation of the tomb in which his remains are
said to have been found in 1190. It had always been assumed that the
abbey precinct was the scene of the earliest Christian settlement of
Glastonbury. It was, and is, believed by many people that the wattle
church destroyed by fire in 1184 (page 129) was of very early origin.
It is perhaps historically unlikely that Christianity reached Glastonbury earlier than the fifth century. Dr Radford believes that there was
a Christian monastery there in Arthurian times (*i.e.*, the late fifth
and early sixth centuries), and that the great ditch found below the
abbey ruins was the boundary of this. It was reasonable, therefore, to
assume that the wattle church, Arthur's grave and the ditch represented
the pre-Saxon religious settlement. The foundations of a stone church
discovered in the earlier excavations were claimed to be those of the
Ill. 75   Saxon church built by Ini in the late seventh or early eighth century
and added to by Dunstan.

Although much circumstantial evidence has been brought forward
to support these hypotheses, no dark-age archaeological material has
been discovered in the abbey excavations, either past or more recent.
There are pieces of Roman pottery and other Roman finds, but they
are all in the clay brought to the site in medieval times. There are
few enough objects which can be attributed even to the earlier Saxon
period, but of the fifth–sixth centuries there are none. Notably
absent are sherds of imported Mediterranean pottery of classes A and
B, dated *c*. 470–*c*. 670, and characteristic of Arthurian or dark-age settlements, especially monastic ones, throughout western Britain.

Dr Radford was the first to define the origins and probable dating
of these wares, which he found in his pre-war excavations at the

PERIOD		DATE	FINDS
PERIOD 0	UPPER PALAEOLITHIC	c.20,000-10,000 BC	Flints
	MESOLITHIC	c.10,000-5,000 BC	Flints
	NEOLITHIC	c.5,000-2,000 BC	Flints, stone axe
	ROMAN	c.43 AD- c.400AD	Pottery, tile
PERIOD 1	DARK AGES or SUB-ROMAN	c.470 - c.650AD	Imported Mediterranean pottery
			Iron and bone objects
			Bronze head
			Crucible fragments
			Roman tile fragments
PERIOD 2	LATE SAXON	c.800 - 1100 AD	Pottery, stone, iron, bronze, bone
PERIOD 3	LATE SAXON MEDIEVAL	c.1000 - 1500 AD	Pottery, stone, iron, bronze, coins, bone
PERIOD 4 (Miscellaneous)	POST MEDIEVAL	c.1500AD to present	Gold, silver, bone, clay pipes / John Rawls' grave

Ill. 79. Chronological chart of the occupation of Glastonbury Tor.

Celtic monastery of Tintagel; but neither from these excavations nor in the collections from earlier digs at the abbey site is there a single sherd. Yet such pottery certainly reached Somerset. It has been found at the hill-fort of South Cadbury (see pages 134, 142); at the Congresbury hill-fort near Weston-super-Mare; at the Roman town of Ilchester; and, as described in the following pages, elsewhere in the Glastonbury area itself, on the Tor. The discovery of Mediterranean pottery of the Arthurian period on the Tor serves to underline its absence from the much larger excavations at the abbey. Such negative evidence is not, of course, conclusive, especially in view of the other evidence described by Dr Radford. But it does show that any discussion of the links between Arthur and Glastonbury must take into account places other than the abbey.

A similar view was taken by the Chalice Well Trust in relation to the origins of Christianity in Glastonbury. The primary function of the Trust is to safeguard the Chalice Well and the area around it, which it believes to have been the scene of very early Christian activity, and to develop it as a religious centre. Pursuing these aims, the Trust decided in 1960 to sponsor archaeological research on sites in and

Ill. 105

Ills. 87 , 90.

Ill. 77

around Glastonbury, to try to substantiate the persistent traditions that Glastonbury was the scene of Christian evangelical activity as early as the first century A D. It was clear that the whole background of Glastonbury was relevant to this aim: the geological, topographical and climatic setting; the prehistoric and pre-Christian settlements, particularly their religious aspects; and the development of the area in Christian times, culminating in the emergence of the great abbey. Any Arthurian connection with Glastonbury is obviously important in this search for evidence of early Christianity.

The first excavation in this series sponsored by the Chalice Well Trust was in 1960, at Chalice Well itself, where slight indications were found of prehistoric and Roman occupation. The Tor, one of the most dramatic features of the Somerset landscape, was chosen as the next objective. It was dominated by the tower of the medieval chapel of St Michael, and its proximity to the great spring of Chalice Well suggested that here might be the nucleus of any pagan religious activity in Glastonbury, and this in its turn might have acted as a spur to early Christian missionaries. In the event, there was little evidence of prehistoric or Roman occupation, but there was an important settlement there in Arthurian times. This was followed by a late Saxon and early medieval monastic settlement of the tenth–twelfth centuries, and finally by the medieval church dedicated to St Michael, of which the tower alone has survived.

Before describing the dark-age remains found on the Tor, it is necessary to say something of the general background of the Glastonbury 'island' and of the topography of the Tor itself.

The plan shows the configuration of the 'island' and the relationship of the Tor to the abbey and other local sites. Recent work on the peat deposits around Glastonbury has shown that there have been many changes in water level and vegetation since Neolithic times. Towards the end of the Roman period, there were changes in the relative sea and land levels, which brought the sea (at the highest tides, at any rate) to the 18-feet contour. Such a level would cause most of the north Somerset plain to be flooded, leaving Glastonbury isolated except for the higher ground to the east linking it with the Shepton Mallet area. Conditions are unlikely to have changed substantially by c. 500; any discussion of Arthurian Glastonbury must therefore envisage the 'island' as approachable by land only from the east; otherwise by water or through very wet and marshy ground.

There is evidence of prehistoric occupation of the whole area from Mesolithic times onwards. The lake villages at Glastonbury and Meare, which are substantial settlements protected by marshy surroundings, probably date from the third or fourth century B C, and were apparently abandoned just before the Roman period.

It is still a matter of conjecture how long the Roman way of life characteristic of the fourth century A D survived into the dark ages. To the extent that Roman ideas and techniques continued into the later fifth and sixth centuries, north Somerset may be described as having a sub-Roman culture. But, as will be seen, there is very little that is Roman about the settlement on the Tor. It must, nevertheless, be taken as axiomatic that any study of Arthurian Somerset must be firmly related to the Roman background.

Roman settlement was dense in north Somerset, and there have been numerous finds of pottery and coins in and around the Glastonbury area. They have turned up in the upper levels of the lake-village sites of Glastonbury and Meare, on the western slope of Wearyall Hill near the abbey, at Chalice Well and on the Tor.

For the immediately post-Roman period with which this book is concerned, the only finds are those from the Tor. This important landmark of central Somerset is visible from all directions for up to twenty miles. It rises to a greater elevation (over 500 feet) than any other hill in the area, but its dramatic impact comes from the steepness of its upper slopes, rising out of the general mass of the 'island' in a way quite uncharacteristic of central Somerset.

It is this 'unnatural' aspect of the Tor that has encouraged the widely held belief that it is man-made. It is, in fact, composed of lias strata (Jurassic blue limestone) capped by a mass of hard sandstone which has resisted erosion. The instability of the lower strata has, however, caused severe slipping and fissuring of the summit, which makes interpretation of archaeological features very difficult. The summit is a fairly flat area about 100 feet by 50. The slopes to north, east and south are precipitous and eminently defensible. To the west, they are less steep and there is a 'shoulder' about 200 feet by 100. There are numerous terraces on the slopes; the conventional explanation of these is that they are natural or the result of agriculture, *i.e.*, strip-lynchets; but a theory has been recently put forward by Mr G. N. Russell that they are, in fact, the remains of a three-dimensional maze. The argument is complex, but it is worth consideration; if this were true, it would be of the greatest importance in any consideration of the religious aspects of Glastonbury.

Ill. 78

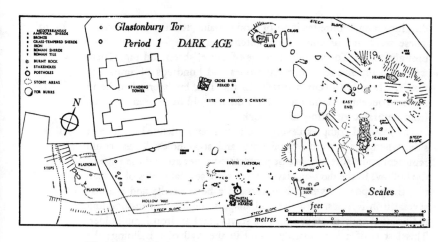

Ill. 80. Plan of dark-age features on
Glastonbury Tor.

The excavation of 1964–66 extended over nearly all of the summit and
part of the shoulder. The earliest dark-age, or 'Arthurian', levels
(Period 1), conventionally dated to the sixth century, were mostly on
the east and south sides of the summit. They may have extended over
the middle of the summit and down over the shoulder; but, if they
did, they have been destroyed by the building operations and rock-
quarrying of the later Saxon and medieval occupations (Periods 2 and
3). The middle of the summit, especially, has probably been levelled
for the medieval church, and there have been many later disturbances.
Where the Arthurian levels are encountered, they are protected by
deep silt, the result of wind and weather.

The plan shows all the features of dark-age date. The two graves
and the pit on the north side of the summit contained no artifacts. The
graves were both of young people, with the heads to the south:
generally a non-Christian arrangement.

The approach to the principal areas of dark-age settlement was
almost certainly from the west (*i.e.*, from the shoulder), up a series of
broad steps cut in the bedrock. These led to a series of 'platforms'
formed by cutting away the bedrock to make it more level. Here
were certainly wooden buildings, though very little remained of
them. The rock level was covered with much dark-age occupation

Ill. 80

Ill. 79

Ill. 84

dirt, including hundredweights of food remains, mainly animal bones. Ill. 93 These were not of animals slaughtered on the spot but of those brought to the Tor as joints: bones of cattle, sheep and pig. There were also much charcoal, burnt stones and hundreds of ammonite fossils. These last occur naturally on the Tor, but seemed to be in greater concentration in these levels than would have been expected from natural weathering of the rock.

The east-end complex lies in a hollow, sharply defined on its east Ill. 85 side, where there were several post- and stake-holes. These could represent some sort of fence or protective barrier around the edge of the hollow. In the dark-age layer, there were several pieces of Roman tile, the purpose of which is uncertain; a bone needle and spatula; several iron ferrules, of a size and shape suitable for iron-shodding the pointed ends of stout sticks or staves; and an iron lamp-holder. This last is of a kind usually found in the wall of a building; the twisted shanks would have been embedded in wood or stonework, and a lamp (of stone, metal or pottery) would rest in the circular end.

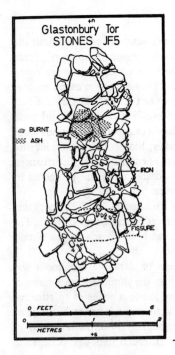

Ill. 81. A drawing of the cairn (*cf. Ill. 86*) found in the east-end complex at Glastonbury Tor.

Apart from this object and the few post-holes, and many patches of burnt rock, there was no definite evidence of a building here, though it may have been based on horizontal timbers which left no trace.

The most curious feature in this area was a cairn, some 10 feet by 4, found as a structure of large boulders, some burnt, lying among the dark-age layer. Carefully cleaned and photographed, it looked like a grave or tomb and aroused high hopes; but it contained nothing at all. Its purpose remains quite enigmatic. Various suggestions have been made: it might be a bench, the foundation for some structure, an 'altar' or a cenotaph (*i.e.*, a grave without a body).

The most important area was that on the south platform. The dark-age layer here lay all along a broad, fairly level shelf, some 4 or 5 feet below the level of the chapel area. This shelf was an artificially cut terrace, with definite edges in places; it originally extended further south but on this side it has been destroyed by erosion. The timber slot shown on the plan, which must originally have held a fairly substantial horizontal timber, has lost its south end; there may have been a wall or fence along this edge as there was round the east edge. On the shelf were many other features, some of which—such as several large post-holes—are clear evidence, along with the timber slot, of a major timber building. No definite plan can be suggested for this area, and there may have been several buildings along the south side, extending as far as the stepped approach at the west end.

Ill. 82. Drawing of the bronze head (*cf. Ill. 94*) found on the south platform at Glastonbury Tor. The details are uncertain as the whole object is badly corroded. The head is one and a half inches high with a core of iron which was presumably part of a larger object.

The most significant features in this area were two hearths. They may have been for normal domestic use (*i.e.*, for cooking or heating), but they appeared to have been basin-shaped; although the associated ash has not yet been examined scientifically, it is likely that they were for metal-working: a suggestion supported by the finding nearby of two fragments of crucibles, which were coated with bronze residues. The hearths would have been used for the extraction of metal, probably bronze, from ores or scrap metal, with the aid of bellows. The nozzle of a bellows might have rested in the small channel to the north of the bigger hearth.

Ill. 91

The other finds from the south platform were few but important. Apart from masses of food bones, there were several more pieces of Roman tile, about a dozen pieces of the imported Mediterranean amphorae (which form the dating evidence for this settlement), a large piece of locally made pottery—thick, coarse and grass-tempered—and the remarkable head. This is of bronze, forming a hollow casting around an iron core which can be seen at the back. The features are of the long 'Celtic' type, with the characteristic long chin and slit mouth. The deep eye sockets may originally have held enamel. Above the face is a domed helmet, with ear flaps on each side. Details are uncertain because the whole thing is very corroded. No parallel has yet been found for this object, nor would it have been easy to date if it had not been found in the same level as the imported sherds. Given a dark-age dating, what was its use? The iron core was presumably part of a larger object, such as a bucket escutcheon or the end of a staff; and the helmeted head was clearly a decorative feature on this object. It was found not far from the crucible fragments and the two hearths, and there is therefore the possibility that it was actually made on the Tor. Conceivably, heads of this type may have been manufactured there in some quantity, and perhaps other metal objects as well.

Ill. 93

Ills. 82, 94

The interpretation of this dark-age settlement is difficult. The remains are slight; there may well have been other features on the summit which were destroyed by the later chapel, or on the shoulder. The complex can be interpreted only from what survives on the south platform and the east end. The settlement is in a place likely to have been chosen for reasons other than those which govern the choice of a 'normal' settlement, such as a good water supply, or easy access to good farming or hunting land. There seem to be only two possible reasons that would cause the Tor to be chosen: religious or defensive, using these words in their widest sense.

Before discussing these alternatives, it is useful to summarise the characteristics of the dark-age occupation. The place is remote, inaccessible, 'inconvenient', a long way from water (though the Chalice Well would have provided an excellent supply at the foot of the hill) and very exposed, though with an excellent view. In the sixth century, there were constructed on the Tor timber buildings set on platforms cut into the rock to provide a level space. They were built into the south and east sides of the summit: the areas fairly sheltered from the prevailing south-westerly winds. The inhabitants ate considerable quantities of meat (or ate it over a long period) brought to the site as joints. They drank Mediterranean wine, or used olive oil, from imported amphorae.* They used Roman tile for uncertain purposes; it was probably foraged from a local Roman building. Within the occupied area, and probably within the principal building, metal-working was done in which crucibles and probably hearths were used. As has been said, the bronze-and-iron head is a rather special find and may have been made on the Tor.

An interpretation of the settlement as a religious site must immediately pose the question: pagan or Christian? Little is known of the process by which missionary activity in the fifth and sixth centuries converted the people of north Somerset. Historically, it is assumed that this area was Christian by the sixth century, though Somerset, archaeologically, is deficient in Christian finds or sites of either Roman or immediately post-Roman times. None of the find-spots in Somerset of imported pottery can yet be shown to be a Christian site, as is certainly the case with such find-spots further west. It is historically unlikely that the Tor was a pagan religious site in this period, though there is nothing in the archaeological evidence to contradict this view; while the north–south burials might appear to support it. The theory of a pagan religious site would be more convincing if there were evidence of a late Roman temple here, such as those which are so common in north Somerset, and mostly on hill-top sites. It may be observed in passing that at one such—Pagans Hill, some twenty miles

*This is perhaps going beyond the strict evidence. It has recently been pointed out that such amphorae were also used for the storage or transporting of other material—including, on one site, raisins and iron nails! Or the sherds may have been used for purposes quite different from those for which they were made.

north of Glastonbury—the temple well yielded finds of even later date (albeit probably derived only from a non-temple use of the site): a seventh-century glass and a bucket. These are among the very few finds of this period in Somerset. But the evidence of the Roman finds on the Tor cannot be stretched so far, and the lack of Roman sherds in the dark-age levels does not suggest continuity from late Roman times. In the absence of a Roman temple, the hypothesis of a sub-Roman or dark-age pagan religious site is unlikely, especially in view of our total ignorance of what such an enclave might be expected to contain.

The second possible religious interpretation is that the Tor was a small Celtic Christian monastic site, perhaps a hermitage. Its remoteness and exposed position might well have made it attractive to early Christian ascetics. Imported pottery is commonly found on early Christian sites elsewhere. Metal-working would be very much in place in such a community. The slight foundations of buildings set on platforms cut in the rock are characteristic of such sites. Yet one piece of evidence suggests that this is not the true explanation: the quantity of meat bones, which is totally at variance with what we know of the dietary discipline of early Celtic monks. Such evidence is not perhaps conclusive; this particular community may not have been orthodox on this point, or may have been remote from any strict example or control. But the meat bones do throw grave doubts on any Christian interpretation.

The other possibility is that the site was defensive or quasi-military, which may be thought the more relevant to Arthurian studies. The steepness of the slopes leading up to the summit, and the excellent view of the approaches in all directions, make the Tor a naturally defensible place. Again, it is not possible to do more than speculate on the character of the occupation or the identity of the settlement's inhabitants until we know more of political and military affairs in sixth-century sub-Roman Somerset.

A defensive interpretation may be thought of in two ways. Firstly, as a small outpost, look-out place, signalling station or the like, manned by a small number of men, subordinate to some more important place and part of a 'system' of linked defensive sites. This interpretation of the Tor in our period is without historical or archaeological support. The buildings and meat bones might suit such an interpretation, but the pottery and metal-working do not.

Secondly, and more probably, the settlement may be seen as the stronghold of a small local chieftain, an eyrie-type fortress. This

Ill. 96

chieftain was probably no Arthur* but someone of lesser stature, though quite important at Glastonbury, and doubtless known to the denizens of Camelot.

This is the concept of the Tor settlement which I favour. The buildings, meat-eating, imported wine or oil, the metal-working and, possibly, the graves—all are consistent with this. The metal-working evidence suggests, indeed, that this was no temporary refuge, to be resorted to only in times of danger, but a permanent residence comparable in its position and size with the craggy, exposed 'palace' sites at Dumbarton Rock, Dunadd and elsewhere. Security against sudden attack would certainly have been the main reason for the choice of site. We must, of course, envisage other buildings on the lower ground of Glastonbury which would be a part of the chieftain's 'estate', such as barns, stables and other domestic structures. This nucleus would presumably have depended, politically, on the allegiance of the people in at least the immediate neighbourhood, and, economically, on the resources of the farming and forest land under its control.

If we wish to put a name to the chief of Glastonbury, it should be Melwas, chief of the *Aestiva Regio* ('Summer Region') whom Arthur besieged in his Glastonbury stronghold and eventually concluded a treaty with, as described by Caradoc of Llancarfan in his *Life of St Gildas* (see page 120 above). If such an identification were acceptable, then perhaps the concepts of 'outpost' and 'stronghold' need not be so mutually exclusive as implied above.

Finally, what of other possible Arthurian or dark-age sites in the Glastonbury area? The Tor excavations were followed in 1967 by the first season of investigations at the chapel of Beckery, just below Wearyall Hill. The traditions of this place are that it was a Christian chapel dedicated to St Mary Magdalene before St Bridget came to Glastonbury from Ireland in 488. Arthur came to the chapel, too, and was rewarded by a vision of the Virgin Mary. The chapel was excavated in 1967. There were two buildings, an outer one of the

*It is, perhaps, not inconceivable that it might have been the lord of Camelot himself. If Arthur was buried at Glastonbury Abbey, he presumably had been a regular visitor there in pursuance of religious duties. However, his impious activities might have made him so much *persona non grata* with the monks at the abbey that he chose not to spend more time there than he had to, and preferred to resort to the Tor where he could eat and drink securely in the company of a few friends.

fourteenth century enclosing an inner one of late Saxon or early medieval date. These were later than timber structures and many graves, which certainly take the site well back into pre-Conquest times. But, apart from a few Roman finds, there was no pottery of pre-Saxon date, such as imported ware. So, unless this should be found in subsequent excavations, we cannot include Beckery in the archaeological evidence for Arthurian Glastonbury.

There remains Ponter's Ball, a massive earthwork of bank and ditch nearly a mile long, spanning the causeway connecting Glastonbury with the 'mainland' to the east. This has not yet been dated, though Dr Bulleid found Iron Age pottery beneath it in his excavation early in this century. Dr Radford has suggested that it might be the outer boundary of a great prehistoric sacred area; but it must at least be considered in any discussion of dark-age Glastonbury, whether pagan or Christian, civilian or military. If the last, it might be thought of as an outer defensive work for our chieftain's stronghold, safeguarding his whole 'estate'. It would be rather easy to by-pass by traversing the marshy land on either side, but it would yet be at least a discouraging obstacle to such activities as cattle-raiding. However, its inclusion in the Arthurian context must await the results of further excavation, and we must be content for the time being with what has been found in the abbey and on the Tor.

7 Cadbury: is it Camelot?

Leslie Alcock
and Geoffrey Ashe

. Ill. 99

SOUTH CADBURY CASTLE, to give the place its full name, crowns an isolated hill about 500 feet high near the Somerset-Dorset border. The hill is composed chiefly, if not entirely, of Inferior Oolite limestone. There has never been a castle here in the medieval sense. The top is occupied, and the name accounted for, by a hill-fort of the pre-Roman Iron Age. An enclosure covering eighteen acres is surrounded by four defensive perimeters, one outside another. Massive banks and ditches, sloping at an average gradient of about 35°, encircle the hill most of the way down to the fields below. Today they are thickly wooded, with patches of nettles and, in the springtime, bluebells and primroses. Three ancient entrances cut through them. On the north-east, a path leads up from South Cadbury village to the one now most used by visitors. On the south-west, there is a much less clear path from Sutton Montis. The third entrance, possibly later than the others, difficult of access and disused, is on the east.

Ill. 97

The spacious grassy enclosure inside the earthwork is by no means flat. It rises, steeply in places, to a summit ridge with a long, level plateau. The highest point commands an impressive view across the low-lying Somerset basin, with Glastonbury Tor twelve miles away toward the Bristol Channel. On the east side, Cadbury Castle faces a recess in the nearby hills, the edge of the higher ground of Wessex. Before the Roman conquest, this district was on the fringe of the territory of the Durotriges and within easy reach of the Glastonbury lake village.

Ill. 96

'Cadbury' is a name of uncertain derivation. Confusingly, there are other hills and earthworks so called. The 'bury' is Saxon. The 'Cad' looks like the principal syllable of a personal name which, if it is not also Saxon, could be one based on the Celtic *cad*, meaning 'battle'. A. W. Wade-Evans proposed the semi-legendary hero Cadwy, or Cado, connected with Somerset in the Welsh *Life of St Carannog*.

PEROID	APPROX. DATE	OCCUPATION	SIGNIFICANT FINDS
NEOLITHIC	3250 BC 2500 BC	Structural nature uncertain	Leaf and <u>petit tranchet</u> arrowheads Polished flint axes Windmill Hill type pottery
BRONZE AGE	1700 BC 750 BC	Late Bronze Age settlement running into Iron Age	Double spiral pin
PRE-ROMAN IRON AGE	500 BC AD 45	Hilltop town with defences Intensive occupation Roman sack followed by abrupt cessation of occupation	Maiden Castle type coarse pottery Glastonbury and Meare Lake Village type pottery Bead rim bowls Bronze Fiddle brooch Roman cuirass hinge and shield binding
ROMAN BRITAIN	AD 250 AD 400	Romano-Celtic temple	Gilt bronze letter 'A'
DARK AGE SUB-ROMAN	AD 470 AD 600	Dark Age defences	Tintagel B amphora sherds Drystone rampart
EARLY MEDIEVAL	AD 1010 AD 1020	<u>Burh</u> and Mint of Ethelred the Unready	Late Saxon <u>Burh</u> rampart Coins of <u>Cadanbyrig</u> (not found at Cadbury)

Ill. 95. Chronological chart of the occupation of South Cadbury Castle.

Not far off is the village of Queen Camel, formerly plain Camel. The belief that Cadbury Castle itself is Camelot can be traced back at least to John Leland, the Tudor antiquary. In 1542, he writes:

At South Cadbyri standith Camallate, sumtyme a famose toun or castelle. The people can tell nothing thar but that they have hard say that Arture much resortid to Camalat.

Leland, however, does appear to have heard a little more than this. He notes tales about a silver horseshoe, 'dusky blew stone' carried off by villagers, and Roman coins turned up by the plough, both on the summit and in fields near the base. Other antiquaries repeat Leland without adding much. But Stukeley in 1724 mentions sling-stones, Roman camp utensils, and the ruins of arches, hypocausts and pavements.

Local Arthurian lore is rich. Some of it, though unrecorded by Leland, was apparently current in his time. The summit plateau at the crest of the ridge is 'King Arthur's Palace'. One of the two widely separated wells in the hillside is 'King Arthur's Well'. It is alleged that at the other, Queen Anne's Well, you can hear when a cover is slammed down on King Arthur's, and vice versa. This idea is one aspect of a more general notion that the hill is hollow. Rumours of a large cavern are numerous and recurrent. Somewhere there is an iron gate, or maybe a golden one, and if you come at the right moment it stands open and you can see King Arthur asleep inside. Some early archaeologists were accosted by an anxious old man who asked them if they meant to dig up the king. But Arthur does not always sleep. On St John's Eve at midsummer, or perhaps on Christmas Eve, you can hear the hoofbeats of the horses as the king and his knights ride them down from Camelot to drink at a spring beside Sutton Montis church.

The Somerset Cam flows by in the middle distance. This is one of the conjectured sites of the battle of Camlann. Close to the western side of the hill, farm labourers once dug up some skeletons of men and boys, huddled together as if they had been pitched into a hasty mass-grave.

Historically, the soundest fact is that from about AD 1010 to 1020, coins were being issued with the mint mark CADANBYRIG. Before that, everything is hazy. In 1890, the Reverend James A. Bennett, rector of South Cadbury, published a paper entitled *Camelot*. Here he summed up the traditions and casually mentioned some digging he had done himself. When he 'opened a hut-dwelling on the plain of

Ill. 101

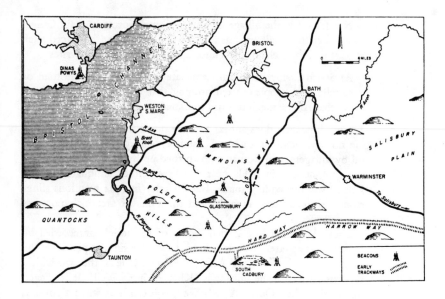

Ill. 96. Map showing South Cadbury
and its environs. The beacons indicate possible line-of-sight communi-
cation between these places

the hill', he saw a flagstone at the bottom, which the workman who
was helping supposed—but not for long—to cover a manhole
leading into the long-sought cave. Unfortunately, Bennett did not say
where the hut was.

The first properly recorded dig was carried out in 1913 by H. St
George Gray, who had also worked on the lake villages. He sectioned
the inner ditch, examined part of the south-west entrance, and
trenched the summit plateau. Near the entrance he found the remains
of a wall. Stone implements and pieces of pottery came to light. The
excavation was neither extensive nor very thorough. But St George
Gray recognised 'late Celtic' pottery and other artifacts akin to those
from the Glastonbury lake village. While he found nothing to support
the Arthur tradition, he expressed a wish to 'learn more about
Camelot, and to solve the many interesting problems which this
wonderful stronghold presents'.

Learning more about Camelot would clearly be a large undertaking. It was unlikely that sufficient interest or funds would be forthcoming till further evidence came to light to support the Arthur tradition and convince archaeologists that it deserved to be taken seriously. This was at last furnished during the 1950s by Mrs M. Harfield and Mr J. Stevens Cox, who patiently collected pottery and flints brought to the surface by ploughing. Dr Ralegh Radford picked out sherds of the significant Tintagel ware, together with a fragment from a Merovingian glass bowl. Commenting on this material, he observed that it provided 'an interesting confirmation of the traditional identification of the site as the Camelot of Arthurian legend'. Pottery of the earlier Iron Age, and of Neolithic type, was also recognised. Meanwhile, the growing of oats on the hill-top led to the appearance, in the summer of 1955, of a rash of crop-marks showing where soil had been disturbed in the past.

Ill. 100

Responding in November 1959 to a proposal for excavations, Dr Radford gave the inevitable answer that, without a sum of money running into thousands of pounds, the site seemed too big to handle. One would wish for buildings, but the eighteen acres supplied no good clues as to where to look for them. At Castle Dore there had been nothing on the surface to show the whereabouts, or even the presence, of the dark-age structures below. However, the project was revived five years later as a result of a magazine article. By then, the financial potentiality was believed to exist. In June 1965, the Camelot Research Committee was formed, with Dr Radford as Chairman and Mr Geoffrey Ashe as Secretary. Sir Mortimer Wheeler later accepted the Presidency. It was composed of representatives of the Society of Antiquaries, the Society for Medieval Archaeology, the Somerset Archaeological Society, the Honourable Society of Knights of the Round Table, and the Pendragon Society. These were subsequently joined by the Prehistoric Society, the Society for the Promotion of Roman Studies, the University of Bristol, the Board of Celtic Studies of the University of Wales, and the Somerset County Council. The representatives included Mr Philip Rahtz and Mr Leslie Alcock, and, outside the list of contributors to this book, Lady Fox and Mr J. G. Hurst. Hence, the committee brought together a number of investigators in the dark-age field, and its programme could be counted as the first serious 'Arthurian' research of a concerted nature. But the terms of reference were strictly confined to the adequate excavation of this one site. The task was entrusted to Mr Alcock, and thereby came within the purview of University College, Cardiff.

A query arose at an early stage as to how much dark-age matter Cadbury was likely to yield. If it lay near the surface, the havoc of ploughing might have reduced its value to near-vanishing point. Learned societies and professional archaeologists would be well satisfied with the Iron Age finds which could be confidently expected. But was the Committee justified in appealing for funds to a broader public, whose interests would be almost purely Arthurian?

It was decided to begin with a reconnaissance on a small scale, and not too costly. This could be financed to a large extent by the learned societies themselves, and there could be no objection to seeking further funds for a 'Quest for Camelot' (as the operation was soon called) if its initial tentative nature was made clear. The Quest soon attracted interest. Money was provided by the British Academy, the BBC, Bristol United Press, Messrs Hodder and Stoughton, the Society of Antiquaries, the University College of South Wales and Monmouthshire, and a number of private donors.

Accordingly the plan went forward. The landowners, Mr and Mrs J. A. Montgomery of North Cadbury Court, gave their permission for excavation, and much help and kindness on the site.

The reconnaissance was carried out from July 15 to August 6, 1966. It was in two phases running concurrently: a survey and a trial excavation. The survey in turn fell into two parts. One of these con- Ill. 97 sisted in making a contour plan of the eighteen-acre interior. Excavators would naturally hope to find traces of buildings. As it was out of the question to dig up the entire enclosure, some guidance would be needed in picking out the most promising areas. The clues from aerial photos, though interesting, were uncertain and insufficient. A contour survey might help both positively and negatively: positively, by showing which portions of the hill-top were the most level and suitable for building; negatively, by showing which portions could be written off because of the steepness of the slope.

From this point of view, the results were disappointing. The contour plan gave an excellent picture of the shape of the interior, with its summit plateau, the sides sloping down from this, and the level zone beside the rampart. It was all too obvious that only one small part of the hill-top, in the south-west, was wholly impossible for building. Nothing suggesting a terrace was detected. Terraces might have been blotted out by medieval and modern ploughing, but there were not even any traces, and on this topic aerial photography had

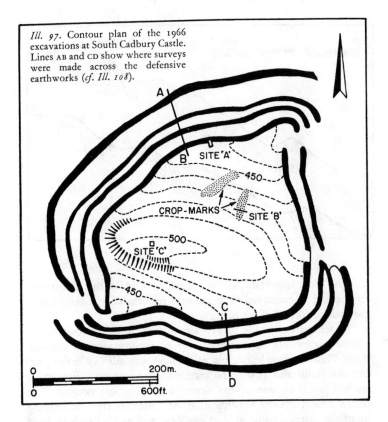

Ill. 97. Contour plan of the 1966 excavations at South Cadbury Castle. Lines AB and CD show where surveys were made across the defensive earthworks (*cf. Ill. 108*).

SITE 'A'

450

CROP-MARKS

SITE 'B'

500

SITE 'C'

450

A

B

C

D

0   200m.

0   600ft.

nothing to add. Excavation was to show in due course that occupants of the hill were not deterred by a mere gradient from putting up houses.

Still, it remained true that the nearly level summit was manifestly the easiest area for that purpose. Brief field-tests were made here with a soil conductivity meter invented by Mr Mark Howell. This device, popularly known as the 'banjo', had its pioneer archaeological trials at Cadbury. It works on a principle analogous to radar. The apparatus is slung from the user's shoulder and carried along parallel to the ground and about a foot above it. A dial shows changes in the conductivity of the soil. The process is fairly rapid and supplies an economical method of plotting irregularities below the surface. The 1966 test gave one impressive, if archaeologically useless, result by detecting a buried fragment of metal: a broken-off scrap of an old

Ill. 110

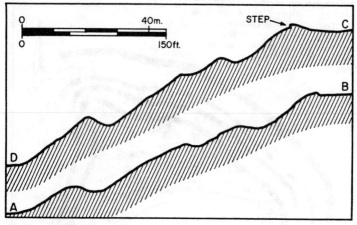

Ills. 108

plough. More important was the cumulative proof that the instrument could be employed to locate such features as post-holes under the shallow topsoil of the plateau.

The second aim of the survey was to take profiles across the defensive earthworks, as a preliminary to cutting sections through them. This was done in two places, on the north side (AB in the plan) and the south side (CD). The sections, especially CD, disclosed a marked break or step in the slope of the topmost rampart. The feature hinted at a late refortification. At some date after the heaping up of the original bank, at least one new wall seemed to have been built on top of it. The present layer of soil masked its presence but was not quite deep enough to conceal it altogether.

As to the 1966 excavations, these could not amount to more than a sampling. The main problem lay in deciding where to take the samples. For future guidance, one of the main tasks would be to determine stratification. Were the soil and its contents in chronological layers with the oldest material at the bottom, and so on up; or had the ploughing and other disturbances created a jumble?

Three cuttings were made at widely spaced points. The first (Site A in the plan) was a square pit 15 feet by 15, just inside the northern rampart, near the foot of the downward sweep from the plateau. Here it might be expected that soil loosened by ploughing, and afterwards exposed to rain, would have drifted slowly downhill over the years and accumulated against the rampart. Toward the close of the season, at the suggestion of Sir Mortimer Wheeler, this cutting was extended into the rampart itself. Site B was a sixty-foot trench laid out across a dark streak prominent on the aerial photos. Site C was another square pit, 20 feet by 20, on a part of the summit plateau rich in crop-marks. The precise location was fixed by thrusting a metal probe down to the bedrock at various places, and choosing a piece of ground where it frequently went deeper than usual, indicating that the bedrock might contain pits, ditches or other artificial depressions.

On a damp grey morning, in the presence of cameras, the first turf was removed from Site A. Digging revealed that the centuries of plough soil washed down the slope had piled up at the bottom, as foreseen. Nothing like stratification appeared till 4 feet below the present surface. There, however, a structural level could at last be identified. It produced pottery of around AD 40–50. Below was a stratified series of Iron Age levels with drainage gullies. The time limit halted excavation at a depth of 8 feet. Pottery at that level was not of the earliest Iron Age, and there was no reason to doubt that the bedrock lay considerably deeper.

The prolongation of this cutting into the rampart proved that refortification had indeed occurred. On top of the decayed pre-Roman earthwork was a bank of black soil, doubtless scraped up from the interior of the fort. On the inner side, this bank was faced (in technical language, 'revetted') with a very poor, mortarless wall of sandstone blocks. On the outside, it was faced with a much more civilised-looking wall, well-laid, mortared and 4 feet thick. The whole added rampart, comprising the earth bank and its two stone revetments, measured about 20 feet from inside to outside, and fully accounted for the step or break in the visible bank within which it had been concealed. A test pit was dug on the line of the southern survey profile, CD. There the outer wall was not found, but mortar streaks in the bank showed where it had once been. On the evidence thus far, it had very likely gone all the way round the hill-top.

The structure could not be dated or interpreted by itself. What was needed—and already largely available when it emerged to view—was a complete time-scheme of the occupation of Cadbury Castle. This was supplied partly by the general character of the other two excavation sites, partly by specific objects found in all three, and partly by facts known from outside sources.

Site B, the trench on the slope, gave further glimpses of the pre-Roman Iron Age. Late in that period (possibly even later), an immense ditch had been dug in that part of the hill, 50 feet wide, 6 feet 6 inches deep. Only a little of it could be uncovered, and its purpose was not established. On its edge the soil was coloured reddish by burnt daub—all that was left of an Iron Age house destroyed by fire. The most significant point about this was the somewhat daunting proof that Cadbury's inhabitants had been willing to build on a fairly steep slope. Hence, many acres which might have been ruled out, or at least consigned to a low priority, still had to be kept in the picture as potential excavation sites. The huge problem showed no sign of narrowing down.

Site C, on the highest patch of the hill, was fruitful but tantalising. It contained several post-holes, clearly defined by the different colour and texture of the soil. Some were very big. They had once contained pillars well over a foot thick, the supports of substantial buildings. But no pattern could be made out, nothing to show the size or plan of these ghostly halls. Like the fortification, they could not be dated on their own testimony. The answer could only come from the actual finds which would give the outline of the hill's history.

What were these finds, and what outline did they sketch?

Cadbury Castle, appropriately for Camelot, was plainly a kind of British Troy. Several layers of habitation covered a long tract of time. First came a Neolithic settlement in the third millennium BC. This had been inferred before 1966 from flint axes noted by St George Gray, fragments of pottery of the sort associated with Neolithic culture at Windmill Hill, and arrow-heads. The 1966 season added a few rims of Windmill Hill pottery, some of them from the top level in Site B, where they had evidently been washed down from dwellings on the plateau. Two more arrow-heads were unearthed, but of a later type than the pottery. The Neolithic part of the story remained shadowy. People had been on the hill, perhaps for a long time, but it was unsafe to say more.

Next came a single clue with large implications. It was a little bronze pin with a double-spiral head like a ram's horns. This resembled Irish pins of the dark age, and was optimistically classed as an 'Arthurian' find . . . until the realisation dawned that the spirals curled the wrong way. The difference of shape pushed it back more than a thousand years. The pin was of an oriental design, with parallels in Greece and Italy during the ninth and eighth centuries BC, and also in Dorset. In British terms, it belonged to the late Bronze Age,

Ill. 95

Ill. 104

a time of Mediterranean contacts expressed more showily in imitative bronze cauldrons. Cadbury Castle failed to yield any cauldrons.

By far the most plentiful finds belonged to the Iron Age, and covered a vast stretch of it. Early pottery items included rims of large, coarse vessels with decorations made by the potter's finger-tips. Next were some rough jars of a type found at Maiden Castle. Occasional fragments with cross-hatched and curvilinear ornament suggested the more advanced Celtic culture of Glastonbury and Meare lake villages, around the beginning of the Christian era. There were also pieces of bead-rim bowls, jars skilfully thrown on the wheel, storage vessels

Ill. 104 and a bronze 'fiddle' brooch. Some of these items could be dated by comparison with Maiden Castle material in what is believed to have been a war cemetery. They belonged to the eve of the Roman conquest, about AD 45.

Much of the pottery of this last Iron Age phase was heavily burnt: a vivid token of the final catastrophe. Roman history records that Vespasian, who conquered southern Britain, took a series of hill-forts by storm. Very probably Cadbury was one of these, and the pottery was burnt when the legionaries sacked the place. They left

Ill. 104 tokens of their own. Excavators turned up a cuirass hinge, part of a shield binding and a very worn coin—a denarius of the Roman republic. After the conquest, the hill-top seemed to have been empty for many years. But below, near South Cadbury church, a valuable supplementary dig conducted by Mr John Laidlaw disclosed what might have happened: the Romans evicted the Celtic population and made them live in a place they could not fortify. Beside the church, people undoubtedly settled soon after the hill-fort fell, and continued to live for a century or more.

Then Roman material began reappearing on the top. The 1966 work yielded some pottery of the third and fourth centuries, two

Ill. 104 coins, and a gilt bronze letter 'A'. As to this last, the theory was proposed after much debate that in the pagan revival during the last decades of Roman Britain, a Romano-Celtic temple had been built on the hill, as at Lydney and Maiden Castle. The gilt letter could have come from a votive inscription, perhaps to Mars.

All these results were fascinating and, to archaeologists, ample justification for pressing on. But journalists also were frequenting the hill and asking questions. So were visitors, who came in such numbers that members of the team had to be detached as guides. Neither the journalists nor the visitors (who dropped a total of over £100 into a collection box on the site) would be satisfied with Ancient

Britons or Romans. Nor would the more literary-minded supporters of the Camelot Research Committee. For them the project would stand or fall by its success in upholding Cadbury's claim to be Camelot. If the reconnaissance could produce nothing from the dark age, the future of the Committee and its plans would be in doubt. Failing the bronze pin, which eventually did fail, a great deal could depend on a tiny minority of finds.

The evidence was slight, but it was enough. As in other places, most of it took the form of Tintagel B pottery: sherds of eastern Mediterranean amphorae like those collected by Mrs Harfield, datable to the dark age and implying a wealthy occupant. Besides these there was a small iron knife, edgeless and misshapen but characteristic of the same period. The most hopeful point about the amphora fragments, beyond the basic fact of their being present at all, was that they occurred in all three cuttings—even on the plateau, where occupation material would have been most subject to drift and to destruction by ploughing. The three trial sites accounted for less than one seven-hundredth of the whole great enclosure, yet 'Arthurian' items were in all three. A single haul might have been put down to luck. The only credible reason for a three-out-of-three success was that the dark-age occupation had been a major one, leaving its traces far and wide. On the analogy of Degannwy and Dinas Powys, it could now be said that a person of importance—an Arthur-type figure, so to speak—had lived in the hill-fort at approximately the right time. If so, the post-holes in Site C might have held the pillars of his hall.

This was not quite the end. When the season's excavation was finished it still did not explain the added rampart. It was clear only that both the stone walls must be comparatively late. The crude inner revetment might conceivably belong to the dark age, the mortared outer one did not. Here the answer was provided by previous knowledge. The coins with the mark CADANBYRIG showed that Cadbury was the site of a mint in the last years of Ethelred the Unready and the first years of Canute, perhaps from 1010 to 1020. This mint was founded away from danger during a time of warfare, and not used for very long. Inherent probability and local tradition agreed in pointing to the hill-fort itself as its location. A mint should imply a *burh*: an inhabited centre with some sort of protective perimeter. The re-fortification revealed by the northern cutting was executed in a manner suitable to a Late Saxon *burh*. It could thus be assigned to the eleventh century. Such an interpretation explained the apparent traces of the same wall going round the other side, and also the

Ill. 105

Ill. 101

Ills. 102,

remnants of walling noted by St George Gray in 1913, when he probably stumbled on the inner end of the gate passage at the southwest of the Saxon *burh*.

Armed with the proofs that Cadbury Castle harboured something like four millennia of British history and prehistory, and that its claim to be Arthur's fortress was now much strengthened, the Camelot Research Committee issued an appeal for funds. About £5,000 was raised from a variety of sources—most of the same that had contributed in 1966, and also the Pilgrim Trust, the *Observer* newspaper, Bristol University and many other organisations and private donors. It is worth remarking that the project never threatened to become dependent on a single sponsor or on subsidies from overseas. It remained a co-operative venture and, though generously helped from America, a British one.

Ill. 109
Ill. 110 The first step taken in 1967 was to look for concealed building sites by another method: a geophysical survey instead of a contour survey. This was an extension of the short test with Mr Howell's soil conductivity meter. Oxford entered the scene and collaborated with Cardiff. At Easter 1967, teams from both universities explored the conductivity of the soil and the magnetic field in a broad belt of ground stretching along the summit ridge. Four different instruments were used, including the 'banjo' itself and a proton-magnetometer, and over 100,000 readings were set down. When plotted on a chart, they showed that the bedrock below the grass and soil was very far Ill. 107 from smooth. It was spotted with a rash of holes that could not all be natural features. The presumption was that they were pits dug in the Iron Age for the storage of food or refuse. Besides these, there were clear signs of half-a-dozen curved trenches—'ring-ditches'—which hinted at the round houses of the same period. Also, in three places, parallel straight trenches and rows of holes suggested foundations and post-holes, marking the outlines of vanished rectangular timber houses, such as might have been built in the dark age or during the Saxon tenure.

The main trouble with these assorted dents in the bedrock was not scarcity but frequency. It looked as if pits and buildings had been superimposed so many times during the three or four thousand years Ill. 111 of settlement as to produce a sort of palimpsest. Some of the shapes alleged by the investigators could only be discerned on the chart by the eye of faith. As it turned out, one of the most remarkable features

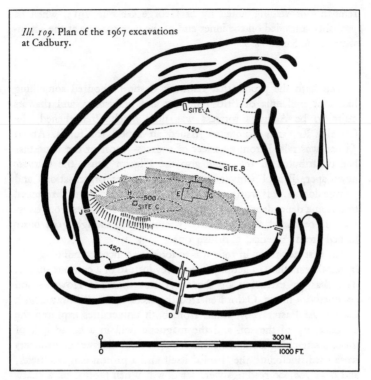

Ill. 109. Plan of the 1967 excavations at Cadbury.

of all was so much entangled with other markings that, although it showed on the chart, its nature was not grasped till actual excavation drew attention to it.

Toward the eastern end of the plateau, however, there was an area where the full subterranean circle of a ring-ditch was so plain as to admit no doubt. A little to the west of this, parallel lines hinted at a rectangular shape. All around, the bedrock was heavily pitted. It was safe to assume that excavation in this area would be productive, that it would yield at least Iron Age matter, and that it might also reveal an 'Arthurian' foundation. The area was accordingly chosen as one of the two main sites for the summer's work. The other was on the southern rampart, where the objective was to cut a complete section through the four banks, from the top of the hill to a point far down the side.

Ill. 111

Six weeks were allotted to the programme, from the middle of July to the end of August. A bigger team was enrolled, partly by selection

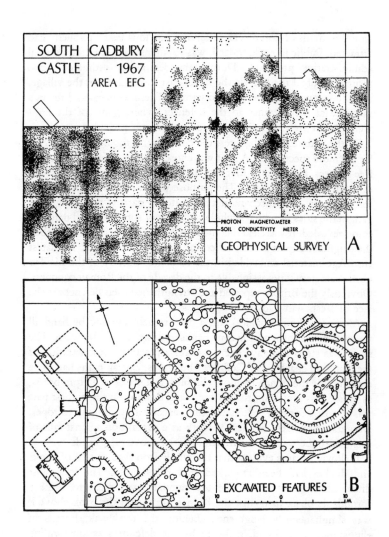

Ills. 110, 111. A geophysical survey, using four different instruments, was made of a broad area of the summit plateau of Cadbury hill before the turf and topsoil were removed. When the readings were plotted on a dot-density chart, an area (*Ill. 110*) near the eastern end appeared a particularly promising site for digging. The full circle of a buried ring-ditch was unmistakable, there were hints of a rectangular shape and the bedrock was heavily pitted. The features found in 1967 in this area are shown in *Ill. 111*. For an interpretation of these features see *Ills. 115, 116.*

from hundreds of volunteers whom the previous year's publicity had attracted. Public interest, indeed, was so intense that it raised unusual administrative problems. During the season an estimated 5,000 visitors climbed the hill via the north-east footpath from the village, including several large organised parties. These were catered for in a marquee at the entrance to the defences, where some of the finds were put on view. A full-time guide service was provided.

Of the main excavation sites, the cut through the ramparts was by far the more spectacular. A spot was chosen where all four banks were free of trees. Here, in the first two days, a mechanical excavator sliced through the topmost bank. The purpose was to obtain a rapid section for guidance. The mechanical cut created a narrow and dangerous gap, in the sides of which a whole sequence of superimposed defences stood revealed. It was clear that the Iron Age occupants had remodelled the original rampart at least twice and possibly four times. The latest Iron Age material embedded in the bank was pottery of the Maiden Castle cemetery type, assignable to the decade of the Roman conquest. Obviously the Britons repaired and strengthened their defences in the face of Vespasian's advance.

Alongside the mechanical cut, a deep trench was dug by hand all the way down through the four banks and the ditches between. The slope was steep and gave every worker a practical demonstration of the daunting character of Cadbury's bulwarks. Zigzag paths had to be made beside the trench to allow climbing in a series of hairpin bends, as on a Swiss mountain road. Ascent and descent on the highest part was almost a form of mountaineering, executed by clinging to ropes. Diggers wore safety helmets at work as a precaution against falls of rock, since the walls of the trench towered above their heads.

Ills. 98, 106, 108

It slowly became evident that the whole Iron Age system of banks and ditches had been reworked at various times. The innermost ditch, immediately below the top rampart, was recut to make a formidable obstacle against the Roman army, and the bank above it was simultaneously heightened. Behind the top bank, hoards of slingstones were found, gathered by the defenders as ammunition but not all expended before the legionaries burst in.

However, the Iron Age history of this rampart was seen to be long and complex, and its complete dissection was postponed. Instead, the team concentrated its efforts on the later phases glimpsed in 1966. These had already singled out Cadbury as a special case among hill-forts, because refortification on a large scale after the Iron Age, as carried out here by the Saxons if no one else, is otherwise unknown in

Britain save at Cissbury in Sussex. Dark-age Welsh chieftains re-occupied them, as at Garn Boduan; but as we have seen in chapter 4, they did not refurbish the old defences. At Cadbury something exceptional had happened. What precisely?

To find out, further cuttings were made through the top bank on the other three sides of the hill. They told a consistent and exciting story.

Ill. 103   The perimeter of the Late Saxon *burh* was easily identified. It rose on top of everything else, with only a shallow earth covering. Its principal feature was a wall of masonry perhaps originally about 10 feet high. Behind this was a bank, normally composed of soil from the interior. In places, where rocks lay near the surface, the builders made use of rock rubble instead. Behind this again there was usually a dry-stone revetment. Hence, the soil or rubble was sandwiched between an inner and an outer stone wall. The resulting rampart was 14 to 20 feet thick, and rose forbiddingly above the old banks and ditches, which must in themselves have looked deterring to an attacker, even in the eleventh century when they were decayed.

As the complete circuit of the hill-top is about 1,200 yards, 'Cadanbyrig' was in the medium-size range of Late Saxon *burhs*. Before 1967, it was assumed that the Saxon mint and *burh* were merely temporary establishments in an emergency. But it is hard to believe that Ethelred would have fortified a temporary centre with 1,200 yards of well-laid mortared masonry. Apparently, in sharp contrast with the normal ways of his time, he meant Cadanbyrig to be a permanent hill-top town. Such a scheme suggests a highly unusual hill—perhaps with unusual associations. And inspection disclosed that, when the Saxons built their rampart, they built it on top of something else more extraordinary still.

Directly beneath it, or, in places, close beneath it with a thin layer of soil between, was another rampart which had also been added to the original one at some date before the Saxons. It was a chaotic mass of
Ills. 112, 113   piled stones and earth which diggers soon christened the Stony Bank. In the cuttings on the north and south of the perimeter, the outer side of this bank had slid away down the hill. But on the west, an observer who climbed over on to the slope and looked at the bank from the outside could trace the bottom course of a stone wall-face. The thing had undoubtedly been a structure, and very big. On the east, to an observer similarly placed, the outside really looked like a wall. Three or four courses of stone lay visibly one above another, over a stretch of 24 feet.

Gaps in the stone about 6 feet apart showed where timber posts had been planted to carry a wooden breastwork. From the upright posts, others had run horizontally backwards to tie the uprights into the body of the rampart. In the southern cutting were plausible traces of a more complex timber structure, perhaps the base of a wooden tower. Such a defensive system of timber, stone walls and earth-and-rubble core was very much in the pre-Roman Celtic tradition . . . only this one could not be pre-Roman.

Ill. 114

It overlay a level containing pottery and slingstones from the time of the Roman conquest itself. Hence it was later than that conquest. But during the heyday of the Empire, the native Celts were not even allowed to live on the hill, much less fortify it. The rubble in the core of the Stony Bank included Roman tiles and blocks of dressed tufa, a porous stone used by the Romans, especially for vaulting. These pieces must have been taken from a demolished Roman building of fairly civilised type. The only candidate was the presumed temple, which would not have been built, let alone pulled down, much before the last generation of the fourth century A D.

The conclusion was patent. Between 400 and 1000, somebody had refortified Cadbury Castle. Furthermore, his style of construction proved him to be Celtic and a restorer of the ways of Celtic forefathers. He was not a Saxon. As the Saxons conquered this part of Somerset in the seventh century, and may have penetrated earlier still, the acceptable range of time shrank to little more than two hundred years. Almost in the middle of it was Arthur.

A more exact inference about this dramatic and unparalleled bulwark would depend on another question. What was the date of the settlement (clearly an important and wealthy one) which it was meant to protect? Of all the inhabitants of the hill, which were within the time range? The simultaneous work on the plateau confirmed the answer already suggested by 1966.

Excavation here soon bore out the geophysical survey and proved its value. When the topsoil was removed, large black patches began to appear against the orange brown of the solid rock, precisely where the instruments had predicted. They showed where rock-cut gullies and pits had been filled in with contrasting material. Over the weeks, more and more features were exposed: post-holes, drainage channels, foundations. These and other remains of human occupancy turned out to be strangely mingled and difficult to interpret. But the previous year's story was steadily checked and amplified.

The Neolithic beginnings were pushed back toward 3000 BC. Pits were noted with red clay in them—the natural soil of the hill-top before ploughing, a process that started in the Neolithic age. The pits contained flints, pottery and a fine leaf-shaped arrow-head. Gullies of the same period hinted at an enclosure or building outside the excavated zone.

After the Neolithic people were gone, the hill was seemingly empty till about 1000 BC. The 1966 pin had given the first indication of Bronze Age inhabitants. More traces of them were now unearthed, including a knife and a spearhead. Metal objects like these could have been lost or broken in the course of hunting, and did not prove permanent settlement. But pottery and loom-weights were found also, making it much more probable. Numerous fragments, and some nearly complete vessels, gave an impression of continuity from the late Bronze Age into the early Iron Age. They furnished profoundly interesting support for a view now widely held, that the Celtic immigrants from the continent, who brought the use of iron to Britain, adopted much of the culture of the pre-Celtic natives. They are thought to have copied them by building round houses, as the Celts of the continent did not generally do; and a small round house which was just discernible on the Cadbury plateau could well have belonged to the Bronze rather than the Iron Age.

This latter period supplied the bulk of the finds. Plainly, the Celtic settlement was flourishing and populous. From the sixth century BC to the Roman conquest, the thousands of pottery sherds ran in sequence without a break. Besides the pottery there were bronze brooches, glass and amber beads, armlets of black shale, spinning and weaving equipment, a piece of a sword scabbard and a few Celtic coins. As expected, storage pits riddled the area. The inhabitants had cut them in the rock and packed them with wicker baskets containing grain and other foodstuffs. When a basket became foul with age it was burnt, leaving a charcoal coating at the bottom of the pit and marks of fire up the sides. Eventually storage was abandoned and the hole was used as a refuse dump or cess pit.

The location of Iron Age buildings was shown by post-holes and an oven. The ring-ditch predicted by the survey proved to be 3 feet deep and 6 feet wide, and enclosed an area 40 feet across. It was a continuous trench, not a circle of close-set post-holes for the base of a building, and no post-holes corresponded to it. The ditch could be construed as a drainage gully, but drainage without a house seemed illogical, and the circle therefore remained somewhat enigmatic.

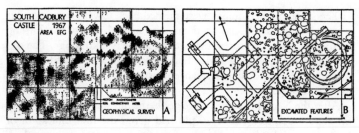

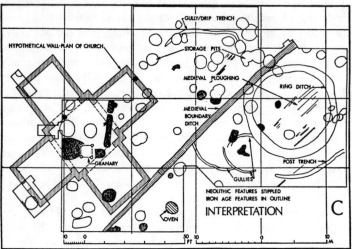

Ills. 115, 116. The dot-density chart, the features unearthed during the 1967 excavations and an interpretation of them.

All these discoveries confirmed Cadbury's ancient importance. None fitted in with the paradoxical rampart. Nor did the 1967 dig on the plateau unearth any further signs of Romans or Romano-Britons. But it did augment the collection of dark-age amphora fragments. As before, these could be assigned to the late fifth or early sixth century A D. The number was small. But the likeliest explanation of this fact was the same as at Degannwy. Imported pottery has been found in large amounts in the hovels of peasants, whereas the kingly stronghold of Maelgwn, more sophisticated and tidier, yielded only half-a-dozen stray scraps. To find this type of pottery, but to find it only sparsely and widely scattered, is good evidence of a rich, com-

Ill. 105
paratively civilised settlement. Such a view accords with the only further object which the summit produced: a gilt bronze button-brooch ornamented with a helmeted head. This could be dated about AD 525–50. But it was Teutonic, not British. Since the major Saxon colonies of that date were nowhere near Cadbury, it is a credible conjecture (though others are also credible) that the Britons who imported the amphorae were powerful enough to loot Saxon belongings or to carry off Saxon slaves.

Nothing on the plateau was later than the Teutonic brooch. Barring some amazing upset, no reasonable doubt was left. The unparalleled rampart was built somewhere about 500, to defend the home or headquarters of a great British chieftain. As if to clinch the matter,
Ill. 113
one sherd of the imported pottery was found lying on the back of it.

Thus the 1967 season brought a vivid success, but not quite in the way anticipated. So far as Arthur was concerned, the main hope had been that excavation would reveal buildings. At the end, those who wished could still believe that some of the post-holes of either year might belong to the dark age. But not a single case had been proved. The best of the straight lines on the geophysical chart turned out to be a medieval field boundary-ditch, not part of an oblong foundation.

One building in the Christian era—or at least the intention of a building—was amply proved. However, this was to be the most puzzling feature of all.

Ills. 115, 116
Near the western edge of the summit site, the surveys had shown what looked like part of a rectangular pattern. When this was uncovered, it proved to be a ditch cut in the bedrock. However, the ditch did not enclose a rectangle. It made several ninety-degree turns without a break, and both ends disappeared under the turf outside the excavation area. For want of a better description, the ditch was called the Zigzag Feature. It inspired several fanciful theories. At first, the most promising was that it was an unfinished practice-trench dug during military exercises in the 1914 war. Veterans, however, objected that it was too wide, and villagers maintained that no troops had ever been on the hill-top.

Toward the close of the season, two questions were being asked with some insistence. First, what about the unknown part of the ditch under the turf? Did it by any chance go round and join up, so as to enclose an area? And secondly, if so, what shape was the area; and in particular, could it be a cross? The section of the feature that had been dug up did suggest a portion of an equal-armed cross about eighty feet from extremity to extremity.

Fresh tests with the banjo and other instruments, followed by systematic use of a steel probe, afforded some support to both guesses. Measurements were then made over the grass to determine where the feature would be if it did indeed trace out a cross. Three small new trenches were dug to find out if it was there. It was.

The Zigzag Feature now became the Cruciform Feature. To all appearances it was a trench for the foundations of a building. Yet this had not actually been built. Irregularities of size implied that even the digging of the foundation was never finished. Two more things could be said with confidence. The width and depth pointed to a masonry building, not a timber one. Also, the angles between the arms of the cross were bevelled off; at each of these four places the foundation was wider than elsewhere, presumably to take the base of a heavier structure. The building, therefore, had been meant to have   Ill. 117

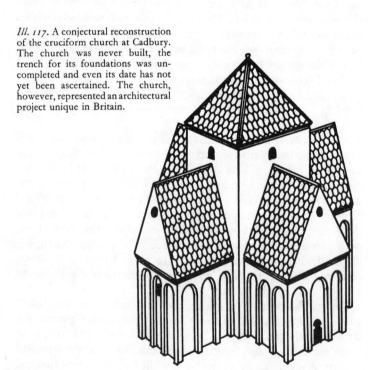

Ill. 117. A conjectural reconstruction of the cruciform church at Cadbury. The church was never built, the trench for its foundations was uncompleted and even its date has not yet been ascertained. The church, however, represented an architectural project unique in Britain.

four equal arms and a central square rising above them, with protruding or buttressed corners. This projected tower could have been square or octagonal. Stone tiles found on the site might or might not have been intended to go on the roof. Whatever the doubts as to detail, there could be no serious doubt as to the purpose of the building. A Greek or equal-armed cross with a central tower could only mean an early church. The orientation was about 30° north of east. But other early churches are just as far off the east-west line.

Such a plan was never common. There are a fair number of churches with roughly equal arms, but surprisingly few where the equality is as nearly exact as it is at Cadbury. The prototype of Greek-cross churches is that of the Holy Apostles at Constantinople, the mausoleum of Constantine, built in 337 and reconstructed by Justinian. In the fourth, fifth and sixth centuries, the plan was followed in various parts of the Christian East, especially for memorial churches housing a tomb or the relics of a martyr. Cruciform chapels were built in Visigothic Spain in the seventh century and, by inference, earlier. The plan was not much favoured among the Anglo-Saxons, but something like it was used by Bishop Wilfrid at Hexham in the eighth century, and by Alfred, more elaborately, in the ninth. Afterwards the familiar Latin cross, formed by a long nave and smaller transepts, supplanted it almost everywhere.

Provisionally, the unbuilt Cadbury church may be dated in either of two contexts. The Greek-cross layout was certainly adopted more often in the fifth and sixth centuries than at other times. The church, therefore, might have been planned as part of the dark-age British settlement. Spain would be a credible source of inspiration if one is needed. Spanish influence on Celtic Christianity can be documented. The absence of a known parallel in dark-age Britain or Ireland is not a grave stumbling-block, since our knowledge of Celtic church buildings is too scanty, and based on too slight archaeological data, to allow any dogmatic statements. The Cadbury building could be 'Arthurian', and if there are no parallels to it in the British Isles there are several in the Mediterranean zone. Moreover, the dark-age rampart has no British parallels either, and the mind that was original enough to conceive this might presumably have conceived the church —though the contrast between the crudity of the former and the sophistication of the latter makes the argument a poor one to rely on.

But the building could also be late Saxon, the intended church of Ethelred's abortive *burh*. The lack of perfect parallels in the eleventh century is a stronger objection, since remains of roughly contemporary churches are plentiful, not only on the continent but in England. However, a somewhat similar church with a central tower was probably built at Sherborne, only six miles away, in the decade before the foundation of Cadanbyrig.

The best argument for a Saxon date is that it explains why such an ambitious building should have been started and abandoned. Ethelred's mint was not used for long. Cadanbyrig coinage was discontinued in the reign of Canute. If the mint was the only reason for the *burh*, we have a coherent story. The construction of two-thirds of a mile of mortared wall absorbed all the available force of skilled masons for a considerable time. A start was made on the church late in Ethelred's reign. Then his death, and the brief and troubled reign of his successor Edmund Ironside, threw the *burh* scheme into abeyance. Canute finally dropped it.

Further excavation, or fresh evidence from other sources, may settle the question of the cruciform church. The results of 1967 left it an intriguing mystery. Neither date is altogether convincing. What is certain is that the plateau, as well as the rampart, has disclosed an architectural project which is both grandiose and unique in Britain: one that bears the stamp of a bold, original, but still anonymous mind.

All being well, the Quest for Camelot will go on. Its archaeological value extends, of course, far outside the dark age, and ensures the support of many scholars who are not concerned with Arthur. But, to most people, Arthur is bound to be the main interest. What did the first two years establish?

To say that the hill-fort was reoccupied at the right time, by a British chieftain of power and wealth, is to say nothing that does not apply equally to sites in Wales. But the lord of Cadbury did at least one thing which the Welshmen did not. He refortified it on a huge scale. So far as we can tell, nobody else in Britain, whether Celt or Saxon, ever did what he did with an ancient stronghold of this type.

To find even approximate analogues we must go to the Rhineland and the eastern Alps. There, during the fourth century, the Celtic people began reconditioning the hill-forts as cities of refuge in the perils of the Empire's decline. They built new walls in a variety of styles, sometimes putting up mortared masonry, sometimes combining dry-stone with timber. A few of these citadels continued to be used during the turmoil of the Germanic folk-wanderings, and new ones were founded, sheltering Christian churches inside the defences.

This continental parallel is at least Celtic, but it is not exact. Cadbury Castle around the year 500 must have been more than a mere refuge. The Saxons were nowhere within many miles. The conclusion is inescapable that it was the fortress of a great military leader, a man in a unique position, with special responsibilities and an unusual temper of mind. To reach this point is to arrive, in effect, at a *dux bellorum*. Nothing has emerged to show what his name was, and we shall be lucky indeed if it ever does. But the question of the name is hardly more than a quibble. The lord of Cadbury was a person as much like Arthur as makes no matter: a person living on a site traditionally picked out as his home, in the traditional period, with resources on the traditional scale, playing at least a part of the traditional role; a person big enough for the legends to have gathered round him. Nowhere else but at Cadbury does Britain supply any archaeological trace of such a person.

One more point must be added, and it opens up vistas. Until lately, historians reconstructing the figure of Arthur were inclined to view him as the last of the Romans. Ambrosius's British revival, in the 460s or thereabouts, was a revival of the Romanised rather than the Celtic element. It was natural to assume that Arthur followed the same line. So, in some degree, he probably did. But the degree seems to have been less than imagined. The dark-age rampart shows no Roman influence whatever. While 'towered Camelot' may well have been a reality, the towers were wooden look-out posts appropriate to Cymbeline rather than Caesar. The *dux bellorum* defended—no doubt consciously and proudly—what Britain retained of the imperial heritage. He may have done it in virtue of some imperial title. But he did it as a Briton. William Blake's oracular utterance is turning out to be a prophetic insight. The stories of Arthur are the acts of the Giant Albion.

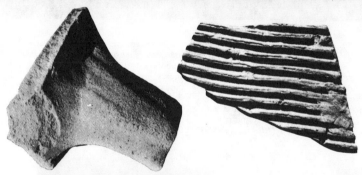

Ills. 87–90. Finds made in the course of excavations at Glastonbury Tor. *Ill. 87,* top, shows sherds and bones *in situ* and *Ills. 88–90,* details of sherds. All of the pieces of imported Mediterranean ware found at the Tor are of Tintagel class B amphorae which has also been discovered at other sites mentioned in the text (*cf. Ills. 54, 105*). The presence of this pottery, which can be dated to the dark age, is the chief source of our knowledge of an occupation of the Tor during the 'Arthurian' period.

Ills. 91, 92. The basin-shaped hearths (*Ill. 91,* top) were found on the south platform at the Tor. The evidence suggests that they were used for metal-working rather than for domestic purposes. The fragments of two crucibles, coated with bronze residues, were found nearby. The bronze head (*Ills. 82, 94*) was found near the crucibles which indicates the possibility that it was made on the Tor. *Ill. 92,* below, shows the iron lamp-holder. This type of holder is usually found in the wall of a building, the shanks embedded in the wall and the lamp – of stone, metal or pottery – resting in the circular end.

Ill. 93. The midden of animal bones found in a fissure in the rock and which dates back to the dark-age occupation of the Tor. The presence of the bones is strong evidence that the Tor was not a monastic settlement during the dark age. Consumption of meat in such quantities is totally at variance with what is known of the dietary discipline of early Celtic monks. The bones do, however, fit in with the explanation that the occupation was defensive in nature: either a small outpost or the stronghold of a local chieftain to which joints of animals were imported for eating.

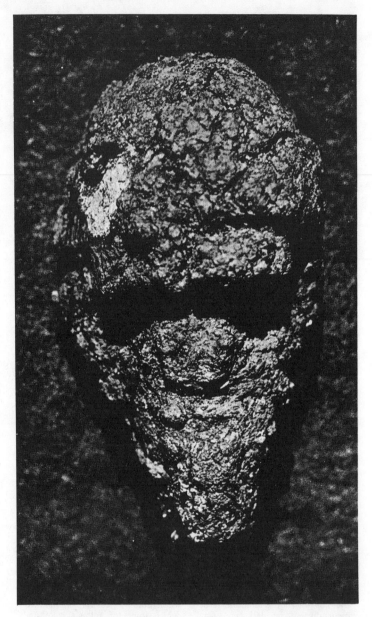

Ill. 94. The bronze head found at Glastonbury Tor (*cf. Ill. 82*). The head obviously served as a decoration, possibly as a bucket escutcheon or the end of a staff. The deep eye sockets may originally have been filled with enamel. Nothing exactly similar to this head has yet been found. It was discovered at the same level as the imported sherds which enabled it to be dated to the dark age.

Ill. 98. Aerial view of the defensive
ramparts which encircle the hill-top
enclosure of South Cadbury Castle.
The cut through the ramparts is
parallel with the line CD on the plan
(*Ill.* 97). The ramparts were first
erected during the Iron Age (700 BC
to AD 43).

Ill. 99. View of Cadbury hill from the south-east. Its wooded slopes are ringed by the banks and ditches of four defensive perimeters. A pre-Roman hill-fort on the summit accounts for the name Cadbury Castle which is given to the hill.

Ill. 100. Aerial view of the summit of Cadbury hill taken in 1955. The dark patches are crop-marks which appeared in the summer of 1955 after oats had been planted on the hill. Such marks occur where the soil beneath has been disturbed in the past and indicate earlier human occupation.

Ill. 101, below. Reverse and obverse
of a coin of Ethelred the Unready
minted at Cadbury by a coiner who
signed himself 'God'. The inscription around the central ornamental
device reads '+GODONCADANBYRIM'.
(of God at Cadbury). The inscription
surrounding the portrait of the king
reads '+EDELREDREXANGLORU.X'
(Ethelred king of the English).

Ills. 102, 103. A section of the Late Saxon revetted wall (*Ill. 102,* above) unearthed in the inner rampart at Cadbury. It protected a *burh,* or inhabited centre, which was the site of the eleventh-century mint, and was originally perhaps as high as 10 feet. The wall was built above an earlier rampart and part of it was demolished, as shown at left in *Ill. 103,* right, in order to examine the older construction more closely. This latter was dated to the fifth or sixth century (see also *Ills. 113–15*).

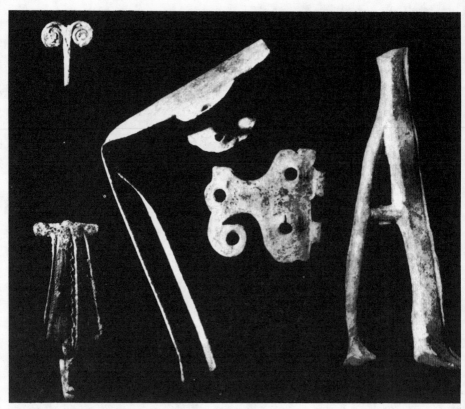

Ills. 104, 105. Finds made at Cadbury which range in time from the late Bronze Age to the Late Saxon period. The bronze pin with double-spiral head (upper left corner, *Ill. 104* above) was originally thought to be dark-age but it is now considered more likely that it was made in the ninth or eighth century BC. The bronze 'fiddle' brooch at lower left belongs to the Iron Age, just prior to the Roman conquest. The two pieces next to it are Roman military bronzes: a cuirass hinge and part of a shield binding. The gilt bronze 'A' is also Roman. It has been suggested that there may have been a Romano-Celtic temple at Cadbury in the third or fourth century AD. If so, the 'A' could have been intended as part of a votive inscription. The three grooved sherds in *Ill. 105*, opposite, are of eastern Mediterranean amphorae of Tintagel class B. The sherd at bottom is from a fine red bowl of Tintagel class A and is also eastern Mediterranean in origin. Sherds brought to the surface of the summit plateau by ploughing provided the first real evidence of dark-age occupation at Cadbury. They were collected in the 1950s and classified as Tintagel ware, suggesting that the traditional association of Cadbury with Arthur might not be wholly legendary. The iron knife at left in *Ill. 105* is possibly Arthurian in date. The other knives are from the Late Saxon age. The gilt bronze button in the centre is pagan Saxon from the sixth century AD.

Ills. 106–108. The cut (Ill. 106, right) made through the lower ramparts on the south side of Cadbury (line CD, Ill. 97) was so deep that workers had to wear helmets for protection against falling stones. Ill. 108, on page 130, shows the two profiles surveyed across the ramparts (lines AB and CD, Ill. 97). Ill. 107, below, is an air view of the top of Cadbury hill showing the 1967 excavations in progress.

Ill. 112. Beneath the Late Saxon *burh* wall at Cadbury the remains of an earlier rampart were found. This mass of stones and earth was named the Stony Bank. It was almost certainly built in the late fifth or early sixth century, the age of Arthur, and its purpose was to defend the home or headquarters of a major British chieftain.

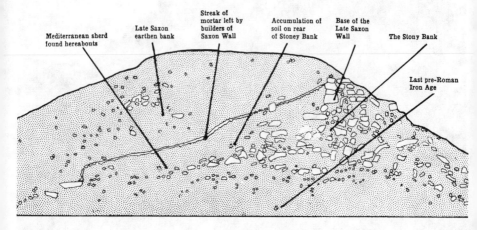

Mediterranean sherd
found hereabouts

Late Saxon
earthen bank

Streak of
mortar left by
builders of
Saxon Wall

Accumulation of
soil on rear
of Stoney Bank

Base of the
Late Saxon
Wall

The Stony Bank

Last pre-Roman
Iron Age

Ill. 113, above, gives a key to what was found in the Stony Bank. *Ill. 114*, below, is a reconstruction of the rampart.

Ill. 119. Trethevy, or Arthur's Quoit in Cornwall. A quoit is the flat stone resting on the perpendicular stones of a cromlech, prehistoric monuments similar to the dolmens of Brittany. By extension 'quoit' has come to be applied to the cromlech as a whole. This burial-chamber, once covered with an earth mound, was probably built and used as a collective tomb *c.* 1800–1100 BC.

Ill. 120. Arthur's Tomb at Camelford in Cornwall. The River Camel is often said to have been the site of the battle of Camlann, from which the mortally wounded Arthur was borne away to be healed in Avalon. If this stone slab does commemorate a battle, it is more probably one fought in 825 during the Saxon conquest of Cornwall.

Ill. 121. Arthur's Stone, Glamorgan, Wales.

Ills. 122, 123. Scotland has a surprising number of Arthurian names and traditions although it is extremely unlikely that the historical Arthur had any connections with Scotland. Aedan, who became king of Dalriada (what is today roughly Argyllshire) in about 574, had a son named Arthur who was killed in a battle. In Stirling, a Roman building (*Ill. 122,* above) was once called Arthur's O'en or Oven. Arthur's Seat (*Ill. 123,* top, opposite) rises beside Edinburgh.

Ill. 125. An inscribed pillar, formerly a cross, in the abbey of Valle Crucis near Llangollen. It was put up in honour of a King Eliseg of the ancient Welsh kingdom of Powys. The inscription is said to show that Eliseg traced his ancestry to both Vortigern and Maximus.

Ill. 124. At low tide ancient field walls are uncovered at Samson Flats in the Isles of Scilly. Areas around these islands, now submerged, were formerly inhabited. Part of the sea-bed between the Scillies and Cornwall is supposed to be Lyonesse where, according to Arthurian romancers, Tristram was born and Galahalt was overlord of a district called Surluse.

Ill. 127, opposite. A dark-age warrior as he might have looked when prepared for battle. The helmet is an iron frame with a brown leather 'cap' inside. The leather cuirass is based on an interpretation of the finds at Sutton Hoo. The shield is based on late Roman examples. The white background is referred to in an early Welsh source and the cross might reasonably be expected on a Christian warrior's shield. The breeches are of brown leather worn over plain linen trousers tucked into brown leather boots. The spear has a polished iron head on a wooden shaft. The sword is of the Roman long-bladed 'spatha' type, which was more effective for slashing than for stabbing. The imperial-red cloak is of wool.

Ills. 128–130. Clothes found at Thorsberg in Germany. By Arthur's time it is likely that Roman styles had largely disappeared and the Britons were dressing in their old fashion, which was probably similar to the dark-age costumes of other nations. The men wore a long tunic (*Ill. 128*), which reached the knees, and breeches or trousers (*Ill. 129*). *Ill. 130* shows a section of the woollen fabric.

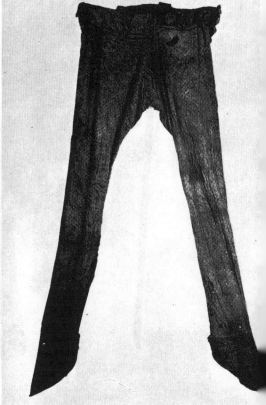

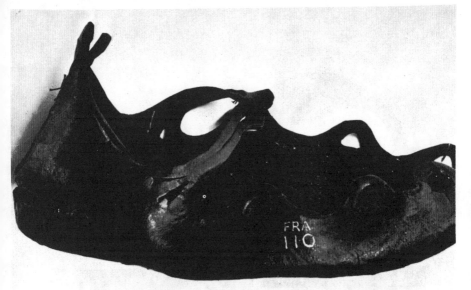

Ill. 131. A leather shoe from Newstead in Roxburghshire. The shoe is
Roman, dating from about the second
century, but is similar to the type
worn in the dark age. The shoe was
closed with a thong drawn through
the loops and tied around the top of
the foot.

Ill. 132. The Franks casket, a whale-
bone box, probably made in Northumbria, dating between 650 and 750.
It is valuable for the clues it gives to
the costume-styles of the Saxons and
possibly the Britons. The warriors
portrayed wear tunics falling to just
above the knee, garments resembling sleeved jackets and cloaks or
mantles fastened at the shoulder.
Some of the men wear puttees, others
are bare-legged or wear hose. The
women wear long tunics reaching to
their ankles and longer mantles with
hoods which can be drawn over
their heads. This side of the casket
shows on the left an episode from
the story of Wayland the Smith, and
on the right the adoration of the
three kings. The label in runic
characters above their heads reads
'Magi'.

Ills. 133–135. In Arthur's age jewellery, which had come under both
Celtic and Roman influences, was
predominantly Celtic in design. A
distinctive item of Celtic jewellery
was the torque, an open necklace.
Ill. 135, opposite, is of one of the
finest examples extant, dating from
c. 50 BC. It was dated by a small gold
coin found in one of the terminals.
Fashioned of twisted gold wires, it is
part of the Snettisham treasure.
Torques may still have been worn in
dark-age Britain. Brooches of pen-
annular Celtic pattern were part of
Arthurian costumes. The example

shown in *Ill. 133*, top, is sixth-century. It was found at Pant-y-saer in
Anglesey and resembles the brooch
reconstructed from the lead die found
at Dinas Powys (*Ill. 56*). *Ill. 134*,
lower, shows a brooch which is part
of the treasure found on St Ninian's
Isle, Shetland. This dark-age treasure
hoard consisted of a miscellaneous
group of objects buried at the level
of a Pictish pre-Norse church. The
hoard probably represented the
movable wealth of the foundation
and thus included gifts from the
community which would explain the
large number of brooches.

Ills. 137–140. The Teutonic invaders of Britain brought with them their own culture and taste in artifacts which existed beside that of the native Britons. Ill. 140, opposite, shows a sixth-century Rhenish glass claw-beaker which was found at Castle Eden, County Durham. Sherds of Teutonic glass were found at Dinas Powys where they had been brought to be melted down and refashioned into ornaments to suit the Celtic taste. The Lullingstone bowl (Ill. 137, centre) and the Winchester bowl (Ill. 138, below) are bronze hanging bowls from the Saxon period. They were made, however, by the Britons for their Saxon conquerors and are of Celtic design. Their existence demonstrates the continuance of Celtic craftsmanship and style following the conquest. The Lullingstone bowl, the decoration of which is appliqué, was found in an Anglo-Saxon grave in Kent, along with pottery and weapons. The Winchester bowl has three escutcheons soldered to the bowl which are enamelled in a Celtic design. It dates from c. 600 and was also found in an Anglo-Saxon grave, along with a knife and a lance. It is similar to bowls found at Sutton Hoo. The drinking horn (Ill. 139, opposite), the rim of which was set with jewels, is Anglo-Saxon and was discovered in a burial-mound at Taplow, Buckinghamshire. Both Anglo-Saxons and Celts used drinking horns. The Welsh *Culhwch and Olwen*, describing a feast at Arthur's hall, says that 'Knife has gone into meat, and drink into horn'. The burial-mound at Taplow was erected, probably in the sixth century, over the body of a dead chieftain named Taeppa. Implicit in the manner of the burial is the belief that his body would con-

137

138

tinue in the next world in the same fashion in which he lived in this one. Finds made in the mound are second only to those from the Sutton Hoo ship-burial in showing the degree of splendour to which early Anglo-Saxon civilisation attained.

139

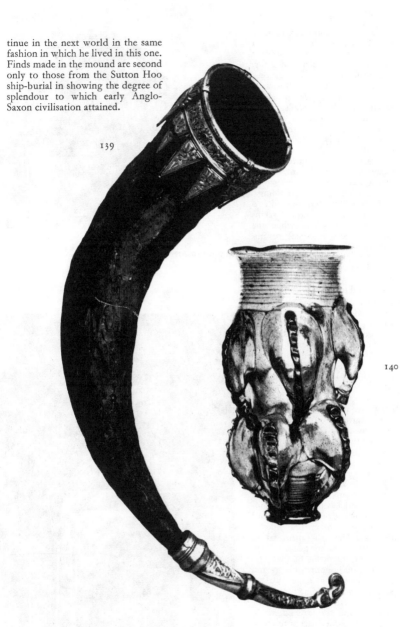

140

Ill. 141. A reconstruction of a Saxon weaver's hut, found at Bourton-on-the-Water. Modern excavators have identified a few house-sites of the early Saxons. The dwellings were small, rough-and-ready affairs, perhaps about seven feet high with walls of mud and straw in alternate layers. The homes of the dark-age Britons were probably similar. The ground-plan of the largest house in a settlement at Sutton Courtenay, south of Oxford, shows that it was of three rooms which were, however, separate buildings. One room apparently served as a kitchen and a third room seems to have been added when the family increased in size or importance. The floor of the kitchen rose six inches over the long period in which it was used, owing to the accumulation of sherds and rubbish.

Ill. 142. A twelfth-century tithe-barn at Harmondsworth, Middlesex. It shows the type of construction used in the Middle Ages for halls and churches as well as barns. A Saxon lord's hall, the centre of the settlement or *burh*, was probably constructed on similar lines and so probably were the halls of the greatest British chieftains. Within such a hall an open hearth ran down the centre between the pillars and smoke escaped through holes in the roof. The walls were hung with arms or perhaps woven hangings. There were benches along the walls on which the lord's retainers, separated by rank, sat while they feasted and listened to the minstrel. The seat of the king or lord was half-way down one side of the hall. His spokesman sat in front of him and the queen or lady at his side. Opposite him was the seat next in honour. In large and important *burhs* there was a separate small building for women and children known as the 'bower' and the women might attend the earlier part of the feasting in the great hall, the lady and her daughters bearing round the ale. The men's arms were always within easy reach in the event of a surprise enemy attack or a brawl resulting from the heavy drinking at the feasts.

Ill. 143. An eighth-century Pictish slab cross from Invergowrie, Angus. St Columba went as a missionary to the northern Picts in the latter half of the sixth century. By the eighth century the Pictish kingdom extended from Caithness to Fife, and carved memorial stones and crosses are a characteristic feature of its culture.

Ills. 144–146. The Irish Church was the creation of the British Church but after the Saxon conquest they followed different paths. British churchmen became narrowly ascetic while Irish churchmen became scholars and missionaries, and Ireland became the most cultivated land in western Europe. The Irish gradually assumed the lead in Celtic religion. St Columba, with twelve disciples, founded the monastery on the island of Iona in about 563. He converted the Picts in important parts of northern Scotland and established monasteries there. The house at Iona was the mother house and its abbots were the chief ecclesiastical rulers, superior even to bishops. *Ill. 145,* below left, shows a stone cross from Iona. The house-shaped Monymusk Reliquary (*Ill. 144,* above left) was made about 597, the year of Columba's death, and is considered to be that known as the Brechbennock of St Columba. *Ill. 146,* opposite, is an eighth-century Irish cast-bronze plaque of the Crucifixion, possibly intended as a book cover.

Ill. 147. The monastery at Lindis-farne, or Holy Island, Northumber-land was founded in 635 by St Aidan, who came from Iona at the request of King Oswald to preach to the Northumbrians. The monastery was destroyed by Danes in 793 but re-built. In 875 the monks, fearing the return of the Danes, fled taking the body of St Cuthbert, the sixth bishop of Lindisfarne. The monks eventually settled in Durham.

Ill. 148, opposite. The boy Arthur draws the sword from the stone in Walt Disney's film of T. H. White's book *The Sword in the Stone.* The infant Arthur was given by his father King Uther to Merlin who in turn entrusted the baby to Sir Ector to raise, and he was brought up with Ector's son Kay. On Uther's death the succession to the crown was dis-puted by many lords. The arch-bishop of Canterbury, on Merlin's

advice, called all the lords together in London at Christmas in expecta-tion of a miracle which would demonstrate the rightful king. The lords obeyed and after they had heard mass together they discovered that a stone had appeared in the churchyard. Resting on the stone was an anvil and in the anvil was a sword bearing (in Malory's version) the legend, 'Whoso pulleth out this sword of this stone and anvil, is rightwise king born of all England'. As none of the lords was able to move the sword, the archbishop declared a tournament on New Year's Day at which all knights might compete in the hope that God would indicate who was the rightful owner of the sword. Among the knights who attended the jousting were Sir Ector and his son Sir Kay, accompanied by the youthful Arthur. Kay discovered that he had for-gotten his sword and sent Arthur

for it. Arthur, however, found nobody at home to give him Kay's
sword so he decided to take the
sword from the stone for his foster-
brother. Arthur easily drew the
sword from the anvil and presented
it to Sir Kay who recognised it for
what it was and, showing it to his
father, declared that he himself was
rightful king. Ector, however, realised that Arthur was the king. The
sword was put back into the anvil
and only Arthur could withdraw it.
As the lords were reluctant to have
an unknown boy as king, the test was
repeated – always with the same
result – at Twelfth Night, Candle-
mas, Easter and Pentecost until
finally, at Pentecost, Arthur was
crowned.

149. The Camelot of romance is
a great castle of the high Middle
Ages, in sharp contrast with what
archaeologists have reconstructed
and conjectured about dark-age
chieftains' dwellings. The scene is
from the film *Camelot*, based on the
musical made of T. H. White's *The
Once and Future King*.

8   *Extending the Map*

Geoffrey Ashe

HAVING GONE SO FAR, the search will surely go further. To some extent the logic of archaeology points the way forward with fair precision, at Cadbury and elsewhere. But the opening up of entirely new sites will often have to await accidental finds, cogent enough to draw archaeologists' attention and persuade them to invest time and money. Without that kind of support, such clues as local legends and place-names are dubious guides. Yet we have seen, amply, that they are not to be despised. Several pieces of the traditional Arthurian map have turned out to be, after a fashion, valid. This result may now justify an attempt to sketch the map as a whole, both for its own interest and also to see what hints it offers for further research.

Ill. 118   At the outset a distinction is needed. Some Arthurian sites are genuinely traditional, others are not. A little guidance is given by the scatter of Celtic place-names. In east and south-east England, their number is small. Anglo-Saxon conquest here was swift and permanent. The Britons were killed, enslaved or expelled, except in isolated pockets, and the settlement was generally a new beginning by a new people. Further west and north is a swathe of counties where the course of events was not so simple. The invaders progressed more slowly. Or they advanced, withdrew and advanced again, the second time in a less exterminatory spirit. As a consequence, British place-names are found among Saxon ones. Further on yet is the Celtic fringe where the conquest was late and not overwhelming or, as in Wales, never happened at all. This is where the old Celtic names predominate. This also, generally speaking, is where the detailed Arthur topography may mean something. It does extend outside but, in most cases, only as romantic or literary fancy. Malory's equation of Astolat with Guildford need not be taken seriously.

At the end of the fringe lie the Isles of Scilly. These include the islets of Great and Little Arthur. Part of the sea-bed between the

Scillies and Cornwall is supposed to be the lost land of Lyonesse, the British Atlantis. According to legend, Lyonesse was above water in Arthur's time. Romancers say Tristram was born there, and Galahad was overlord of a district called Surluse. In Cornwall itself, Tintagel and Castle Dore stand on firmer ground. We already know what they have and have not divulged. As Ralegh Radford observes, Castle Dore has a small cluster of significant place-names around it. Tintagel, too, branches out into a neighbourhood lore. Some of this is spurious (it is hard to excuse giving the name 'Vale of Avalon' to the rocky ravine down to the beach), but some is at least picturesque, as when we are told of a pond from which the Round Table rises if you watch for it on the right night. The impressive cavern under the castle, where the sea roars in at high tide, is Merlin's Cave, and there are rock-hollows called Arthur's Chair, Arthur's Quoit and Arthur's Cups and Saucers.

Ill. 119

The small and battered hill-fort near Padstow, identified as Arthur's stronghold of Kelliwic, has a fairly solid claim. The River Camel is often stated to be the scene of the battle of Camlann. Slaughter Bridge on the river—with the stone slab of 'Arthur's Tomb'—may commemorate a battle, but it is more likely to have been the one fought in 825 during the belated Saxon conquest of Cornwall. Other parts of the county supply a hill called Bann Arthur, and fancifully named natural features—such as Arthur's Chair and Oven (noted by the visiting French priests in 1113), Arthur's Hall south-east of Camelford, Arthur's Bed and Arthur's Hunting Seat—with or without a prefixed 'King'. On Bodmin Moor is Dozmary Pool, one of the places where Excalibur was thrown away. Off Mousehole is Merlin's Rock.

Ill. 120

Devon is nearly blank except for Blackingstone Rock at Hel Tor, where Arthur met the Devil. Somerset has, of course, Cadbury Castle and Glastonbury. A dark-age causeway is said to run through the former marshlands from one to the other. Those who maintain that Camlann was fought beside the Somerset Cam are also inclined to say that the wounded leader was carried to Glastonbury along the causeway, and it is sometimes called by his name. The *Life of St Carannog* points to Dunster as the centre of Arthur's activities at the time of the saint's arrival. Up the coast is a solitary hill, Brent Knoll. This once belonged to Glastonbury Abbey. According to a chronicler, it was previously the property of Arthur, who gave it to the monks.

The early literary sources contribute battle sites—Badon, Glein, Linnuis and the rest—but most indicate, at best, ill-defined areas rather than specific places. For Mount Badon the choice of Lidding-

Ill. 25

ton Castle, with its adjacent Badbury, is a modern theory which may be plausible but lacks any traditional background. Some prefer Badbury Rings in Dorset. There are at least three proposed Camlanns, Camboglanna in Cumberland being better than the other two etymologically but perhaps not historically.

Nennius is more exact about two folklore 'marvels' or *mirabilia* which he notes in his appendix. One is located at Ercing (Archenfield) in Herefordshire.

> There is a burial mound near a spring which is known as Licat Anir, and the name of the man who is buried in the mound is Anir. He was the son of Arthur the soldier, and Arthur himself killed him there and buried him. And when men come to measure the length of the mound, they find it sometimes six feet, sometimes nine, sometimes twelve, and sometimes fifteen. Whatever length you find it at one time, you will find it different at another, and I myself have proved this to be true.

Charles Williams described that final throw-away line as one of the 'mind-shattering things' which we occasionally encounter in history. Unfortunately, the precise site is uncertain. (Hereford also has a cromlech called Arthur's Stone.)

Nennius's second Arthurian marvel is in 'Buelt', *i.e.*, Builth, Brecknockshire.

> There is a heap of stones, and on the top of the heap one stone bearing the footprint of a dog. When they hunted the boar Troit, Cabal which was the dog of Arthur the soldier, put his foot on that stone and marked it; and Arthur afterwards piled up a heap of stones and that stone on top, on which was the dog's footprint, and called it Carn Cabal. And men will come and carry away that stone for a day and a night, and the next morning there it is back again on its heap.

The tale of Arthur's boar-hunt is told at length in *Culhwch and Olwen*, but sheds no light on the homing stone. Nennius does not claim to have tested this.

The 'marvels' take us round into Wales. Brecknockshire itself adds an Arthur's Chair between two peaks, an Arthur's Hill-top, an Arthur's Table. Caerleon, besides the literary legend in Geoffrey of Monmouth, is said to have a cave where some of the knights lie Ill. 121 sleeping till their leader calls them. Glamorgan has another Arthur's Stone, another cave, and Guinevere's Monument at Llaniltern.

1 *Lyonesse*
2 Mousehole
3 Merlin's Rock
4 Padstow
5 *Kelliwic*
6 CORNWALL, Bann Arthur, Arthur's Bed, Arthur's Hunting Seat, Arthur's Quoit
7 Tintagel
8 Merlin's Cave
9 Camelford
10 Arthur's Hall
11 Bodmin Moor, Arthur's Chair
12 Dozmary Pool
13 Bodmin
14 Golant
15 Castle Dore
16 Fowey
17 Morwenstowe
18 Dunster
19 Carhampton
20 GLAMORGANSHIRE, Arthur's Stone
21 Llantwit Major
22 Llancarfan
23 Dinas Powys
24 Caerleon
25 Malmesbury
26 Dyrham
27 Bath
28 Congresbury
29 Brent Knoll
30 Glastonbury, *Avalon*
31 South Cadbury, *Camelot*
32 Queen Camel
33 Ilchester
34 Badbury Rings
35 Maiden Castle
36 Badbury
37 Swindon
38 Liddington Castle
39 Windmill Hill
40 Dorchester
41 Reading
42 Guildford
43 Amesbury
44 Winchester
45 Cissbury
46 Dover
47 Canterbury
48 Aylesford
49 Crayford
50 London
51 St Albans
52 Cirencester
53 Gloucester
54 Lydney
55 Monmouth
56 HEREFORDSHIRE, Arthur's Stone
57 BRECKNOCKSHIRE, Arthur's Chair
58 St David's
59 Llyn Barfog
60 Llangian
61 Aberdaron
62 Castell Odo
63 Garn Boduan
64 Careg-y-llam
65 Dinas Emrys
66 CAERNARVON, River of Arthur's Kitchen
67 Bangor
68 ANGLESEY, Arthur's Stone
69 Pant-y-saer
70 Degannwy
71 Dinorben
72 DENBIGH, Round Table
73 Flint, Arthur's Hill
74 Chester, *City of the Legion*
75 Eddisbury
76 Valle Crucis
77 Llangollen
78 Old Oswestry
79 Breiddin
80 *River Glein*
81 Lincoln
82 *Linnuis*
83 York
84 Catterick
85 Whitby
86 Jarrow
87 Newcastle
88 NORTHUMBRIA, King's Crags
89 Camboglanna
90 Carlisle
91 CUMBERLAND, Round Table
92 *River Tribruit*
93 *Forest of Celidon*
94 LANARK, Arthur's Fountain
95 Dumbarton, *Astolat*
96 DUMBARTONSHIRE, Ben Arthur
97 STIRLING, Arthur's O'en
98 Edinburgh, Arthur's Seat
99 PEEBLES, Merlin's Grave
100 Melrose
101 Perth
102 ANGUS, Arthur's Fold
103 Garvock
104 KINCARDINE, Arthurhouse

Ill. 118. Map of Britain showing sites mentioned in the text.

Names in *upper and lower case italics* on the map refer to conjectured and legendary sites. Where a number occurs under a COUNTY name, between parentheses on the map, it refers to Arthurian topographical sites in that county too small to be precisely located on the map and listed opposite.

Carmarthen has yet another cave and several more Merlin features, including an Arthur's Pot, a rock which the wizard shaped for cooking. Merioneth provides two Arthurian lakes: Bala, the source of the Dee, where Kay lived at a spot called Caergai; and Llyn Barfog, where Arthur slew a monster and his horse left a hoofprint on the rock. In Caernarvon, by Marchlyn Mawr, is a cave with a slightly different story. It contains Arthur's treasure, a source of dazzlement to the wanderer who sees it, and of disaster to the pilferer who touches it. Another cave near Snowdon houses more slumbering knights. The same county has a River of Arthur's Kitchen, cairns of Arthur and also Tristram, and, as noted, Dinas Emrys. In Anglesey are another Arthur's Quoit, a cave where Arthur sheltered during a war, and a stone Round Table. There is a similar Round Table in Denbigh. Flintshire has Arthur's Hill and another hoof-printed stone.

Northern England adds a little: a Round Table and an Arthur's Seat in the Cumbrian Border country; King's Crags near Sewingshields in Northumberland, with an Arthur's Chair from which the king threw a boulder at Guinevere on Queen's Crags; an Arthur's Hill near Newcastle and an Arthur's Well at Waltoun-Crags. Variants of the 'sleep' motif are found at Alderley Edge in Cheshire, Threlkeld in Cumberland and The Sneep in Durham.

Scotland is surprisingly rich in this respect. It has a further alleged cave, in the Eildon hills south of Melrose, which competes with Cadbury Castle for the honour of housing Arthur himself. Arthur's Seat rises beside Edinburgh, and in Dumbarton is the mountain Ben Arthur. Lanark has an Arthur's Fountain; Stirling, another Arthur's O'en and a questionable earthwork Round Table; Peebles, a Merlin's Grave. Angus produces an Arthur's Fold, another Arthur's Stone, another Arthur's Seat. A cairn at Garvock in Kincardine is called Arthurhouse, and Perth has local associations with Guinevere and Modred.

Ill. 123

Ill. 122

The place-names which actually have 'Arthur' in them often apply to natural features rather than human structures. As the case of Shakespeare's Cliff might suggest, the name is of dubious value as a guide to research. It occurs, indeed, over the Channel in Brittany, where Arthur is unlikely to have lived. It even occurs in the sky. Some Cornishmen call the Great Bear 'Arthur's Wain'. We could not safely infer that the *dux bellorum* anticipated the astronauts. Nevertheless, the name may help to focus attention on areas where other clues possess value. This has happened in Cornwall itself.

What prospects emerge for further discovery? To begin where the map does, it is probable that the full story behind the Lyonesse legend has yet to be told. Cornish tradition on the subject is a medley of popular and antiquarian lore, rather like the mythology of Cadbury Castle. Some of it must be false, but some of it bears at least a slight relation to fact. It is worth examining a little more fully.

In ancient days, we are told, Lyonesse was a country spreading westward from Land's End. The Isles of Scilly were joined together and linked with the mainland. Over a broad expanse, most of it low-lying, were fair-sized towns and a hundred and forty churches. The Cornish name for this region is Lethowstow. It was engulfed by the sea quite suddenly. A man named Trevilian got away by jumping on horseback and riding madly just ahead of the waves; the arms of the Trevelyan family depict a horse coming out of water. Elizabethan antiquaries, such as Camden, collected reports current in the sixteenth century. The reef of the Seven Stones, where the *Torrey Canyon* met with disaster in 1967, was said to be the remains of a town called the City of Lions. Fishermen declared that their nets brought up fragments of masonry and windows. Camden heard circumstantial accounts of a lighthouse far west of anything standing in his own time.

Much of this fantasy can be dismissed. The question is whether it

Ill. 126. The coat of arms of the Trevelyan family.

all can. The inundation legend is found in other parts of north-western Europe, where heavy seas have been pounding at the coasts for thousands of years. Rumours of such legends, conveyed to the Mediterranean along Mycenæan trade-routes, may have helped to inspire the myth of Atlantis. Ammianus Marcellinus, a Roman historian, testifies that they were part of the druids' lore in the first century B C. Brittany has its story of Ker-Is, the sunken city, and Wales has its 'Lost Cantref' in Cardigan Bay. Encroachments of the sea did occur, though presumably not so suddenly as the legends imply, and in most cases long before Arthur. Thus, the Dogger Bank used to be inhabited land. Stone implements have been dredged up from it. The Straits of Dover were not breached till after 6000 B C, and the water was gaining and altering the coastline for several millennia after that. Indeed, the formation of the Zuider Zee and the erosion of Dunwich are, geologically speaking, things of yesterday.

In Cornwall, it is known that Mount's Bay was above water long after the first human settlement in that area. It contains remnants of a forest, and stone axes were seemingly being made on what is now the sea-bottom between 1800 and 1500 B C. Such facts, however interesting, still do not lead to Arthur's Britain, but the Isles of Scilly may perhaps do so. In 387, the pretender Maximus, 'Prince Macsen', used that remote spot as a place of banishment for a heretic. The historian who records the sentence refers not to the 'Isles' of Scilly but to the 'Isle': *Sylina Insula*. The implication is that the group was then a single island with no dividing channels—or, at any rate, that there was one clearly predominant island, as is no longer the case.

And, in fact, we have good reason to think so. At low tide, in the sand-flats between the present islands, rows of stones can be seen which are manifestly ancient walls. On St Martin's, huts have been found with floors below the modern high-water mark. One dates from the early Iron Age. Another, a circular dwelling, belongs to the Roman period. When sifted in 1948 it was found to contain pottery of the third and fourth centuries A D. The island of Old Man was split in two by the sea in recent times, and here, also below high-water mark, is a stone grave where excavation revealed two Roman bronze brooches made in the first century.

Ill. 124

With the growth of submarine archaeology as a technique, the many wrecks in the dangerous Cornish sea have already lured expeditions. The tale of Lyonesse is unlikely to lead anyone to similar treasures, but it could lead to further glimpses of dark-age Britain.

On mainland Cornwall, the two major sites at Tintagel and Castle

Dore are probably fully known. The third is Kelliwic. Allusions to it as a dwelling of Arthur's can be traced far back—to *Culhwch and Olwen*, for instance—and it may still have a story to tell. Cornish archaeology undoubtedly has. Work on small dark-age sites not associated with Arthur has supplemented the picture and will continue. But Arthurian names will probably give no further help, unless the Camel is indeed Camlann.

As we move eastward, the results at Glastonbury and Cadbury strengthen the other claims of Somerset. Arthur's so-called causeway connecting the two has yet to be properly explored. Local antiquaries have traced part of it near South Cadbury, and a reconnaissance in 1967 suggested that several sections might be mapped out. Besides the causeway, and the further sites around Glastonbury proposed by Philip Rahtz, Dunster and Brent Knoll have both become slightly more interesting. Arthur's legendary status at Dunster as the junior colleague of Cadwy fits in curiously well with the theory that Cadbury is Cadwy's Fort. Did Arthur occupy Dunster and then move to Cadbury on the death of his senior, its original lord?

Brent Knoll is known to have been inhabited in early times. Arthur's connection with it rests on an assertion by property-minded monks and is thus, in itself, poorly supported. However, the hill attracted some fresh attention after the 1966 season at Cadbury. It was pointed out that three hills had now been identified as dark-age royal sites—Cadbury, Glastonbury Tor, Dinas Powys—and that these lay nearly along a straight line, crossing low country and the sea. Brent Knoll, moreover, was close to the same line, and could be seen both

Ill. 96

from the Tor and from Dinas Powys. This visual chain of four hills, three at least of them occupied in the same period, suggested the 'signalling' theory mentioned by Philip Rahtz (p. 119). Such an arrangement between Arthur and the lords of the other hills would have been in keeping with Nennius's statement that the *dux bellorum* fought alongside the kings of the Britons. A beacon experimentally lit at Cadbury was picked out without trouble by observers on the Tor. At Brent Knoll, and at Dunster also, there is not enough at present to make the site look promising, but there is enough to save it provisionally from being dismissed.

Nennius's battles are too vague to supply much practical guidance. Even if we were satisfied that Linnuis is Lindsey, we could not dig up half Lincolnshire looking for burials or weapons. The names might assist in the future interpretation of chance finds, and it would be interesting to know what is concealed inside the earthworks of

Liddington Castle. As for Nennius's 'marvels', they take us toward Wales. There, and in the Marches, Leslie Alcock has pointed out the geographic imbalance of archaeology thus far. Much remains to be found outside Gwynedd. The Arthurian names and legends may not offer any direct help, but they do cluster in shapes that could reflect some historical fact. There is a Brecknock-Hereford-Monmouth-Glamorgan-Carmarthen group, and a Merioneth-Caernarvon-Anglesey-Denbigh-Flint group. The block of country between is an Arthurian near-hiatus like Devonshire. In the southern area was the monastery of Llancarfan which produced the Arthurian Saints' Lives. The findings in Somerset reinforce the belief that that part of Wales had an authentic tradition which the Llancarfan monks drew upon. With patience, clues might be disentangled. As for Nennius's elastic grave in Herefordshire, anyone who can explain his statement will have earned the right to follow it up.

An unsolved riddle, Welsh but not solely so, is the meaning of the term 'Gewissi' which figures in early medieval Welsh contexts. At the abbey of Valle Crucis near Llangollen stands an inscribed pillar, Ill. 125 formerly a cross. It was put up by the royal family of the kingdom of Powys—east-central Wales plus part of Shropshire—in honour of a King Eliseg or Eliset. If a long-accepted reading is right, the inscription shows that Eliseg traced his descent from a son of the notorious Vortigern by Sevira, a daughter of Maximus. After that pretender's fall his daughters became imperial wards, and the marriage of one of them to a British noble might well have been part of a treaty devolving authority on to him. Vortigern would have been younger than his bride, but not absurdly so.

Now, however, Geoffrey of Monmouth reappears on the scene. He tells a story implying that Sevira inherited rights in the Powys area derived from her own mother, Maximus's British wife. Through Sevira a title, which Geoffrey gives as *dux Gewissi*, was apparently transmitted from her own forebears to her husband Vortigern. Geoffrey's narrative is in harmony with the Valle Crucis inscription yet could not be deduced from it: one of his curious hints at unknown source-material. But the third part of the problem is the strangest. The founder of the Saxon dynasty in Wessex (and the ancestor of all English royalty) is said to have been a chief named Cerdic, who landed on the shore of Southampton Water in 495. Cerdic's name is not Saxon but British; his father's name in his pedigree is Elesa, which is like the Eliseg in the Powys dynasty; and the West Saxons are referred to in early sources as Gewissi or Gewissae.

The trail from the Valle Crucis pillar appears to lead, if it leads anywhere, to a phase of British-Saxon fraternisation and intermarriage in the fifth century, before the débâcle. Geoffrey indeed says there was such a phase, and inflates Vortigern's employment of Saxons as mercenaries into a ruinous friendship with them. Later that century, at all events, we seem to be confronted with a man of mixed blood who bears a British name, has a title which establishes an obscure link with a British family, yet leads a Saxon war-band against the Britons.

Whether or not any more can ever be squeezed from these cryptic hints, they show the need for collation of facts from many sources. The same is true of the north, where literary research has outrun archaeology to the point of building up an unresolved tension. Arthur's first fame is in a different place from his home. In northern England and Scotland, as in Wales, the map suggests that there is more waiting to be discovered which will harmonise the data.

Outside Britain, in other Celtic lands, Ireland has already supplied many sidelights. Irish romances help to explain what is happening in the Arthurian stories. Irish archaeology elucidates the findings of British archaeology. The process may be expected to continue. It would be surprising, however, if Ireland were to go beyond this interpretative role, except perhaps in Church matters. There remains Brittany. Here the only visible prospect is a speculation, and far-fetched, but not to be entirely passed over. It concerns the British equivalent of Homer, whom literary logic demands in vain.

To survey the progress of dark-age archaeology in relation to legend is to see a parallel with the work of Schliemann, Evans and their successors in the Aegean world. The great poetic fables of classical Greece were drawn, like the motifs of Arthurian romance, from the tradition of an heroic age several centuries earlier. The events were supposed to have happened, roughly, between 1500 and 1100 BC. But the gap between that age and the classical literature was not empty. In it stood the vast double edifice of the Homeric epics, reflecting the former and supplying characters and themes for the latter. Homer appeared to give a true portrait of the heroic age, and Schliemann began the excavation of Troy in a naïve confidence that he did.

Archaeology has not confirmed the portrait in detail, or proved the existence of Agamemnon or Helen. But it has shown that more or less the right sort of society did flourish in the right places at the right time; that the school of thought which made Homer a weaver of fiction, and Troy a dream city, was mistaken; that the art of Aeschylus, Sophocles and Euripides was grounded in a reality, however remote. Thus far, the quest for Arthur's Britain has yielded results of much the same kind. There is a dark-age Fact underlying the medieval Legend. But the parallel breaks down on a very large absence. We have no Celtic Homer midway between Arthur and the romancers, no great source-book for the Legend which is similarly close to the Fact.

The whole picture would become clearer if such a source could be shown to have existed, a literary bridge over that immense gap. Furthermore—if we could only trust Geoffrey of Monmouth—it did. The problem is whether he actually possessed the 'ancient book in the British language' given him by Archdeacon Walter. The easy course is to write his statement off as a lie. But perhaps it is not. In at least one instance (an account of a Roman massacre beside the Walbrook in London), a story of Geoffrey's, with no known literary antecedent, has been supported by excavation. A purely oral tradition surviving nearly a thousand years is a hard thing to admit. But if it was written down and Geoffrey read it, where was it written down? Again, medieval Welsh authors produced over fifty chronicles or 'Bruts' based on his *History* and telling portions of the same tale—yet not precisely the same. Careful comparison gives hints of another original.

Geoffrey wrote as a Welshman, and doubtless to glorify and comfort the Welsh. But if he was spinning his *History* out of his head, he could have played up Wales more than he does. Apart from the placing of Arthur's birth in Cornwall, several chapters lay a stress on the related promontory of Brittany which is puzzling. Was the ancient book actually in the Breton language, and the Celtic Homer a Breton? As we saw, there are separate reasons for thinking that the figure of the romantic Arthur—the crowned king who fights on the continent and does not die—took shape in Brittany rather than Britain. Conceivably an epic or saga composed in that country was a common source both for Geoffrey himself and for the Arthurian lays which spread through Europe before his time and to which Chrétien de Troyes acknowledged a debt. On the historical side, this epic would have embodied the south-western version of Arthur rather than the Welsh or northern, because it was from Devon and Cornwall that the emigrants to Armorica came. These are the regions which are linked in the Tristram story.

Even if the epic existed, we are unlikely to recover it after so many years. But it is just possible that manuscript matter of Breton origin might, somewhere, and perhaps in conjunction with other clues, shed fresh light on a process that is still deeply mysterious.

9   Life in the Arthurian Age

Geoffrey Ashe
with Jill Racy

THOUGH WE LACK a British Homer, we can still do our best to supplement archaeology from other sources: from the literature that does exist, from parallels among non-British peoples, and so forth. And indeed we shall not go much further toward a clear picture of the society of the time if we can form no mental image of the living human beings who made it up. To begin with, how did the Britons dress? Archaeology by itself can reveal jewellery and metal, items that do not rot away to nothing, but has less to say on perishables. In the next few pages this topic is examined.

This section on costume is by Jill Racy.

Since it is Arthur himself and, of course, those who followed him in his daily life with whom we are primarily concerned, it would be appropriate to consider first how the well-dressed warrior appeared. With the knowledge and skills gained during the years under Rome, and adapted to the needs of a land which knew a hard climate, Arthur and his men would have presented an efficiently clothed front to any enemy. These were men well-armed and fitted out for battle. The continuing imperial contact at least up to the time of Ambrosius, and the Gallic link through Armorica even after that, would have helped them to keep up with current ideas in weapons and armour. The resemblance between the Cadbury fortification and those in the Rhineland certainly points to influence of this kind.

The warrior probably wore more or less the male civilian costume— of which more later—but with the additions necessary for the fighting man. These can be reconstructed from scattered phrases in Aneirin's *Gododdin*, eked out and interpreted in the light of Anglo-Saxon descriptions and the military archaeology of the Empire. Over the outer tunic would be a leather tunic, over which would be a coat of mail. The finds on the Welsh sites, such as Dinas Powys, prove that

Ill. 127

there was no lack of skilled craftsmen in parts of Britain who would have been able to make mail in the form of metal rings. The mail coat was worn with a leather belt at the waist. Under it the leather tunic hung down to about the knee. Warriors might also have worn some sort of leg protection, such as leather breeches. To judge from evidence in Teutonic lands (for instance, the Nydam ship in Denmark) it is possible that some form of puttees or gartering was worn.

The helmet was an item which had been degenerating for some time. By the fourth century, the Roman infantry apparently seldom wore helmets. The barbarian auxiliaries did not like them, and preferred to protect their heads by wearing their hair long. As for cavalry helmets, there was a trend towards making them of pieces riveted together. In a letter written in 474, the Gallic author Sidonius Apollinaris refers to 'the flexible cheek pieces of the helm'. A specimen discovered at Worms was constructed in sections including neck and ear guards riveted on. Another found in Derbyshire hints at a simpler British type—in essence, a leather cap covered with metal.

British weapons included the long-bladed Roman sword known as a *spatha*; a spear with wooden shaft and diamond-shaped iron head; possibly daggers, axes and slings. For his own protection the warrior carried a large oval, or round, whitewashed shield.

The Roman Eagle was now supplanted by the Dragon. To judge from continental evidence, weapons were sometimes decorated with emblems representing dragons and other strange animals, as well as the common geometrical motifs. An example of animals, in the form of two dolphin-like creatures which strongly resemble the dragon, occurs on a buckler depicted on a disc found at Geneva.

As already mentioned, the military equipment was worn and carried in addition to the everyday costume worn by men generally. This would have varied from area to area and from tribe to tribe. (Gildas expressed his disgust at the scanty costume of the Picts.) Basically, however, clothing would be much the same. The traditional costume of the British Celts can be reconstructed from descriptions or references in classical authors. During the third and fourth centuries, there was a tendency towards Roman fashions among the upper classes. But, by Arthur's time, it is probable that the Britons had largely reverted to their old style of dress. Some light is shed by remains of the dark-age costume of other nations found in a partly preserved state in peat bogs in Germany, Holland and Denmark.

Men's dress was based on three main garments: a simple tunic, long breeches or trousers and a warm cloak. The tunic, which reached to

Ills. 128, 129
130

Ill. 132

the knees, had long or short sleeves and a plain round neck. It was pulled on over the head. Several tunics could be worn at once if the weather was cold. This outer tunic was usually of wool. Furs or pelts were also used for outer garments. Leather belts were worn round the waist.

A man of high rank would most likely have worn an undergarment or *camisia* (rather like an undershirt) which would be of linen. As it had to be imported, linen was a material which only the wealthy could afford. Flax was now cultivated in Gaul, but a finer form of linen was also available from Italy. Because of the unsettled state of commerce which was the result of the barbarian invasions, trade in textiles was limited to supplying those who were rich enough and high enough in rank to allow themselves the luxury of costly and rare materials.

Ill. 129   The breeches or trousers were the 'barbarian' garment called *braccae* by the Romans. They were fastened in a primitive manner with rawhide thonging which was threaded through the waist and tied. They were similarly tied at the ankles. Although these breeches were often without further adornment, it is likely that rough puttees or even cross-gartering, also of rawhide, may have been added to hold the material close to the legs. Breeches were of wool cloth, and in colder climates, of fur and skins. As with the linen undershirt, a man of high rank might wear a form of short underbreeches or loin cloth. Among the remains of garments found in the continental peat bogs, shorter knee-length versions of the breeches have been discovered. With this shorter style it was usual for a form of leg and foot covering to be worn. There is no certainty that this garment was adopted by the Britons, but we can assume the possibility.

The cloak was roughly four to five feet across and was either rectangular or circular. It was of wool, fur-lined wool or skins. A

Ill. 133   brooch or fibula was used to fasten it together on the chest or right shoulder. Many different kinds of these fibulae have been discovered in Ireland and western Britain.

Ill. 132   Women's costume was probably very much as described by the Roman historian Dio Cassius in his account of Boadicea. Women wore an ankle-length tunic which, like the man's, had long or short sleeves and a round neck. It was worn with or without a leather belt. A well-to-do woman might easily have worn a more elaborate form

Ill. 134   of belt with plaques or brooches, with the addition of a purse and possibly a small dagger attached. Over the tunic a three-quarter-length gown could be worn. This was either short-sleeved or sleeveless. With these outer garments there may have been some slight surviving

Roman stylistic influence, at least among the upper classes. Underneath the outer clothes were one or more short under-tunics or *camisiae*, the number depending on the weather. These would be of linen if the wearer was of high enough rank to afford it. The woman's cloak was the same as the man's and fastened in the same manner.

The clothing of the very poor of both sexes consisted simply of rough woven tunics and pelts. Since such animals as the bear, wild boar and wolf were then found in Britain, it was possible to obtain a large fur or hide and pin it over the shoulder with a primitive form of brooch.

Shoes for both sexes were simple. The most primitive resembled moccasins and were made of a single piece of rawhide, cut large enough so that when a thong was drawn through the edge it could be tied round the top of the foot, rather like a mobcap. Sandals of Roman inspiration were also made.

Ill. 131

Both men and women wore their hair long and flowing. The women's hair, of which they were extremely proud, reached to their waists or even further. The men usually wore beards. As a rule the people went bareheaded, except in cold weather when a small cap of fur or wool, rather like a Phrygian cap, would be worn. Women of rank wore a gold fillet round their foreheads. The dark-age archaeology of Teutonic lands has supplied razors, combs and scissors, and all three are mentioned in an Arthurian context in *Culhwch and Olwen*.

Knowledge of techniques of spinning, weaving and dyeing were probably brought in very early times from Europe and even from as far off as the eastern part of the continent. Since the remains of cloth with a diamond design of some complexity have been discovered near the Nydam ship, it is not unreasonable to assume that such skills were known among the Celts. Rough wool clothes in plain colours, stripes or even a checked pattern had been woven in Britain for some centuries. It has been suggested that the check design was the origin of the more complicated pattern which today we know as the plaid.

Ill. 130

It is clear that there was a considerable knowledge of dyeing, and even perhaps of the use of some substance which would act as a crude method of making the colours fast. Bright colours were worn, and vegetable dyes are known to have been in use since the Bronze Age. Red was a favourite colour, obtained from the madder root. Yellow was obtained from saffron flowers or from the stalks and leaves of weld. Blue came from woad, and green from a weed which is now called 'dyer's greenweed'.

Jewellery, like everything else, had come under both Roman and Celtic influences, though by Arthur's time the Celtic was predominant. Ornaments of bronze, iron and gold were decorated by incising or embossing, with stones and coral and enamel. There are many good examples from Ireland and more fragmentary specimens from Wales. The dark-age inhabitants of Glastonbury Tor may have worked with enamel. Other jewellery found in Kent dates from the early phase of Teutonic conquest, and may have been made by British slaves. It was natural that the higher the wearer's rank, the more precious the metal used and the more skilled and elaborate the workmanship. Design was often big and simple, though the unique and well-known Celtic type of design was intricate and beautiful with its stylised animals and birds and writhing serpentine shapes.

A distinctive and highly valuable item of Celtic jewellery was the torque, an open necklace, usually heavy and with knobbed ends. The British Museum has a superb example made of twisted gold wires, which is part of the Snettisham treasure dating from the first century B C. Others have been found in France and many of these are decorated with geometric motifs, stylised heads, spirals in relief and strange animal shapes. Torques may still have been worn in dark-age Britain. Fibulae or brooches, together with pins, bracelets, armlets, rings and bead necklaces, were certainly in everyday use. Bronze hand mirrors had been used before the Roman conquest and very probably still were.

Although we do have a certain amount of solid information concerning the culture of the Britons in the fifth and sixth centuries A D, there is plainly much that we can still only conjecture. For this semi-barbaric period the phrase 'dark age' is still all too appropriate. But with the search for knowledge widening all the time, it is not too much to hope that in due course we shall discover and piece together enough recognisable remains of an Arthurian wardrobe to set our minds at rest as to what really was high fashion in those far-off days.

When we take leave of everyday objects and turn to institutions, religion and art, our information tends to become equivocal. It needs careful interpreting, especially because of doubts over date. While Welsh literature supplies many assertions about the dark age, and writings said to have been composed in it, they can never be taken uncritically at face value and must sometimes be dismissed altogether. At best, they reveal only a minority of the people: nobles, courtiers, priests. But the revelation is better than nothing; in fact, much better.

Those two major sources, the early Welsh poetry and laws, are not only valuable but related, as are the family trees, triads and remnants of miscellaneous prose which eke them out. For a long time, the courts of western Britain were the island's only centres of patronage for a learned class. In that class the bards were key figures, and more than mere entertainers. They corresponded roughly to the *filid* of Ireland who had taken over the scholarly and educational functions of the moribund druids. *Filid* not only composed laureate-type eulogies and elegies like the court minstrels of other lands; they were also the custodians of saga, genealogy, poetic rules, even ordinary law. In Britain, as in Ireland, the bardic calling was far from irresponsible. It served the needs of the kings and aristocracy. Property and power depended on the poetic word. Pedigrees had to be right, traditions had to be sound, customs and precedents had to be correctly transmitted. The bards who immortalised the famous confirmed the status of their descendants, and were honoured members of the household.

As a result, the royal secretaries and codifiers of law worked in concert with literary men. It was a fruitful co-operation. On the one hand, the literary men respected the lawyers and took an interest in their profession: Welsh romances have a sprinkling of legal terms, like Elizabethan plays. On the other hand, the lawyers themselves acquired a rich and lucid vocabulary, with many literary touches. Fragments of early codes now lost have gone into the tenth-century *Laws of Hywel Dda*. Historians have remarked that most of the basic words are Celtic, not Latin, and hence do not suggest a strong Roman influence. The general reader may prefer to linger over items like the penalty for killing or stealing the cat that guards a royal barn. The thief is to pay a fine assessed by measurement of the cat:

Its head is to be held downwards on a clean, level floor, and its tail is to be held upwards; and after that, wheat must be poured over it until the tip of its tail is hidden, and that is its value.

To this edict (which would seem to raise difficulties if the animal is still alive) some cat-fancying clerk has added a note on the points to look for when judging one:

It should be perfect of ear, perfect of eye, perfect of teeth, perfect of claw, without marks of fire, and it should kill mice, and not devour its kittens, and should not go caterwauling every new moon.

The dark-age society of Wales seems to have been divided into free tribesmen who claimed descent from an original conquering stock, and an unfree populace comprising most of the families with whom the free admitted no blood relationship. The unfree had fewer rights and did most of the heavy agricultural work. Also there were slave labourers, not in large numbers, who were the property of the wealthy. In the parts of Britain more influenced by Rome, the pattern may have been somewhat different, but there is no reason to doubt the existence of regional social pyramids of much the same kind.

At the apex of each pyramid was a chief or king. His title was hereditary, but not necessarily from his father. Every king enjoyed a certain freedom of choice in appointing a successor from among his male kin. Complications may have been introduced by the wish to ground legitimacy on a tie of blood with Maximus or some other person who had been part of the imperial scheme. Several Welsh genealogies look plausible even as far back as the fifth century, but farther back still we wander into a region peopled by unlikely ancestors borrowed from Roman history. A genuine confusion at this level over the identity of the Empress Helena, Constantine's mother, underlies the long-standing belief that Constantine was partly British and could be counted, after a fashion, among the princes of Britain. The Picts in the north had a rare custom of inheritance in the maternal line, and the Britons, who intermarried with them, sometimes allowed succession to go through the female. However, a woman apparently could not reign herself. As time passed, a regular succession from father to son tended to become the norm.

Around each king was a band of noble retainers. The relation foreshadowed feudalism in a very loose sense, with the nobles looking to the sovereign to uphold their local rights, and rallying round him in time of war. But the ties were personal, to the man rather than the office. The king's position depended on his lineage and his own prowess. If his court bard failed to stress the former, or keep the warriors convinced of the latter, the whole system could become unstable and seek a new centre. Then the king might succumb to a stronger rival, or try to enhance his prestige by victories. Hence, in part, the quarrels and inter-British wars lamented by Gildas in the middle of the sixth century. No organised state could exist. Each kingdom was held together—so far as it was held together—by an ever-shifting network of obligations and by the *esprit de corps* of the nobles. They prized such virtues as courage, honour, generosity, faithfulness. They lived close to their chieftains, feasting with them to the accompaniment of music, dressing finely and making a proud display. They were fond of the chase. We have a glimpse of one of them in a song sung by a nurse to a child:

> When thy father went a-hunting
> With spear on shoulder, and cudgel in hand,
> He would call his big dogs,
> 'Giff, Gaff': 'Catch, catch!' 'Fetch, fetch!'
> In his coracle he would spear a fish . . .
> When thy father went up the mountain
> He would bring back a roebuck, a wild boar, a stag,
> A spotted grouse . . .

The sole bond that transcended personal and dynastic loyalty was religion. Most Britons were nominally Christian, the upper class almost solidly. Their faith did not much affect their morals, but it did affect their relationship with the Church. Even such powerful kings as Maelgwn of Gwynedd made religious retreats and endowed monasteries. Patronage of this kind helped the Church to flourish and attract some of the highest talent of the age.

The Celtic Christianity of Britain and Ireland, almost cut off from the world outside, had a character of its own, disclosed in the Saints' Lives and other ecclesiastical literature. Later indeed, when the Synod of Whitby brought its practices into conformity with Rome, the controversy was so violent as to start historians on a false trail. There is still a lingering impression that the Celts anticipated the Greek Orthodox in schism, or even that they were proto-Protestants. This impression is quite wrong. The Church in Britain was Catholic, and never ceased to recognise Rome as the spiritual capital. Thanks to a firm ruling by St Patrick, the same was true in Ireland. The Celts' undoubted idiosyncrasies arose partly from divergence during the long chaos of the later fifth century, and partly from a feature already noted: that their Church was based on monasteries rather than dioceses, with authority vested in abbots rather than bishops.

Ills. 144, 145, 146

Bishops were never done away with. They were needed to ordain priests and thereby keep up the apostolic succession. But otherwise they were not held in much esteem, nor was the secular priesthood. British and Irish monks, by contrast, were allowed a scope and freedom of movement denied to their continental brethren, and this freedom was widely exercised because of their responsibility toward ill-defined 'parishes' covering vast areas. According to a triad, the

Ill. 136. A chart for calculating the date of Easter, made in 1011 by the monk Byrhtferth. The Church in Celtic Britain was Catholic and recognised Rome as its spiritual capital. When the Celts came into dispute with. Rome, in the seventh century, one of the matters of dispute was the method of fixing Easter.

three great communities of sixth-century Britain were Amesbury, Glastonbury and Llantwit Major, each of which had a 'perpetual choir' reciting the liturgy round the clock. Whatever the precise historical weight of this triad, such monasteries must have extended their ministry for many miles round. There are accounts of monks, like St Sampson, who gave up fixed residence altogether. At various times Sampson was in Wales, Cornwall and Brittany.

The monks' contempt for worldly goods restricted the Celtic Church on the artistic side and impelled parts of it toward a barren asceticism. But their originality and comparative liberty gave it unusual qualities in other respects. Married men, for example, were admitted freely to the priesthood. They were expected to live apart from their wives after ordination, and the married clergy was recruited, in practice, from older couples who separated by mutual consent. But there was no feeling that men with a true religious vocation were beings apart, or that a candidate's fitness could be called in question by contact with women. The status of the women themselves, if they too turned toward a religious calling, was higher than elsewhere. Where the monk was so important, his counterpart the nun was likewise important.

When the Celts finally clashed with Rome's representatives, long after Arthurian times, the dispute raged round two matters of discipline: the method of fixing Easter, and the shape of the tonsure. (Other monks shaved a round patch on top of the head, the Celts shaved a broad band from ear to ear.) These details were mere rallying-points in a more profound conflict of will, temperament and philosophy. In both cases the word 'heretic' was flung back and forth with no visible justification. In both cases, the spokesmen threw out hints at secret traditions of a dubious sort, deriving from Simon Magus or the Apostle John. Among the Irish at least, and their northern ecclesiastical colonists in the orbit of Iona, the seeds planted by the Briton Patrick had unquestionably burst into strange blossoms. The monks preserved apocryphal books which Rome disliked. They taught formulae for conjuring the angels. They even contrived to salvage druidic notions. St Bridget, the namesake of a pre-Christian goddess, was saluted in poetry as the Mary of the Gael, a reincarnation of the Mother of Christ and, in some highly uncanonical sense, a priestess.

Whether such eccentricities were found in the Britain from which Ireland was evangelised, it is hard to say. But Celtic Christianity always had an air of oddness, a 'Sense of Something Else', as it has been called. Uneasiness in its presence, inability to get the hang of it, is the best explanation of the strange virulence of the Roman party. Irregularities of doctrine which the pope tried to pin down as revived Pelagianism were observed in the north in 634; and long after Rome's official victory, the disturbing philosopher John Scotus Erigena appeared out of what can hardly have been a vacuum. The Grail story may or may not owe a debt to some specific tradition of paganised Christianity or Christianised paganism; it certainly reflects, among much else, a medieval feeling that the dark-age spiritual lore of the British Isles had an elusive and peculiar flavour.

In the absence of clerical support, and lay patronage also, the visual arts languished. The Britons had no known sculpture except inscribed crosses on stones. Here the barbarous Picts completely outshone them. The Irish in due course produced splendid manuscripts covered with labyrinthine designs; but even they were weak on representative art and could seldom manage a good human figure. British architecture (subject to the query raised by the cruciform foundation at Cadbury) was confined to the simple structures of stone or wood already described. Occasionally the Celts dug out storage cellars, called 'fogous' in Cornwall and 'weems' in the Scottish Lowlands.

The art which did flourish, because of its exponents' importance to the ruling class, was poetry. Most of the early Welsh verse is in four medieval manuscripts. Among what purports to be of the dark age, enough actually is so to allow a few generalisations. The poems are meant to be recited to an audience, with instrumental accompaniment. They are in strict and complex native metres, implying a still earlier process of development. Latin influence shows in the stanza form and the use of rhyme. There is virtually no direct narrative. Most of these dark-age items are poems of praise, celebration or lamentation. The bards assume that the hearers know what they are singing about. They allude without explaining.

Gildas refers to royal minstrels before 547, at the court of Maelgwn. But the oldest extant Welsh poetry dates from the later sixth century, and is the work of a school of bards in Rheged, the Cumberland area. Nennius names five: Talhaern, Bluchbard, Cian, Taliesin and Aneirin. More than a dozen poems by the last two have been identified. Most are in praise of Urbgen or Urien, the most successful of Rheged's monarchs, and his son and successor Owein. Their setting is the warfare of the northern Britons against the Angles and, unhappily, against each other. Further verse of much the same type is ascribed to Myrddin—from whom Geoffrey of Monmouth got the name Merlin —and Llywarch Hen, 'the Old'.

Taliesin wandered widely, and had more than one royal patron. He sang at the court of Powys in eastern Wales. The legendary *Story of Taliesin* makes him begin his bardic career at the court of Gwynedd. There, as an impudent and precocious boy, he confronts the flattering bards whom King Maelgwn already has in residence. They view him with disfavour, but he bewitches them so that they can say nothing but 'blerwm blerwm'. Then he utters a long and baffling rigmarole. It looks like a riddle, and has been so construed by Robert Graves, who offers an incredibly ingenious answer in his study of poetic myth *The White Goddess.*

> My original country is the region of the summer stars . . .
> I was with my Lord in the highest sphere,
> On the fall of Lucifer into the depth of hell;
> I have borne a banner before Alexander;
> I know the names of the stars from north to south;
> I have been on the Galaxy at the throne of the Distributor;
> I was in Canaan when Absalom was slain;
> I conveyed Awen to the level of the vale of Hebron; . . .

> I was instructor to Eli and Enoch . . .

> I have been three periods in the prison of Arianrhod;
> I have been the chief director in the work of the tower of Nimrod . . .

> I have been in Asia with Noah in the Ark,
> I have witnessed the destruction of Sodom and Gomorrah.

So it goes on for forty lines, with Taliesin claiming to have lived in many places and periods, usually in distinguished company. Some have detected the druidic idea of reincarnation. Or Mr Graves may be right in seeking a cryptographic meaning. However, the poem can be viewed as a satire on the pretensions of bards who claimed superhuman knowledge and inspiration. The nearest analogue is the irreverent American ballad 'Ten Thousand Years Ago', discovered by the Lomaxes and revived in the folksong of the 1960s. In any case it is not, as it stands, the work of the real Taliesin. What the legend surely communicates, if it communicates anything historical, is the faint echo of a shock. The poet makes his mark as a mischievous teenage innovator for whom modern parallels are not hard to find.

In the authentic verse composed during his Rheged phase, Taliesin has settled down and joined the Establishment. He extols the kings' hospitality and martial deeds. *The Battle of Llwyfein Wood* celebrates a victory won by Owein over the Angles. *The Death Song of Owein* recalls vividly how he left his enemies' bodies lying staring-eyed on the field:

> His keen-edged spears were like the wings of the dawn . . .
> The host of broad England sleeps
> With the light in their eyes.

Taliesin's language is fairly simple, but curt and disjointed. He conveys a series of sharp, evocative images rather than a sequence of thoughts. The same style appears in Llywarch Hen. When King Urbgen was slain, his head was cut off and carried away, perhaps to avoid defacement. In a lament Llywarch imagines himself as its bearer. Each brief stanza begins 'A head I carry', slightly varied, with a phrase contrasting the glory of the hero in life. Lastly:

> A head I hold up which once sustained me . . .
> My arm is numb, my body trembles,
> My heart breaks;
> This head I cherish, formerly cherished me.

As with Taliesin and Llywarch, the best poetry of Aneirin is sombre and poignant. Aneirin's great work is the *Gododdin* mentioned previously, which contains the oldest literary allusion to Arthur. Toward 600, a body of British noblemen assembled in Manau Gododdin, the country beside the Firth of Forth, to attack the Angles. After a period of court attendance and military exercises, they rode the long distance to Catraeth (Catterick in Yorkshire) and met the army of the Northumbrian king. For several days they struggled against impossible odds till nearly all were dead. Aneirin himself rode with them, and was one of the few who escaped.

Gododdin is a kind of epic-elegy in a hundred and three stanzas, mourning for the fallen. Parts are not by Aneirin, but a great deal is. He never describes the battle directly, yet a picture of the warriors and the action slowly emerges.

> The men went to Catraeth, strenuous was their army, the pale mead was their feast, and it was their poison; three hundred men battling in array, and after the glad war-cry there was silence. Though they went to the churches to do penance, the inescapable meeting with death overtook them. . . .
> The men went to Catraeth with the dawn, their high courage shortened their lives. They drank the sweet yellow enticing mead, for a year many a bard made merry. Red were their swords (may the blades never be cleansed), and white shields and square-pointed spear-heads. . . .
> The men went to Catraeth, they were renowned, wine and mead from gold cups was their drink for a year, in accordance with the honoured custom. Three men and three score and three hundred, wearing gold necklets, of all that hastened after the flowing drink none escaped but three, through feats of sword-play—the two war-

dogs of Aeron, and stubborn Cynon; and I too, streaming with blood, by grace of my blessed poetry. . . .

The men went to Catraeth in column, raising the war-cry, a force with steeds and blue armour and shields, javelins aloft and keen lances, and bright mail-coats and swords. He led, he burst through the armies, and there fell five times fifty before his blades— Rhufawn the Tall, who gave gold to the altar and gifts and fine presents to the minstrel. . . .

The warriors arose together, together they met, together they attacked, with a single purpose; short were their lives, long the mourning left to their kinsmen. Seven times as many English they slew; in fight they made women widows, and many a mother with tears at her eyelids. . . .

It is grief to me that after the toil of battle they suffered the agony of death in torment, and a second heavy grief it is to me to have seen our men falling headlong; and continual moaning it is, and anguish. . . . After the battle, may their souls get welcome in the land of Heaven, the dwelling-place of plenty.

10 Arthur and English History

Geoffrey Ashe

GODODDIN, with its air of a requiem for lost glories, raises an obvious question: whether Arthur's Britain is now dead, a topic of purely antiquarian interest. Events that happened a long time ago are relevant or otherwise according to their effects. By unearthing this buried dark-age society and tracing its achievements, are we bringing to light only a Celtic aberration that made no difference, or a creative epoch that moulded the life of Britain ever afterwards? Arthur's legacy will always be important as legend. But can we say that it is important as history—important enough (for example) to justify any major rewriting of school textbooks?

The verdict will depend on a more careful assessment of the aftermath than was made in chapter 2. At first glance, the Arthurian Fact, however resounding, seems empty. We have to admit also an Arthurian Non-Fact and an Arthurian Anti-Climax. Only by defining these, and assessing their weight, can we decide whether the Fact was blotted out by its sequels.

The Arthurian Non-Fact was summed up by the Anglo-Saxon historian Bede, who is acute on this point although he appears to know nothing of Arthur personally. When the Britons had peace and the upper hand after their success, they made no attempt—none, at any rate, of which we have record—to assimilate their halted opponents. This, in the dark ages, would have meant primarily a Christian mission. The British Church failed to launch one. It evangelised Ill. 143 the Pict and the Scot, but it left the third enemy, the Anglo-Saxon, alone. The saints of Wales laboured in other fields, and Britons in general were willing to let the Teutonic pagans go to perdition.

So far as there was any religious response to the heathen presence, it took a form which the sermonising book of the monk Gildas discloses all too plainly. Many of the more ardent Christians treated the invasion as a divine punishment for British sins, and tried to atone

177

by a restrictive, inward-looking penance. The chief name here is, regrettably, St David. Born in Pembrokeshire during the first quarter of the sixth century, he had a purely religious education; despite King Voteporix's Roman title, there is no sign that the classical curriculum survived in those parts. David was ordained and began a wandering mission, probably going through parts of Herefordshire and staying at Glastonbury, but never approaching the Saxons' country. Then he founded a monastery of his own at Menevia, the place now called St David's. His monks performed the usual pastoral duties. But their abbot imposed a rule of extreme rigour, with self-mortification as its aim. He copied the harsh practices of the ascetics of Egypt, making no allowance for a less helpful climate. His own diet was bread and water, and he harnessed the monks to ploughs like oxen, condemning them to the hardest of labour to expiate the public guilt.

Ill. 52

Given personal virtue and force of character, people of David's stamp are sometimes remarkably successful at winning disciples. He had both qualities, and his tough, introverted ideals were spread through Wales by a medley of imitators: Gudwal, Rumon, Cybi, Deiniol and many more. Welsh Christian dynamism and culture flagged. The daughter-church of Ireland, though looking to David among others for guidance, soon surpassed it in both. When David died, St Augustine, sent from Rome by Pope Gregory, was perhaps already in Kent converting Saxons. Augustine invited the Welsh clergy to join his mission, and they refused. Thenceforward they were isolated.

Besides the preoccupation with guilt and penitence, we can glimpse another aspect of British failure in Gildas's 'Complaining Book'. This is the main witness to the Arthurian Anti-Climax. Gildas himself came from the north. He lived at Llancarfan for several years, on more or less friendly terms with its founder St Cadoc. His alleged quarrels with Arthur, and also with St David, may or may not be historical. Certainly tradition agrees with Gildas's own writings in giving the impression of a very difficult person. He probably spent some time at Glastonbury and in Brittany, though the belief that he founded the monastery at Ruys, where Peter Abelard was abbot in the twelfth century, may be based on a confusion of names.

At any rate, during the 540s he wrote his *Liber Querulus de Excidio et Conquestu Britanniae*, which we have glanced at more than once. His biographers call him 'the Wise', *sapiens*, like the erudite King Cadman of Gwynedd, and the book does reveal a considerable survival of

Ill. 51

Roman learning. But the mind that harbours it is old-fashioned, backward-looking, with an aroma of being left over. Gildas presupposes Rome, and imperial citizenship, in a Church governed by bishops, and he plainly fears that his contemporaries are tossing all he cares for on to the scrap-heap. He thinks in Latin, transcribes scriptural texts from the Vulgate, bases his conception of history on the learned fathers Eusebius and Orosius, quotes Virgil and echoes other Roman poets. But one gathers that he feels himself to be surrounded by barbarians.

Mount Badon, he declares after his embittered historical retrospect, put an end to foreign but not to civil wars. For a while, evidently, these wars were merely local affrays and Britain flourished. Gildas's post-Badonic phase of prosperity and order supplies the basis for the legend of Arthur's reign. But when a generation grew up that had not been involved in the struggle and took the peace for granted, Britain's moral and political cohesion began to dissolve. Rulers ignored the danger from outside, and the social order succumbed to feuds, fragmentation and irresponsibility.

Camlann may have been the first serious breach, though Gildas does not name the battle. He does murkily disclose the first step in a well-recognised process. Arthur's Britain, unable to maintain a united front, broke up into three sub-Britains, none of them saving more than a fraction of the full heritage. Very gradually the term 'British', though still employed (by Bede, for instance), became less apt to the Celtic people than the terms 'Cymry', meaning 'fellow-countrymen', and 'Welsh', from the Anglo-Saxon for 'foreigners': words implying an ethnic bond instead of a claim to the Island of Britain. A sort of northern Wales stretched from the Pennines far into Scotland, its terminus just beyond Dumbarton, the Fort of the Britons. Wales proper contracted toward its medieval limits. West Wales was the peninsula from Somerset to Land's End, with its scattered islands. Within these areas there were further divisions.

In the 540s, when Gildas writes, a much larger extent of Britain is still British. But the men of the fringe are plainly in the ascendant and setting the tone, at least in the evil sense that concerns Gildas. He denounces their injustice, their perfidy, their wars against each other, their private crimes, their sexual misconduct, their patronage of self-seeking favourites and cacophonous bards, and their pretence of putting things right by almsgiving and pious gestures.

Of more interest to the modern investigator is a series of specific upbraidings addressed to five named kings. These are Constantine of

Dumnonia, ruling from Somerset westward; Aurelius Caninus, the unworthy heir of Ambrosius Aurelianus, apparently in Gloucestershire and south-east Wales; Vortiporius of Demetia or Dyfed, the Voteporix of the Carmarthenshire monument; Cuneglasus or Cinglas, a descendant of Cunedda, in central Wales; and—the most important —Maglocunus or Maelgwn of Gwynedd, the lord of Degannwy Castle. The last is the only one for whom Gildas's savage phrases add up to anything like a portrait. He is tall, talented, a former pupil of St Illtud, a ruthless and successful power-seeker, alternating his crimes with spells of penitence which are sincere but do not last.

Can we accept Gildas's dismal sketch of mid-century British affairs? The account of Maelgwn is supported by several Saints' Lives and poems, and by the evidence that this king and his successors claimed hegemony over others. Gildas, however, is supposed to have had family ties with Gwynedd. A query hangs over his much vaguer abuse of those outside. Doubt is deepened by his version of Britain's earlier history, which is not only muddled but fundamentally warped by his reading the present back into the past; also by the curtness of his reference to Mount Badon, on his own showing a key event. His silence as to the victor's identity is a problem which is not solved, but made worse, by denying Arthur's existence. If clerical rancour has spoilt his narrative at this point, it may have spoilt it at other points. To confuse matters further, he drops in what could be an oblique allusion to Arthur, after all, in his address to Cuneglasus. According to him, that prince was once the charioteer of a person nicknamed 'The Bear', which 'Arthur', by a Celtic pun, was sometimes interpreted as meaning.

Gildas is not so much untrustworthy as uneven. His work looks like an irritating mixture of knowledge and ignorance, with too few signs to show where one stops and the other starts. Careful study of his historical chapters bears out this impression. He omits much that should go in, he perpetrates appalling howlers, yet sometimes he is curiously well-informed. Thus, his story of the two Roman rescues of Britain between 388 and 446 could not have been taken from any known book, yet is now seen to be credible, and his mention of cavalry in the second rescue but not the first is a striking touch. On military events—the course of land operations after Maximus against Britain's invaders, and the related diplomacy—he does not do badly. Although a monk, he is better briefed here than he is in the history of the Church. It has been conjectured that he knew some military document drawn up by, or for, a field-commander, and that in his account of the previous century and a half he has relied on this where he can and on hearsay and imagination for almost everything else. Certainly, Gildas is an unsatisfactory witness. But the broad picture of collapse, recovery and decline is sound; and his forebodings of doom were quickly fulfilled.

The year 547 brought a disaster which Gildas doubtless considered the judgement of God. An epidemic of Persian origin, the Yellow Plague, reached the Channel and crossed it. Perhaps because of the contact with Gaul through Brittany, it struck the Britons more fiercely than the Saxons. Its victims included Maelgwn. Legend relates that he shut himself in a church when semi-delirious, peeped out through a keyhole, saw the Plague as a monster closing in for the kill, and dropped dead. With the king of Gwynedd gone, no ruler was left who could even pretend to a real paramountcy among the Britons.

About five years later, the Saxons were on the move again. Their first major encroachment was in Hampshire, and the record thereafter is of British retreat, with some pauses but few counter-thrusts. National debility and division may not have been the only causes. A theory proposed by the novelist Alfred Duggan is that Arthur had succeeded partly by using large horses imported from the continent, and that the Britons failed to keep up the breed, so that they soon had only the insular type, smaller and less formidable. Whatever the truth about their horses, the Britons found no more outstanding men except in the north, whereas their enemies did. King Ceawlin of the West Saxons reversed the verdict of Mount Badon.

Ceawlin started by conquering most of Hampshire and Berkshire. In 571, his brother Cuthwulf overwhelmed a British enclave in Buckinghamshire. Meanwhile, Ceawlin had induced (not without violence) several of his Saxon neighbours to acknowledge him as overlord. In 577, he marched west and won a battle at Dyrham, killing three allied British kings, taking Cirencester, Bath and Gloucester, and breaking through to the Bristol Channel. This campaign was decisive. It destroyed whatever may have been left of the Romanised civil life of the Gloucestershire region, and it cut off the Devonian promontory, which henceforth became merely West Wales.

The West Welsh were by no means finished. They fought a long series of rearguard actions. Central Somerset held out till 658, Devon till 710, Cornwall till 825. But Ceawlin caused another mass flight to

Ill. 28

Brittany which permanently depressed the importance of the whole area. It was shortly after his victory that the Britons of Cambria and the north began to call themselves Cymry. They never applied that term to the waifs of the south-west, whom they no longer counted as fellow-countrymen.

As for the Angles at the other end of the British front, their equivalent of Ceawlin was Aethelfrith, king of Northumbria. He had to cope with a tougher opposition. The British states of the north were entrenched behind barriers of hill and wild country. A broad extent of the Scottish Lowlands formed the kingdom of Strathclyde, ruled by descendants of the fifth-century *gwledig* Ceredig from their capital at Dumbarton. Most of the Lowland Picts were still under British authority. Eastward around the head of the Firth of Forth was Manau Gododdin, the base of the expedition mourned by Aneirin. Part of what is now Yorkshire—the Pennine hill country—remained British under the name of Elmet, and the Cumberland area was Rheged, where the court gave its hospitality to the famous bards.

Before Aethelfrith's accession in 593, there was a flash of recovery when King Urbgen of Rheged and King Rydderch of Strathclyde almost ended Teutonic settlement in the north. Urbgen drove the Angles into the sea near Lindisfarne. But the Britons' feuds were again Ill. 147 fatal to them. Urbgen was assassinated, and his son Owein, though an able commander, failed to complete his work. Aethelfrith managed, during the first decade of his own reign, to subdue a portion of Rheged. The position was briefly complicated by Scottish intervention. Aedan, the king of the Scots who had colonised Argyll, had British sympathies and dynastic links; he even named one of his sons Arthur. In 603, he marched against Aethelfrith under the delusion that Northumbrian rebels would help him. He was routed, however, at an unidentified place called Degsastan. Welsh legend ungenerously makes him a traitor. While such stab-in-the-back fables can be discounted, it is a fact that Rheged crumbled, while Elmet was swallowed up in Northumbria, and Strathclyde became ineffectual.

In 616, Aethelfrith achieved his counterpart of the battle of Dyrham by crushing a Welsh army at Chester. Several hundred monks came from the great community at Bangor to pray for a Christian victory. When the purpose of these non-combatants was explained to the pagan Aethelfrith, he said that praying to their God was morally no different from bearing arms. Like Jeremy Cruncher's wife in *A Tale of Two Cities*, they were 'flopping agin him'. He therefore opened his attack with a massacre of monks, turning on the disconcerted Welsh soldiers afterwards. His success divided the Cymry of Wales from the northerners, completing the separation of the three sub-Britains. Except for a vengeful counter-blow in 632 by Cadwallon of Gwynedd, which burned itself out after a moment of bewildering triumph, the Cymry never came back. England henceforth was England.

This being so, the question must be asked again: how should we regard the Arthurian Fact as a portion of history? Was it merely an accident that did no more than delay the inevitable, or had it any lasting effect? Is Arthur a part of what we are today in any more than a literary sense?

The shortest and simplest answer is that even the delay made a difference, because the Anglo-Saxons who finally won were no longer the murderous pirates of the fifth century. They had had time to settle, to organise, to study the arts of peace and to absorb something of the culture and moral outlook promoted by Christian missions. Civilisation never entirely perished in Britain. The Celts held out against the Teutonic savages till they had ceased to be savages.

But there are subtler considerations. The long, complex train of events which led to a united England was profoundly affected by its own length and complexity, and by the main cause of these: the fact that Celtic Britain, however split and downgraded, was always an entity to be reckoned with. Even in their early onslaught, the invaders were not quite uninfluenced by that stubborn presence. The hereditary chiefs who carved out the first Teutonic kingdoms took no notice of Britain's administrative boundaries, except perhaps in Kent; yet, although they did not adopt the British map, they did adopt the concept of Britain. A series of Anglo-Saxon kings who claimed paramountcy over their colleagues, beginning in the late fifth century with Aelle of Sussex, assumed the title 'Bretwalda'. It means Britain-ruler, and envisages Britain as a whole. Where it came from is uncertain. It sounds like a minstrel's phrase, comparable with 'deed-doer' and 'bracelet-giver'. At any rate the minstrel (or whoever it was that coined it) thought of the ex-Roman land as one country, and was possibly saluting Aelle as rightful claimant to the power of the fallen Vortigern. Bede translates Bretwaldaship into Latin as *imperium*.

So the idea of Britain survived in Britain. Similarly, the idea of Gaul survived in Gaul. But in Gaul, the Frankish conquest that laid the foundation of the renamed kingdom of France was far quicker and simpler than the making of a united England. Clovis, the Frankish monarch, was master of nearly all the country by 510. In Britain, the Arthurian rally prevented any such thing from happening. Aelle did not become a Clovis. For some decades, the idea of a Teutonic Bretwaldaship went into abeyance, and Anglo-Saxondom remained broken up into small units. Each ruling family turned into a local dynasty. Each tribe struck root and turned its attention to agriculture and forest clearance. At least twelve kingdoms flourished at various times: Kent, Sussex, Wight, Wessex, Essex, East Anglia, Lindsey, Mercia; Bernicia and Deira, the two parts of Northumbria; and the states of the Hwicce and the Magonsaetan.

Arthur, so to speak, atomised Anglo-Saxondom. After Mount Badon, recovery and coalescence could only be gradual. These petty realms were too small, their growth in population too slow, their means of overseas recruitment too limited. No king was prominent enough to renew the claim to Bretwaldaship till Ceawlin of Wessex, who considered himself supreme as far as the Humber. But the Bretwaldaship, once reasserted, proved to be a potent abstraction around which an English monarchy could take shape. It never became the prerogative of any one royal house, and it carried a notion of legitimacy and consent as distinct from pure brute force. Aethelbert of Kent, who had no great material resources, was Bretwalda after Ceawlin. So in his turn was Raedwald of East Anglia. Aethelfrith of Northumbria, that strong warrior and expansionist, was not. His successor Edwin was. Edwin not only headed most of the Anglo-Saxon kings but exerted a protectorate over some of the Welsh, and had a standard of Roman type borne before him. Two more Northumbrians were Bretwaldas, and then the title passed to the Mercians, ruling in the Midlands. It was acquiring a constitutional meaning. By 796, five of the minor states had become Mercian provinces, and the heads of their dynasties were no longer called kings but *subreguli* or even *duces* —dukes.

The final phase began when the Bretwaldaship returned to Wessex in the person of King Egbert. The *Anglo-Saxon Chronicle* describes how he achieved that status. Kent, Surrey and Sussex 'submitted to him'. The king of the East Angles 'sought his protection'. Northumbria, after a West Saxon military demonstration, 'offered him submission and peace'. The Welsh were 'reduced to humble submission'. Egbert's Bretwaldaship was based on armed force, but it was no mere obliteration of weaker sovereigns. Treaties were signed, benefits conferred, obligations assumed. Egbert's heir Alfred the Great was served and immortalised by a Welsh secretary, and the

Cymry acknowledged him as Protector of all Christians in the Island of Britain. He maintained Wessex's independence against the Danish invasion. After his victory, the growth of the West Saxon realm into the kingdom of England was fairly rapid.

It was a growth conditioned by all that had gone before, by centuries of unconscious political education. Alfred's Wessex could absorb Welshmen as well as Anglo-Saxons and make them willing liegemen. In 920, his son Edward received the submission of Constantine, king of Scots, of the Welsh king of Strathclyde, and of the Scandinavian ruler of York. He had not crushed them in war. They acknowledged in him an elaborately evolved central dignity. By the time the Normans arrived, everything had been digested. A sense of community held together English and Scandinavians and many Celts. The medieval state which emerged was a mixture of institutions, Anglo-Saxon, Welsh, Breton, Danish, Frankish, Norman and even Flemish.

It is a complicated story, and its complication is precisely the point. The process affected the product. Each of the small units endured long enough to have its own character, laws and idiosyncrasies. When big kingdoms did eventually absorb little ones, the local witans or assemblies stood up for their rights. As a result, Anglo-Saxon law-making never became legislation in the sense of a code imposed from above. It was largely a written standardisation of existing customs. So far as the ordinary man's life was regulated by public authority, it was regulated by small shire-courts and hundred-courts where everybody knew everybody, rather than by royal edicts. This is the root of the English conception of the Common Law.

Feudalism developed in England as in France, but its dynamics were different. Clovis the Frank created a single monarchy in his own lifetime, and feudalism took shape later as the nobles drew away from the Crown and usurped its powers. The tendency of France was to fall apart, and at last only absolutism could keep it united. In England, the national monarchy arose from a slow process of fitting together, spread over many lifetimes. The feudal earls were the descendants of former sovereigns. The basis of their position lay in a partial surrender of their power to the Crown, an acceptance of responsibility to it. The logic of the monarchy was centripetal and constructive. Even the worst civil wars never threatened to tear England apart.

All this can be traced back to that shattering Arthurian blow which prevented Anglo-Saxon unity for hundreds of years, and meant that in Britain a post-Roman successor-state arose in a way that was unique. On the face of it, there is nothing here which Arthur himself could have foreseen or intended. It would be pleasant to think that he did try to draw the Saxons into some combined system, and that the British failure to give a lead toward unity was his successors' rather than his own. Evidence is lacking. Nevertheless, he set the enemy on a road that led to distinctive and genuine political virtues: solidarity, balance, a capacity for adjustment and creative reconciliation of interests. As George Orwell remarked, there is at least this to be said for the English, that they are less inclined than most people to kill each other for the sake of factions and causes. However multiple the reasons, the slaughter at Mount Badon is not wholly unrelated to the rarity of slaughter in later times.

An unconscious, roundabout influence of this kind, however vast, may not be very satisfying to the seeker after Celtic survival. But another influence also was active in the long work of England's formation. We can go beyond the statement that Arthur delayed the Saxons' triumph till they were on the way to civilisation themselves. Although the credit for civilising them has to be shared, although the task was shirked by the Britons of the sixth century, it was partly a Celtic achievement after all.

At first, the signs were adverse. Decades of warfare virtually ruled out any social continuity between Celt and Saxon, or direct native influence on the new people. The Saxons seldom moved into British farms or villages. Generally they broke virgin ground and left the wreckage of rural Britain alone, as they did the ruined cities. There was some copying of Celtic jewellery, clothing and pottery; or more likely, these articles were made for the conquerors by British slaves. But borrowings on the whole were scanty. Few Celtic words got into the English language. In the areas colonised during the first hundred years, even Celtic place-names were seldom preserved.

Ills. 137, 138

Far to the west, however, new and potent forces were slowly gathering. The British Church might be turning inward, but its creation, the Irish Church, stood firm. Mount Badon ensured that the Saxons would never ravage the smaller island. Behind the military barrier the saints went to and fro in peace. For some time, in spite of their preoccupations, the Britons were still the teachers rather than the taught. David and Gildas both played a part in the instruction of Irishmen. A chapel in Galloway, built by the Briton St Ninian long before, became the nucleus of a college for Hibernian clerics. Then the balance tipped. The Irish pupils did not go the narrowly ascetic way

Ill. 142

of their British masters. They became scholars and missionaries. Soon Erin was the most cultured land of Western Europe: the only one, for instance, where any appreciable number knew Greek. Gradually

Ills. 144, 145

the Irish assumed the lead in Celtic religion. St Columba crossed to Scotland in 563, founding the Iona community and evangelising the northern Picts. Monks from Iona spread through the Hebrides and, south of the Clyde, joined hands with British apostles such as St Kentigern.

The Celtic tendency for abbots rather than bishops to predominate was taken further. In Scotland, the abbot of Iona was the bishops' official superior. The importance of the wandering monks, the absence of a fixed hierarchy, continued to give the Church elasticity and ardour. The Irish, with a youthful-spirited zeal which had expired almost everywhere else, tramped over Europe restoring scholarship and stimulating jaded minds. St Columbanus of Leinster founded monasteries in the Vosges and the Apennines. Irish monks entered pagan Germany. One, named Ferghil or Virgil, became bishop of Salzburg and caused a stir by teaching that the earth is round and that other inhabited worlds exist.

Even when Irishmen did choose the path of penitential retreat, they were apt to do it in a startlingly enterprising manner. Many sailed out in highly seaworthy curraghs seeking a 'solitude in the ocean', a marine equivalent of the hermit's desert. By doing so they almost accidentally explored the northern Atlantic. Irish settlements were to be found in the Orkneys by 579, in the Shetlands by 620, in the Faeroes by 670, in Iceland by 795. There is some evidence that Irish monks reached Greenland and had a dim knowledge of America before the Norsemen. The saga of the sea-pilgrims produced the extraordinary tale of St Brendan's Voyage, which has connections with Brittany and the Grail theme, and is counted by one medieval authority as part of the Matter of Britain.

When the papal mission to Kent arrived at Canterbury in 597, the Celtic Church was flourishing in a huge arc alongside Anglo-Saxondom. St Augustine was aware of the Welsh Christians at least, and tried to enlist their aid. A conference was held at Aust on the Severn. But the differences of practice which had grown up during separation presented an obstacle. The Welsh mistrusted Augustine; and he put them off by a lack of courtesy which they construed as a bad omen. Rebuffed, he withdrew. Despite the legends afterwards fostered about him (still by no means dead), his success was confined to restoring two or three ecclesiastical centres in the south-east and Christianising the aristocracy of Kent and Essex—many of whom relapsed. The English Church grew, in the end, round Canterbury because Canterbury supplied a headquarters through which Rome was prepared to work. But its progress for more than fifty years was due mainly to Celtic influence flowing in from the other direction. After St Augustine himself, there is no record of a single Christian advance among the Anglo-Saxons which was incontestably the unaided work of his successors.

In Northumbria, the Bretwalda Edwin and many nobles were converted by Paulinus, who was sent from Canterbury; but the Briton Rhun, a bishop of Rheged, is said to have helped, and in any case the Church in Northumbria was almost destroyed by the Welsh inroad of 632. Its restorer was King Oswald, who had fled to Iona and returned as a Christian on the Celtic model. Oswald invited the kind and humble St Aidan, a Scot, to preach in his kingdom. The two travelled together, Aidan preaching in Gaelic and Oswald interpreting. The Northumbrian Church was now governed from Lindisfarne. Its first saints, such as Chad and Cuthbert, were purely Celtic in inspiration, and it was they who converted the Mercians of the Midlands and repaired the wreck of Augustine's mission in Essex. Historians have claimed Aidan rather than Augustine as the true Apostle of England. The Synod of Whitby in 663 brought Northumbria into harmony with Canterbury and fully under Rome's jurisdiction. But the north kept its character. Oswy, the Northumbrian king who presided at the Synod, married a British princess, probably the grand-daughter of Urbgen of Rheged, whose territory and people were thereby peacefully absorbed. The Anglo-Celtic scholarship that culminated at Jarrow in the person of Bede was the richest in Western Europe. Alcuin, head of the school of York, became an adviser to Charlemagne and had a hand in the foundation of the Holy Roman Empire.

Wessex too embodied Celtic as well as Teutonic culture. Wessex has a special interest, since the United Kingdom eventually grew from it and all the sovereigns are descended from its royal house. That house, as already observed, has a puzzling Celtic tinge from the outset. Its alleged founder Cerdic bears a British name, and the term 'Gewissi' or 'Gewissae' which is applied to his people seems to be connected in some mysterious fashion with Vortigern and Maximus. It used to be argued that Cerdic was probably mythical in any case, because the nucleus of Wessex was a settlement in the upper Thames valley, and no traces of early Saxons had been found in southern Hampshire, along the line of advance which the *Anglo-Saxon Chronicle* attributes to Cerdic. However, the unearthing of early burials near Southampton Water and Winchester has refuted this objection. Cerdic's heirs were doubtless a martial stock who fought their way to the Thames and imposed their rule on unwarlike peasants living there.

The West Saxon ruler who achieved this was very likely Ceawlin, the same who revived the Bretwaldaship and routed the British kings in the west. But the map of the territory he conquered shows another side of him. Saxon place-names beginning 'Weala', Welsh, prove that the former people were allowed to exist in organised communities. Throughout much of the West Country, moreover, the proportion of Celtic place-names is high. From Ceawlin onward, annihilation and oblivion were no longer the Saxon watchwords. In the seventh century, princes of Wessex were marrying princesses of Wales, and another West Saxon king bore a British name, Ceadwalla.

West Saxon Christianity itself had a mixed origin. The first missionary, Birinus, came under papal auspices. In 635, King Cynegils was baptised with the Iona convert Oswald as sponsor. His pagan successor Cenwalh became a Christian while in East Anglia, where an Irishman, Fursey, was one of the leading figures in the Church. Cenwalh founded the see of Dorchester-on-Thames with an Irish-trained priest as its bishop. The Church in Wessex was educated by yet another Irishman, Maelduib, whose pupil St Aldhelm developed an Anglo-Celtic scholarship comparable with that of the north. Aldhelm in turn taught Boniface, the Apostle of Germany and restorer of the Church in Gaul. The same Aldhelm was a trusted adviser of the West Saxon King Ini, who reigned in the early eighth century and enlisted his West Welsh subjects in his own service—even in his bodyguard. Under Ini, the laws of Wessex gave these Welshmen a recognised, if unequal, status. They were no longer merely the aborigines.

Ill. 75 One of Ini's most famous acts was his enlargement and enrichment of Glastonbury. That Celtic foundation had been swept into the West Saxon kingdom in 658 by Cenwalh, who conquered central Somerset. In his conduct toward Glastonbury, Cenwalh set a notable precedent. He made it a place of reconciliation between the two races and the two Christian traditions. The British abbot stayed in charge, and although Saxon monks gradually replaced Celts, the community did not become entirely Teutonic. It attracted Irishmen, for whom it was a centre of pilgrimage and a school. As we have seen, some of them asserted that St Patrick was buried there. Glastonbury is spoken of in a ninth-century document as a place where 'the Scots' (that is, in the old sense, the Irish) 'used to resort' as to a sanctuary of their own. This may account for a strange passage in one of the Grail romances, where the author says that Joseph of Arimathea lies buried in 'the abbey of Glays in Scotland'. At Glastonbury, for the first time, the English adopted a major Celtic institution and made it their own in a spirit of collaboration. Here, in a sense, the United Kingdom was born.

The fact is eloquent. Whatever the truth about Glastonbury's origins and its links with Arthur, it was a place where Arthur's Britain lived on and remained a reality after the Saxon conquest. Continuity was unbroken. It was far more than a continuity of traditions and fables. Glastonbury's august prestige kept it alive afterwards through the horrors of the Danish invasion, when all the other monasteries were blotted out. The Danes sacked Glastonbury, too, but royal aid and protection saved the abbey from ruin and preserved it as an estate of the king. Within its enclosure, the Irish toiled to restore the buildings and library, and English monks were in due course able to resume communal life.

In 943, King Edmund appointed his friend St Dunstan as its abbot. Dunstan was a man of varied gifts and administrative genius, and still young. He refounded Glastonbury as a Benedictine house in the grand manner. Besides enlarging the church and refashioning the graveyard in the way that was to have such a strange bearing on the story of Arthur, he set the monks to work on imaginative projects. They reclaimed marshland for farming, set up a glass factory, copied books, learned music and gardening. Both these last activities were under the care of a monk named Ethelwold, who became Dunstan's principal helper. It is said that the abbot had a dream of a tree covering Britain with its branches, which bore the cowls of monks instead of fruit, and a large cowl at the top was Ethelwold's. For ten years Glastonbury was fulfilling that dream as the school of the English nation, with Ethelwold carrying an enlightened monastic revival through the counties recovered from the Danes. Educationally, architecturally, artistically, the 'Isle of Avalon' laid the groundwork of medieval England. Before the Norman conquest, at least four of its monks became archbishop of Canterbury.

Glastonbury was, and is, great enough not to need the more dubious legends that have clustered round it. To this day, Arthur's

Britain can still be found there, if the Holy Grail cannot. The magic survived the dissolution of the abbey in the sixteenth century, and the destruction of its fabric. In 1908, the Church of England bought back the site from a private owner. The rich archaeological sequel has already been partially described. However, Glastonbury was no mere corpse for dissection. It became a goal of pilgrimages again, both Anglican and Roman Catholic. In 1961, the suggestion was put forward that this national shrine and temple of reconciliation might fittingly become a centre of Christian reunion. Within four years the idea had borne fruit. The bishop of Bath and Wells allowed Roman Catholics to celebrate Mass in the abbey for the first time since the Reformation, and began restoring the crypt of the Old Church as a chapel for all denominations.

The spell goes on. Enthusiasts have predicted that Glastonbury's future, in some way which cannot yet be foreseen, will be greater than its past. That is the sort of hope which inspires the Chalice Well Trust, the sponsoring body of the Tor excavations. Archaeology, of course, produces the most concrete results. But many who have taken part in Glastonbury's renewal find themselves exploring the mystery by other paths. To act thoughtfully in these surroundings is to ask questions, and to ask rightly is to discover. The quest which this book surveys would not have moved into the high tempo of the 1960s without the impulse given by people whose first Arthurian concern was the resurrection of Avalon.

11 *The New Matter of Britain*

Geoffrey Ashe

REDISCOVERY has come also through action of other kinds. Medieval imagination created an Arthurian Britain with a life and logic of its own. In the twentieth century, writers have begun turning back to history, digesting the results of the search, probing the emergent reality instead of the dream. A new Matter of Britain is taking shape and becoming part of the search itself, if only as a catalyst and an awakener of minds.

The original Matter did, of course, go on after Tennyson's *Idylls*. But it could never be as before, and it was soon visibly moving toward the modern transition. So far as the *Idylls* had any direct literary sequels, they were handlings of the Arthurian themes which Tennyson himself had been shy of. By far the most important, and the most alluring to other poets, was the story of Tristram and his loves. This, predictably, was the Arthurian theme which Swinburne made most of. His *Tristram of Lyonesse* appeared in 1882, in some degree a retort to the Laureate. It is a long, verbose, carefully researched poem, full of Swinburnean ardours and sea-imagery. The same legend reappeared, variously interpreted, in further poems by Laurence Binyon and E. A. Robinson (the latter's being a Pulitzer prize-winning work) and in plays by J. Comyns Carr, Arthur Symons (under the influence of its treatment by Wagner), Thomas Hardy and others. Lancelot and Guinevere also attracted several writers who felt, justly, that Tennyson had left a good deal unsaid.

These poems and plays, while obviously far from negligible, marked a breaking-up rather than a continuation. The same could be said of the two Wagner music-dramas on Arthurian subjects. None of the authors re-evoked Arthur's Britain in a large sense. Each simply took it for granted, the English and Americans more or less in Tennyson's terms, as the background of the plot. That assumption was safe. Almost anybody who read Swinburne, Binyon or Hardy would also have read Tennyson, enough at least to know what sort of world he portrayed. But when two poets did make a fresh attempt to realise an Arthurian milieu as a whole, the result was no longer purely romantic or legendary. The Tennysonian trail was petering out. Awareness of history, of the Celtic tradition behind Geoffrey of Monmouth, of current research and dimly perceived probabilities, was beginning to press in.

John Masefield's *Midsummer Night and Other Tales in Verse*, published in 1927, is a cycle which prunes away much of the romantic proliferation and restores Arthur himself to the centre of the stage. Masefield mixes the medieval legends, the older Welsh poems, historical fact and inventions of his own, in a remarkable amalgam. He employs several metres, often with a light, ballad-like effect that escapes from the Tennysonian stateliness. His sketches of character and psychology have a pointed economy of language that is most welcome after some of the other literature.

The climax is *Badon Hill*, in which Saxon pirates come raiding up the rivers into the west of Britain. They are surprised and slaughtered, historically, by Arthur—aided, however, by the unhistorical Lancelot. Masefield follows the victory with an allegorical version of the Otherworld Quest in that cryptic Welsh poem *The Spoils of Annwn*. He goes on to develop the folk-tale of Arthur asleep in a cave. The account of the decline and downfall of Arthur's kingdom presents the familiar characters in an altered plot. Masefield closes with an acknowledgment that he has altered it, and outlines the more familiar version.

His drama *Tristan and Isolt* is bolder in its return to the roots. Arthur is a Romano-British commander who comes to King Mark with Kay and Bedevere to seek help against the Saxons. Even the triadic pig-stealing affair is brought in. Masefield is the only major writer with the audacity to do this.

The same spirit of adventure, the same readiness to bring together different strata of the legend, appears in a very different poet, Charles Williams. His two volumes *Taliessin through Logres* (1938) and *The Region of the Summer Stars* (1944) are so subtle and personal that they require a commentary. It was supplied after Williams's death by C. S. Lewis, who knew him well and understood what was in his mind. The basis of his conception is a colossal symbolic image recalling Blake, in which the Roman Empire is seen as a human figure, with meanings attached to various regions. Logres—idealised Britain, with a name of Celtic provenance—is the Empire's head and the true abode of its soul. The feet of the giant figure are in a vaguely Asiatic limbo which is a place of lies and death. West of Britain stretches the 'sea-wood' of Broceliande, and beyond a part of it, but a part only, is the Grail Castle. To go the right distance is to discover the Grail, or at any rate its general whereabouts, but to go farther is to be in danger of losing one's way and coming round to the oriental abyss. The map expresses a spiritual tension, a need for diagrammatic precision and the right answer.

The bard Taliessin (spelt with a double s and shifted backward in time) is the chief character. His mission is to find the secret by which Arthur's Britain or Logres can become, as in Tennyson, an earthly kingdom of God and dwelling-place for the Grail. But as in Tennyson, when the experiment is tried, the harmony of spirit and flesh breaks down. Only the Grail-achiever Galahad entirely fulfils the ideal. His departure is not, as in the older versions, an abandonment of those who have failed. 'Joy remembered joylessness.' But the failure has happened, the joy is absent. The Quest destroys the Round Table, the Grail is never brought back, and Logres sinks into mere Britain.

Williams's writing is tightly packed, serious, musical, evocative and very, very difficult. He drew inspiration not only from literature and Christian mysticism but from Collingwood's theory of Arthur. The imperial setting, and events such as the battle of Badon, give the cycle a foundation in history as well as imagination. Arthur's realm is an afterclap of Rome, reaffirming a civilisation betrayed in the West by its own decadent representatives.

None of that description would fit *The Once and Future King*, T. H. White's exuberant best-seller. Here the visionary kingdom, full-blown, makes what may turn out to have been its farewell appearance.

Ill. 149   The musical *Camelot* was adapted from this, and the film of the musical was almost contemporary with the first major finds at Cadbury Castle. Public relations, in fact, forged a link between the two.

White was a solitary, tormented, but forceful man, with a dislike for the twentieth century and a profound knowledge of animals and outdoor sports. He retired from a teaching post to plunge into authorship and antiquarian learning. His eccentric mixture of interests, coupled with a weird and glorious sense of humour, produced in 1938 the first of his Arthurian tales. Neither this nor its sequels could be said to follow on from Tennyson. He went back to Malory and branched off from there.

Ill. 148   *The Sword in the Stone* deals with Arthur's boyhood and his education by a Merlin who is based on the author himself. For this part of the king's career there were no real precedents to draw on; Spenser had the same notion, but treated it in a totally different manner. The result with White was a prodigy of comic invention. Three more stories followed, graver in tone and far more strictly constrained by Malory. All four were published in 1958 as a tetralogy, *The Once and Future King*—White's perfect translation of the phrase *rex quondam rexque futurus* said to have been inscribed on Arthur's tomb. Unlike *The Sword in the Stone*, the complete tetralogy is not for children. It contains much amatory and political matter, and scenes of bizarre gruesomeness. *The Sword* itself, as it reappears in this later context, has been rewritten in the interests of harmony and severely damaged.

White's Merlin (he makes the wizard more of an independent creation by spelling the name 'Merlyn') goes on being a key figure after he ceases to be a tutor. He has a knack of remembering the future and forgetting the past. In the first book this is simply a joke, and later he is still apt to discourse of Mafeking and top hats. But his multiple time-scale becomes thematic. In *The Once and Future King* the realm of the Arthur of romance is, at long last, explicitly divorced from history as commonly understood. It is an ideal Platonic cosmos where the entire expanse of the Middle Ages is present at the same time. It sums up medieval Europe. Actual monarchs, such as Henry III and Louis XI, are spoken of as fictitious. They are mere shadows or feeble expressions of the Arthurian archetype. White goes farther than simply dismissing history. He inverts it. King Arthur is a quintessential Plantagenet with Saxon serfs, and the Celts are his chief enemies.

Within this enchanted ground, White's achievement is vivid and definitive. The Malory characters not only live afresh, legitimately developed: they give the impression that no other writer will ever develop them any further. White said he invented very little, and in a sense this modest remark was true. But he had a genius for building up meagre hints. The best of him shows in such superb touches as the babu English of the Saracen knight Palomides; the eventual and ironical triumph of the public-school Quixote Pellinore; the *de trop* ineptitude of Elaine; and the bit of dialogue where we confront an issue evaded ever since Wace:

'You could never sit a hundred and fifty knights at a round table. Let me see. . . .'

Merlyn, who hardly ever interfered in the arguments now, but sat with his hands folded on his stomach and beamed, helped Kay out of the difficulty.

'It would need to be about fifty yards across,' he said. 'You do it by $2\pi r$.'

Less happy are several passages where White interweaves the chivalric vision with ideas about international peace and the rule of law. These strike a pacifist, cosmopolitan note which is scarcely in keeping with the heraldic atmosphere. But there is never any lasting doubt as to where we are. We are in an immense crystal sphere of imagination that is shattered at a precise moment, with one of the memorable shocks of literature:

'Mordred is using guns.'
Rochester asked in bewilderment: 'Guns?'
'He is using the cannon.'
It was too much for the old priest's intellects.
'It is incredible!' he said. 'To say we are dead, and to marry the queen! And then to use cannon. . . .'
'Now that the guns have come', said Arthur, 'the Table is over. We must hurry home.'
'To use cannons against men!'

In White's eyes, the search for an historical Arthur belonged to the modern, unknightly, iconoclastic world of the guns. Once, in passing, he tells the reader that for him Arthur is no Celt, no 'distressed Briton hopping about in a suit of woad in the fifth century'. But even his denial marks a transition. The crack has opened and nothing will close it. The New Matter of Britain, the rediscovery in art and creative writing, is a product of the search White despised. Others have not despised it. While in no way under-rating the grandeur of the Legend, they have come to terms with the Fact and seen that the 'distressed Briton' possesses an interest of his own.

The pioneer of this trend was Alfred Duggan, a fertile original as odd in his way as White, but calmer. Lord Curzon's stepson, grievously handicapped by wealth, Duggan wasted his time at Oxford in what looked like an alcoholic haze, but wasn't. For years he did little but flirt with Marxism, read and travel. He lost his money and served humbly and honourably in the Second World War, only turning to writing in his forties. The historical novels which he then produced are all in the same style: lucid, exact, quietly entertaining, but reverent in the right places. Great knowledge is carried and communicated with a deceptive, throw-away ease. Duggan follows Robert Graves rather than Walter Scott: the stories are centred on actual people and events, rather than imaginary plots in period settings.

His foray into dark-age Britain, *Conscience of the King* (1951), compelled him to invent more than he did in his other fiction. The 'king' and narrator is not Arthur but Cerdic, and the novel is a black comedy tracing his rise to sovereignty over the West Saxons. Arthur is seen at a distance through Cerdic's eyes as a formidable enigma, the sole British leader who gives him pause. Almost the only thing about him which Cerdic is ever certain of—by painful but not disastrous experience—is his use of cavalry. It is through Cerdic that Duggan puts forward his interesting theory of a British failure to keep up the breed of horses.

After Alfred Duggan came Meriol Trevor, later to achieve solid success as a biographer of Newman. Her novel *The Last of Britain* appeared in 1956, before the cardinal absorbed her attention. This too avoids any attempt to introduce Arthur in person. It is set in the 570s, when the Britons are still under the spell of his rally without grasping that its force is spent. Most of the plot concerns intrigues at the courts of the British kings who died fighting Ceawlin of Wessex, and the climax is the Saxon victory of 577. Gildas (a distinctly idealised Gildas) is depicted as still alive on the eve of the collapse. He represents the Christian and Roman heritage, and dies symbolically at the right moment. In the end, the Glastonbury monks are left preserving all that is worth preserving, and beginning the work of reconstruction by the conversion of a Saxon hostage.

As a novel, *The Last of Britain* scarcely carries the impact it might. The atmosphere is too futile and negative, the effect is too wan. The world-weary people at Bath and Gloucester are like the world-weary people whom we find anywhere in the later Roman Empire, only rather more so. No serious effort is made to capture the flavour of Celtic life, and nothing is said about the Welsh saints, the Irish scholars or the Cumbrian poets. But the striking thing about the book was that it should have been written. It marked the trend, and it acted as a stimulus.

Further glimpses of the Celtic dark age, still without Arthur, were afforded by Bryher in *Ruan* (1961) and by Anya Seton in *Avalon* (1965). The former is a small masterpiece of meticulous and restrained evocation, the latter is a frankly popular but well-researched novel about Anglo-Saxons, which brings in Glastonbury again. Both Bryher and Anya Seton make use of the Irish legends of Atlantic voyages.

Meanwhile, we first meet Arthur as a character in *The Long Sunset* (1955), a play about the passing of Roman Britain, by R. C. Sherriff of *Journey's End* fame. It makes him an ambiguous barbarian warlord to whom, with Gawain, the remnant of imperial power is transferred. This is historically sound for the earlier successor-chiefs like Cunedda. But to place Arthur in 410 seems too violent a stretching of the data. He reappears in a novel, *The Great Captains* (1956), by the poet Henry Treece. Here everything Roman perishes with the death of Ambrosius, and Arthur is a murky, sinister Celt from the pagan borderland. His exploits are largely fraudulent; the hero, so far as there is one, is Modred.

It is no slur on these peripheral or off-beat items to say that the New Matter of Britain produced its first central work in *Sword at Sunset* by Rosemary Sutcliff, a writer of children's stories who entered the adult field through fascination with the history discovered in the process. Her long novel came out in 1963 as the fruit of much study and thought. Warmly praised by Alfred Duggan, it reflected not only the speculations of Collingwood and other scholars, but also the more popular, less purely academic inquiry datable from the late 1950s, which was soon to find a focus at Cadbury.

Arthur himself is made the narrator—a bold course for a woman writer to take. His career is very much as suggested in this book, and therefore need not be described. Rosemary Sutcliff locates Badon at Liddington, drawing on the advice of a professional soldier to get the battle right. After the triumph, Arthur's soldiers crown him as emperor. He spends the rest of his life in uneasy but partially successful attempts to give Britain a stable peace. At the end, his own achievement is plainly doomed, but there are dim foreshadowings of his immortality in legend and of the new state which will arise from the chaos.

Lastly (for the moment), 1967 brought a junior version of Arthur's story by George Finkel, *Twilight Province*.

A project which has hovered for many years without ever coming firmly to earth is that of an Arthurian Festival. Doubtless there was no hope of staging one in an endurable form till all hankerings after sham-medieval pageantry were safely in limbo. Here too the 1960s have witnessed, at least, some experiments. Their roots lie far back in one of England's more peculiar cultural failures.

Readers of the later editions of Shaw's *The Perfect Wagnerite* may be perplexed by his reference to a nascent English Bayreuth at Glastonbury. Shaw was only the most famous of several famous supporters behind a Glastonbury Festival, launched in 1914 and continuing in the 1920s, which is now almost completely forgotten. Laurence Housman was also concerned in this, and John Cowper Powys took a hint from it (though not more than a hint) for his strange, enormous novel *A Glastonbury Romance*. The Festival's demise was due to the shortcomings of its founder and master spirit, the composer Rutland Boughton, remembered today only for his opera *The Immortal Hour*. At Glastonbury he did a surprising amount with a piano and no orchestra, in a poorly appointed hall. But he was inadequate simply as an artist. His Arthurian music-dramas are dead. The Rutland Boughton Trust, which holds the copyrights, revived one of them in later years (*The Queen of Cornwall*, based on Hardy), but its reception was tepid.

Rutland Boughton's personal quirks did him no good, and Glastonbury has chosen to know nothing of him. One of his more disruptive qualities was a left-wing outlook which could take curiously graceless forms (he once refused to conduct at a performance of *The Immortal Hour* because King George v was there). The Arthur cycle, in his hands, kept its Tennysonian panoply yet ended with a peasants' revolt and a red dawn in the east. It was another symptom of dissolution and regrouping. In 1963 and 1964, the Glastonbury Festival was revived as a mainly local effort. For the second of those years one of the events was a kind of drama-documentary, *The Glass Island*, with a frankly historical Arthur presented through the technique of the television interview.

Lack of resources and lack of interest prevented the revival from going further. For the moment at least, the Glastonbury Festival passed into abeyance. By far the most effective pursuit of the same idea occurred at the well-established Bath Festival in 1967. Here, the main programme is regularly supported by 'fringe' events, with a theme which is different each year. In 1966, for example, they were centred on William Beckford of Fonthill, and included an oriental reception based on his novel *Vathek*. In 1967, the interest roused by the Cadbury excavation inspired an Arthurian motif.

Barbara Robertson, for some years the organiser of the fringe programme, wrote the script for a dramatic *King Arthur* pageant with music. This was performed in the open air, in the centre of Bath beside the abbey church. It was a highly original attempt to show history and legend together, and suggest the relation between them. A double stage was used: a simple scaffold construction with little scenery, evoking a touch of the medieval mystery-play atmosphere. The upper stage was Legend, the lower, History. On the lower set a group of writers, such as Gildas and Chrétien de Troyes, debated what had happened. Beside them the *dux bellorum* and other drab-looking dark-age figures enacted scenes of Saxon invasion. On the set above, the legendary persons moved in bright contrast: Merlin, the Grail knights, Morgan le Fay. A staircase at the back enabled characters who figured in both actions to pass from one to the other.

Coloured lights, professionally deployed by TV technicians, created bold effects. The cast was composed of staff members and students of the Old Vic Theatre School in Bristol. After rehearsal, the speeches were recorded at the Bristol TWW studios, together with music. At the actual performance the tape was run through, greatly amplified. The actors mimed to it without the difficulty of projecting their voices in the open. Despite a number of tricky problems, the play was performed four times during June with no serious mishap.

Meanwhile the fringe programme was anchored to fact by the inclusion of two lectures (given by Leslie Alcock and Geoffrey Ashe), with guided coach expeditions to Cadbury and Glastonbury. Michael Owen, the curator of the Roman Bath Museum, set up a special dark-age exhibition. Festival visitors were able to buy an unprecedented souvenir: a map of Arthurian Britain, with pictures and captions explaining both the history and the legends, compiled by I. F. Roberts and G. W. C. Revels.

During 1967, the Bath Festival, the much-filmed Cadbury dig, and also a skilful TV documentary by the Canadian Bruce Parsons, took the quest for Arthur's Britain into the realm of public awareness and mass media. Can we draw any conclusions as to the results so far, and the implications?

This, perhaps: that objective research has not borne out either the credulous romantics or the ultra-sceptical professional scholars. But, as at Troy and elsewhere, it has shown that the credulous were slightly less wrong than the extremists of the destructive party. To compare the critical scholarship of today with that of fifty years ago, or indeed much less, is to note a series of quiet shifts and concessions. In the specific case of Cadbury Castle, one can hardly help observing that in books published at about the same time by professional scholars and by amateurs, it was the scholars who ignored or belittled it, the amateurs who mentioned it and urged excavations.

The naïve believers have no right to claim that they have been vindicated. They have not. Excavation shows that we go wrong if we take the legends literally. But it also shows that we go more wrong if we refuse to take them seriously. This is the same lesson that follows from the work of Schliemann and his successors, whether in Ilium, Crete, Mycenae, the Middle East, India or Mexico. The Victorian historian E. A. Freeman, no pro-Celt, made the point memorably when discussing one aspect of the Matter of Britain: 'We need not believe that the Glastonbury legends are records of facts; but the existence of those legends is a very great fact.'

Unfortunately, there is as yet no method of taking-seriously-without-taking-literally that can even pretend to be systematic or lead reliably to the truth. Hence, the reconstitution of dark-age Britain has struggled forward (and will probably continue to struggle forward) through a tangle of wild guesses and futile disputes. Forward, nevertheless, it goes. Thanks chiefly to Cadbury, the alliance of archaeologists, literary scholars and responsible amateurs is at last becoming a reality, and more and more students are undertaking dark-age research. A lunatic fringe still has to be contended with. But even here, it is fair to remark that some of the major archaeological work owed its inception to unacademic zealots whom all too many scholars dismissed. In this field nobody has a monopoly of truth, or credit.

To live with the Arthurian theme for long is to feel that the prophecy of Arthur's Return means something, though it may be hard to say what. An answer, possibly, has now begun to take shape. As the exploration of national roots goes on, there are signs in Britain of a new disposition to ask, 'What are we, how did we come to be so, where are we meant to go from here?' Inquiry in depth is injecting a fresh element into the national scene, an element of reappraisal. From this a new and acceptable patriotism, a new sense of national vocation may surely come. The quest for Arthur's Britain cannot be the only factor in such a renewal, but it can be—indeed, it already is—a stimulus. One day we may discover that the Fact has been more truly potent than the Legend, and that King Arthur has returned, after all, by abdication.

General Events

367	Saxons, Picts and Irish attack Britain.
369	Imperial rule restored, but henceforth a rapid decline of towns and villa economy.
383	Maximus (the 'Prince Macsen' of Welsh and Cornish legend) proclaimed emperor by British army.
387	Maximus moves British troops to the Continent.
388	Maximus defeated and killed, but British link with Empire remains weakened.
395 ?	Niall, High King of Ireland, sacks cities of western Britain.
399	Stilicho clears Britain of barbarians (the first 'rescue' described by Gildas ?).
First half of 5th century	Cunedda, from the north, takes over a large part of Wales. Other chieftains in western and northern Britain claim succession to imperial power.
402	Stilicho withdraws troops from Britain.
405 ?	Niall killed at sea. Irish threat to Britain henceforth much reduced, though some Irish settlers remain, e.g. in south Wales.
407	Constantine III (the 'Bendigeit Custennin' of Welsh legend, and king of Britain in Geoffrey of Monmouth) proclaimed emperor by British army. Goes to Gaul taking most of the remaining regular forces.
410	Great Saxon attack on Britain. The regional councils or *civitates* rebel against Constantine. Britain autonomous within the Empire; provisional *de facto* recognition by Emperor Honorius.
418 ?	Possible imperial expedition to Britain and partial re-occupation (the second 'rescue' described by Gildas ?).
421	

Chronology

A query after a date means that this is attested only by an unreliable early document, but is defensible enough to be worth including. A few such dates have been adopted in the text, usually with some qualification.

Religion

367	Celtic pagan revival about this time (Lydney, etc.).
369	
383	
387	
388	
395 ?	
399	
First half of 5th century	Missionary and literary activity by British Christians. St Ninian converts some of the Picts. Pelagius teaches in Rome. Possible settlement of monks or hermits in Glastonbury area.
402	
405 ?	
407	
410	
418 ?	
421	Agricola introduces Pelagian doctrine into Britain.

General Events

425   No imperial forces or administration in Britain after this date. Vortigern probably beginning to rise to prominence. Saxons in Cambridgeshire.

429   Defeat of combined raid by Picts and Saxons.

432?
440   Extensive Saxon raiding.

446   Unsuccessful appeal of *civitates* to Aëtius (according to Gildas).

447   Vortigern predominant.

450   Angles, Saxons and Jutes settling in Thanet and elsewhere about this time as auxiliary troops, with Vortigern's permission.

455?   Hengist seizing territory in Kent. Battle of Aylesford.

457?   Battle of Crayford. General Anglo-Saxon revolt about this time and sacking of lowland Britain. Flight of refugees to Armorica (which thus begins to become 'Brittany') and to Spain. Collapse of British economy.

461?   Death of Vortigern. After this, a gradual British recovery under the remnant of the Romanised citizenry led by Ambrosius.

470   Seaborne British army joins Armorica settlers in campaign to restore authority of Emperor Anthemius in Gaul. Ambrosius's counter-offensive against Anglo-Saxons beginning now or a little later.

477?   Aelle, the South Saxon leader, lands near Selsey.

480–90   Probable lull; St Germanus's biographer speaks of Britain as prosperous.

495?   Cerdic, the West Saxon leader, lands from Southampton Water.

500   Angles and Saxons on Humber, in north Lincolnshire, in East Anglia, Essex, Middlesex, Sussex, Hampshire, and advancing from the Wash toward the upper Thames; Jutes in Kent and New Forest. British migration to Armorica continuing (and throughout this century), but some success at home in containing the invasion. Arthur among the British leaders.

508?   Cerdic defeats Britons in Netley Marsh.

516 or '18?   Britons under Arthur win great victory at 'Mount Badon', probably regaining lost ground in Thames valley and north-west of London. After this, a phase of British ascendancy and comparative peace, with some Saxons returning to the continent.

537 or '39?   Battle of Camlann. Death of Arthur.

425	
429	St Germanus in Britain to combat Pelagianism, apparently favoured by Vortigern's 'Celtic' party.
432?	St Patrick begins his Irish mission.
440	
446	
447	Second visit of St Germanus. (Possibly a little earlier than this date.)
450	
455?	
457?	
461?	
470	Faustus, a British bishop, perhaps a son of Vortigern, prominent in Gaul. British Church now virtually cut off but regaining vigour.
477?	
480–90	
495?	
500	St Illtud at Llantwit Major during first quarter of 6th century. Many disciples and strong forward movement of Church in west.
508?	
516 or '18?	Gildas, Cadoc, David and other important ecclesiastical figures active during the next half-century. Britons assisting Irish Christianity. Monastery at Glastonbury on present site.
537 or '39?	

General Events

545	The five kings denounced by Gildas ruling over western Britain about this time, Maelgwn of Gywnedd being the most important.
547?	Yellow Plague. Death of Maelgwn.
552?	West Saxons resume advance. British defeat at Salisbury.
563	
570–600	Oldest surviving Welsh poetry: Taliesin, Aneirin, Llywarch Hen, Myrddin ('Merlin'). Urbgen of Rheged drives back the northern Angles.
571?	Saxons overrun British enclave in Buckinghamshire.
577?	British defeat at Dyrham. Loss of Bath, Cirencester and Gloucester. 'West Welsh' isolated.
593–603	Aethelfrith of Northumbria gaining ground in the north. British defeat at Catterick (*Gododdin*).
597	
603	Aethelfrith routs Aedan, King of Scots.
616	Aethelfrith defeats Welsh at Chester, cutting off Wales from the north.
632–33	Welsh invasion of Northumbria defeated. End of effective British challenge to Anglo-Saxons.

Religion

545	
547?	
552?	
563	St Columba founds Iona.
570–600	
571?	
577?	
593–603	
597	St Augustine in Kent.
603	Welsh bishops refuse to co-operate with Augustine.
616	
632–33	After this date, Celtic missionaries are active in most of the Anglo-Saxon territory.

Bibliography

General Bibliography

This list contains no works of creative literature later than Malory. Thus, for example, Spenser and Tennyson do not appear, though a few relevant books about them do. All the chief literary works after Malory are mentioned in the first and last chapters of the text, and it would be inflating an already long catalogue to list such works here.

On the other hand, several books are included which are semi-popular, speculative or, for various reasons, unsatisfactory. Some might include my own in this dubious class. But where so much is uncertain and liable to rethinking, rigid academic tests cannot be applied without loss. Serious students who use this bibliography will be able, after a little practice, to judge for themselves when they are on safe ground.

ADAMNAN, *Life of St Columba*, ed. and trans. William Reeves, Edinburgh 1874.

Anglo-Saxon Chronicle, ed. G. N. Garmonsway, Dent, London 1953; Dutton, New York 1953.

Annales Cambriae: see WADE-EVANS II, and WILLIAMS, Hugh II.

ASHE, Geoffrey: I *King Arthur's Avalon*, 1957, rev. edn, Collins, London 1966; Dutton, New York 1958. II *From Caesar to Arthur*, Collins, London 1960. III *Land to the West*, Collins, London 1962; Viking Press, New York 1962.

BABCOCK, William H., *Legendary Islands of the Atlantic*, American Geographical Society Research Services, New York 1922.

BARBER, R. W., *Arthur of Albion*, Pall Mall Press with Barrie & Rockliff, London 1961; Barnes and Noble, New York 1961.

BARING-GOULD, S. and FISHER, John, *Lives of the British Saints*, 7 vols., Cymmrodorion Society, London 1907–13.

BEDE, *History of the English Church and People*, trans. Leo Sherley-Price, Penguin, Harmondsworth 1955.

BENNETT, J. A. W. (ed.), *Essays on Malory*, Oxford University Press, London and New York 1963.

BIELER, Ludwig, *The Life and Legend of St Patrick*, Burns, Oates and Washburn, London 1949.

BLAIR, Peter Hunter, *An Introduction to Anglo-Saxon England*, Cambridge University Press, Cambridge 1956; New York 1959.

Brendan, Voyage of St: see ASHE III, BABCOCK, O'DONOGHUE.

BRINKLEY, Roberta F., *Arthurian Legend in the Seventeenth Century*, Johns Hopkins Press, Baltimore and London 1932; new edn, Octagon Press, New York 1966.

BROMWICH, Rachel: I 'Cantre'r Gwaelod and Ker-Is', in Fox, Cyril and Dickins, Bruce (eds), *The Early Cultures of North-West Europe*, Cambridge University Press, Cambridge and New York 1950.   II *Trioedd Ynys Prydein* (the Welsh Triads, with translation and notes), University of Wales Press, Cardiff 1961.

BROOKE, Dorothy, *Pilgrims Were They All*, Faber and Faber, London 1937.

BRUCE, J. D., *The Evolution of Arthurian Romance*, Johns Hopkins Press, Baltimore 1923; 2nd edn, Peter Smith, Gloucester, Mass. 1958.

BULLEID, A. and GRAY, H. St George, *The Glastonbury Lake Village*, 2 vols, Glastonbury Antiquarian Society, Glastonbury 1911 and 1917.

BUTLER, Alban, *Lives of the Saints*, rev. and ed., H. Thurston and D. Attwater, Burns, Oates and Washburn, London 1956; P. J. Kenedy, New York 1956.

Cambridge Ancient History, Vol. XII, Cambridge University Press, Cambridge 1939.

Cambridge Medieval History, Vol. I, Cambridge University Press, Cambridge 1911.

CARADOC OF LLANCARFAN: see WILLIAMS, Hugh I, and TATLOCK.

CHADWICK, H. M. and CHADWICK, N. K., *The Growth of Literature*, Vol. I, Cambridge University Press, Cambridge 1932; Macmillan, New York 1932.

CHADWICK, N. K.: I 'The Celtic Background of Anglo-Saxon England', *Yorkshire Celtic Studies*, Vol. III, 1946.'   II 'The Lost Literature of Celtic Scotland', *Scottish Celtic Studies*, August 1953.   III *Studies in Early British History* (ed.), Cambridge University Press, Cambridge and New York 1954.   IV *The Age of the Saints in the Early Celtic Church*, Oxford University Press, London and New York 1961.   V *Celtic Britain*, Thames and Hudson, London 1963; Frederick A. Praeger, New York 1963.

CHAMBERS, E. K., *Arthur of Britain*, Sidgwick and Jackson, London 1927; Barnes and Noble, New York 1964.

CHAMBERS, R. W.: I *England Before the Norman Conquest*, Longmans, London 1926. II *Beowulf—an Introduction*, Cambridge University Press, Cambridge 1932; Macmillan, New York 1932; 3rd edn, Cambridge University Press, New York 1959.

CHILDE, V. Gordon, *Prehistoric Communities of the British Isles*, Chambers, London 1940.

CHRÉTIEN DE TROYES, *Eric and Enid*, trans. W. W. Comfort, Dent, London 1914; Dutton, New York 1914; reissued in 1955 as *Arthurian Romances*, Dent, London and Dutton, New York.

COLLINGWOOD, R. G. and MYRES, J. N. L., *Roman Britain and the English Settlements*, Oxford University Press, London and New York 1937.

COMFORT, W. W. (ed. and trans.), *The Quest of the Holy Grail*, Dent, London 1926.

COPLEY, Gordon J., *The Conquest of Wessex in the Sixth Century*, Phoenix House, London 1954; Dent, Toronto 1954.

CROSS, Tom Peete, 'The Passing of Arthur', *Manly Anniversary Studies in Language and Literature*, 1923.

DANIEL, G. E. (ed.), *Myth or Legend?*, Bell, London 1955; Macmillan, New York 1955.

DENOMY, Alexander J., *The Heresy of Courtly Love*, Declan X. McMullen, New York 1947; new edn, Peter Smith, Gloucester, Mass. 1965.

DE PAOR, Maire and Liam, *Early Christian Ireland*, Thames and Hudson, London 1958; Frederick A. Praeger, New York 1958.

DUCKETT, Eleanor Shipley, *Anglo-Saxon Saints and Scholars*, Macmillan, London 1947; Shoe String Press, Hamden, Conn. 1947.

EADIE, John W., 'The Development of Roman Mailed Cavalry', *Journal of Roman Studies*, 1967.

EKWALL, Eilert, *The Concise Oxford Dictionary of English Place-Names*, Oxford University Press, London and New York 1960.

ESCHENBACH, Wolfram von: I *Parzival*, trans. Jessie L. Weston, London 1894. II *Parzival*, trans. Helen M. Mustard and Charles E. Passage, Knopf, New York 1961.

EVANS, Sebastian (ed. and trans.), *The High History of the Holy Grail (i.e. Perlesvaus)*, Dent, London 1910; Dutton, New York 1910.

FASTIDIUS: see HASLEHURST.

FERGUSON, John, *Pelagius*, W. Heffer, Cambridge 1956.

FREEMAN, E. A.: I 'King Ine', *Proceedings of the Somerset Archaeological and Natural History Society*, Vol. XX, 1874. II 'Presidential Address', ibid., Vol. XXVI, 1880.

FRERE, Sheppard, *Britannia*, Routledge and Kegan Paul, London 1967.

GEOFFREY OF MONMOUTH, *History of the Kings of Britain*, ed. and trans. Lewis Thorpe, Penguin, Harmondsworth and Baltimore 1966. See also GRISCOM, and PARRY, J. J.

Germanus, Life of St: see HOARE.

GEROULD, G. H., 'King Arthur and Politics', *Speculum*, January 1927.

GILDAS: see WILLIAMS, Hugh I.

GIRALDUS CAMBRENSIS: I *De Principis Instructione*, Rolls Series, London 1891. II *Speculum Ecclesiae*, Rolls Series, London 1873.

GOUGAUD, Louis, *Christianity in Celtic Lands*, Sheed and Ward, London 1932.

GRAVES, Robert, *The White Goddess*, 3rd edn, Faber and Faber, London 1952; Farrar, Straus and Giroux, New York 1966.

GREENLAW, Edwin, *Studies in Spenser's Historical Allegory*, Oxford University Press, London 1932; Johns Hopkins Press, Baltimore 1932; new edn, Octagon, New York 1966.

GRISCOM, Acton, *The Historia Regum Britanniae of Geoffrey of Monmouth*, Longmans, London 1929.

GREEN, J. R., 'Dunstan at Glastonbury', *Proceedings of the Somerset Archaeological and Natural History Society*, Vol. II, 1861–62.

HAMILTON, A. C., *The Structure of Allegory in the Faerie Queene*, Oxford University Press, London and New York 1961.

HANNING, Robert W., *The Vision of History in Early Britain*, Columbia University Press, New York 1966.

HARDEN, D. B. (ed.), *Dark-Age Britain*, Methuen, London 1956; British Book Service, Toronto 1956.

HARVEY, John, *The Plantagenets*, Batsford, London 1948.

HASLEHURST, R. S. T., *The Works of Fastidius*, Society of SS Peter and Paul, London 1927.

HAWKES, Jacquetta, *A Guide to the Prehistoric and Roman Monuments in England and Wales*, Chatto and Windus, London 1951; Clarke, Irwin, Toronto 1951.

HAWKINS, Desmond, *Sedgemoor and Avalon*, Robert Hale, London 1954.

HOARE, F. R. (ed. and trans.), *The Western Fathers*, Sheed and Ward, London and New York 1954; new edn, Harper, New York 1965. Includes *The Life of St Germanus* by Constantius of Lyons.

HODGKIN, R. G., *A History of the Anglo-Saxons*, 3rd edn, Oxford University Press, London 1952; New York 1953.

HOUGH, Graham, *A Preface to the Faerie Queene*, Duckworth, London 1962; Norton, New York 1963.

HULL, E., 'The Development of Hades in Celtic Literature', *Folk-Lore*, 1907.

JACKSON, Kenneth H.: I 'Once Again Arthur's Battles', *Modern Philology*, Vol. XLIII, 1945–46. II *A Celtic Miscellany*, Routledge and Kegan Paul, London 1951. III *Language and History in Early Britain*, Edinburgh University Press, Edinburgh 1953; Harvard University Press, Cambridge, Mass. 1954.

JAFFRAY, Robert, *King Arthur and the Holy Grail*, Putnam, London and New York 1928.

JERROLD, Douglas, *An Introduction to the History of England*, Collins, London and Toronto 1949.

JOHN OF GLASTONBURY, *Chronicle*, ed. T. Hearne, Oxford 1726.

JOHNSTONE, P. K., 'The Victories of Arthur', *Notes and Queries*, June 2, 1934.

JONES, J. Morris, 'Taliesin', *Y Cymmrodor*, Vol. XXVIII, 1918.

JONES, W. A., 'On the Reputed Discovery of King Arthur's Remains at Glastonbury', *Proceedings of the Somerset Archaeological and Natural History Society*, Vol. IX, 1859.

JONES, W. Lewis, *King Arthur in History and Legend*, Cambridge University Press, Cambridge 1911.

KENDRICK, T. D., *British Antiquity*, Methuen, London 1950; British Book Service, Toronto 1950.

KILLHAM, John (ed.), *Critical Essays on the Poetry of Tennyson*, Routledge and Kegan Paul, London 1960; Barnes and Noble, New York 1960.

LAYAMON: see MASON.

LELAND, John, *Itinerary*, ed. Lucy Toulmin Smith, Centaur Press, Arundel 1964; Southern Illinois University Press, Carbondale, Ill. 1965.

LETHBRIDGE, T. C.: I *Merlin's Island*, Methuen, London 1948. II *Herdsmen and Hermits*, Bowes and Bowes, Cambridge 1950; Humanities Press, New York 1950. III *The Painted Men*, Melrose, London 1954; Philosophical Library, New York 1954.

LEWIS, C. S., *The Allegory of Love*, Clarendon Press, Oxford 1936; Oxford University Press, New York 1936. See also WILLIAMS, Charles.

LINDSAY, Jack, *Arthur and His Times*, Frederick Muller, London 1958; Barnes and Noble, New York 1966.

LLOYD, John Edward, *A History of Wales*, Longmans, London 1939.

LOOMIS, R. S.: I *Celtic Myth and Arthurian Romance*, Columbia University Press, New York 1927. II Nitze's *Perlesvaus*, in *Romanic Review*, Vol. XXIX, 1937. III 'Geoffrey of Monmouth and the Modena Archivolt', *Speculum*, 1938. IV *Wales and the Arthurian Legend*, University of Wales Press, Cardiff 1956. V *Arthurian Literature in the Middle Ages* (ed.), Clarendon Press, Oxford 1959; Oxford University Press, New York 1959.

LOOMIS, R. S. and LOOMIS, L. H., *Arthurian Legends in Medieval Art*, Oxford University Press, London 1938; Kraus Reprints, New York 1938.

Mabinogion, trans. Gwyn and Thomas Jones, Dent, London 1949; Dutton, New York 1949.

MALORY, Sir Thomas: I *Works*, ed. E. Vinaver, Clarendon Press, Oxford 1948; Oxford University Press, New York 1947. II *Le Morte d'Arthur*, modern English rendition by Keith Baines with Introduction by Robert Graves, University Books, New Hyde Park, N.Y. 1962; Ambassador, Toronto 1962.

MASON, Eugene (trans.), *Arthurian Chronicles* (*i.e.*, Wace and Layamon), Dent, London 1962.

MATTHEWS, William, *The Ill-Framed Knight*, University of California Press, Berkeley, Calif. 1966.

MEYER, Kuno and NUTT, Alfred, *The Voyage of Bran*, London 1895–97.

NENNIUS: see WADE-EVANS II.

NITZE, William A., *Le Haut Livre du Graal, Perlesvaus*, Paris 1932–37.

NUTT, Alfred, *Studies on the Legend of the Holy Grail*, London and New York 1888.

O'DONOGHUE, Denis, *Brendaniana*, Dublin 1893.

OMAN, Charles, *England Before the Norman Conquest*, Methuen, London 1938.

PARIS, A. Paulin, *Les Romans de la Table Ronde*, Paris 1868–77.

PARRY, J. J. (ed. and trans.), *The Vita Merlini of Geoffrey of Monmouth*, University of Illinois Press, Urbana, Ill. 1925.

PARRY, Thomas, *A History of Welsh Literature*, Clarendon Press, Oxford 1955; Oxford University Press, New York 1955.

Perlesvaus: See EVANS and NITZE.

PROCOPIUS, *History of the Wars*, 7 vols, trans. H. B. Dewing (Loeb Classical Library); Heinemann, London 1914–40; Macmillan, New York 1914–40.

Queste: See COMFORT.

Reader's Digest Complete Atlas of the British Isles, London, 1965.

REES, W. J., *Lives of the Cambro British Saints*, Abergavenny 1853.

RHYS, John, *Studies in the Arthurian Legend*, Oxford and New York 1891.

RICHMOND, I. A., *Roman Britain*, Penguin, Harmondsworth and Baltimore 1956.

ROBINSON, Joseph Armitage: I *Somerset Historical Essays*, British Academy, London 1921. II *The Times of St Dunstan*, Clarendon Press, Oxford 1923. III *Two Glastonbury Legends*, Cambridge University Press, Cambridge 1926.

RYAN, John, *Early Irish Missionaries on the Continent and St Vergil of Salzburg*, Irish Messenger Press, Dublin 1924.

SAKLATVALA, Beram, *Arthur: Roman Britain's Last Champion*, David and Charles, Newton Abbot 1967; Taplinger, New York 1967.

SCHOEPPERLE, Gertrude, *Tristan and Isolt*, David Nutt, London 1913; Burt Franklin, New York 1963.

SHELDON, Gilbert, *The Transition from Roman Britain to Christian England*, Macmillan, London 1932.

SKENE, William F., *The Four Ancient Books of Wales*, Edinburgh 1868.

SLOVER, Clark H.: I 'William of Malmesbury and the Irish', *Speculum*, July 1927. II 'Glastonbury Abbey and the Fusing of English Literary Culture', *Speculum*, April 1935.

SOZOMEN, *Ecclesiastical History*, Select Library of Nicene and Post-Nicene Fathers, Vol. II, London 1891.

STENTON, F. M., *Anglo-Saxon England*, Oxford University Press, London 1943 and New York 1947.

TALIESIN: See JONES, J. Morris, and SKENE. The 'Story of Taliesin' is in the nineteenth-century version of the *Mabinogion* by Lady Charlotte Guest.

TATLOCK, J. S. P., 'Caradoc of Llancarfan', *Speculum*, 1938.

TENNYSON, Charles, *Alfred Tennyson*, Macmillan, London and New York 1949.

TILLYARD, E. M. W., *Shakespeare's History Plays*, Chatto and Windus, London 1944; Barnes and Noble, New York 1964.

TREHARNE, R. F., *The Glastonbury Legends*, Cresset, London 1967.

WACE: see MASON.

WADE-EVANS, A. W.: I *Welsh Christian Origins*, Aldus Press, Oxford 1934. II *Nennius's History of the Britons*—with *Annales Cambriae*, genealogies etc. (ed. and trans.), Church History Society, London 1938.

WESTON, Jessie L.: I *The Legend of Sir Lancelot du Lac*, David Nutt, London 1901. II *From Ritual to Romance*, Cambridge University Press, Cambridge 1920; Doubleday, Garden City, N.Y. 1957.

WHEELER, R. E. M. and WHEELER, T. V., *Report on the Excavations of the . . . Site in Lydney Park, Gloucestershire*, Quaritch, London 1932.

WILLIAM OF MALMESBURY: I *The Acts of the Kings of England*, trans. J. Sharpe, London 1854. II *De Antiquitate Glastoniensis Ecclesiae*; partly spurious but important; trans. Frank Lomax as *The Antiquities of Glastonbury*, Talbot, London 1908.

WILLIAMS, Charles, *Arthurian Torso*, a fragment edited with discussion by C. S. Lewis, Oxford University Press, London 1948.

WILLIAMS, Hugh: I *Gildas* (*Works*, and the *Life* by Caradoc of Llancarfan, and another Life), ed. and trans., Cymmrodorion Society, London 1901. II *Christianity in Early Britain*, with *Annales Cambriae*, Clarendon Press, Oxford 1912.

WILLIAMS, Ifor, 'The Gododdin Poems', *Transactions of the Anglesey Antiquarian Society and Field Club*, 1935.

Special Bibliographies

TINTAGEL

In General Bibliography see: GEOFFREY OF MONMOUTH, Book VIII, 19. *Perlesvaus*, Branch XX, 10/11.

RADFORD, C. A. Ralegh: I 'Tintagel—the Castle and Celtic Monastery', *Antiquaries Journal*, Vol. XV, 1935, pp. 401–19. II 'Tintagel in History and Legend', *Journal of the Royal Institution of Cornwall*, Vol. XXV, 1942, pp. 24–41. III 'Imported Pottery found at Tintagel, Cornwall', in HARDEN (see General Bibliography). IV 'The Celtic Monastery in Britain', *Archaeologia Cambrensis*, Vol. CXI, 1962, pp. 1–24.

RYAN, John, *Irish Monasticism: Origins and Early Development*, Longmans, London 1931.

THOMAS, Charles, 'Imported Pottery in Dark Age Western Britain', *Medieval Archaeology*, Vol. III, 1959, pp. 89–111.

Tintagel Castle, Official Guide, Ministry of Public Building and Works, HMSO, London 1955.

CASTLE DORE

In General Bibliography see: BROMWICH, Rachel, 11.

RADFORD, C. A. Ralegh, 'Report on the Excavations at Castle Dore', *Journal of the Institution of Cornwall*, new series Vol. I, Appendix, 1951.

Also:

BEROUL, *Romance of Tristran*, ed. A. Ewert, Blackwell, Oxford 1939; lines 2452–7, 2972–95.

HENDERSON, Charles, *Essays in Cornish History*, Oxford University Press, London and New York 1935.

WALES

ALCOCK, Leslie: I 'Castell Odo—An Embanked Settlement on Mynydd Ystum, near Aberdaron, Caernarvonshire', *Archaeologia Cambrensis*, Vol. CIX, 1960, pp. 78–135. II *Dinas Powys—An Iron Age, Dark Age and Early Medieval Settlement in Glamorgan*, University of Wales, Cardiff 1963. III 'Excavations at Degannwy Castle, Caernarvonshire, 1961–66', *Archaeological Journal*, Vol. CXXIV, 1967, pp. 190–201.

Also:

FOSTER, I. W. and DANIEL, G., *Prehistoric and Early Wales*, Routledge and Kegan Paul, London 1965; Humanities Press, New York 1965.

GARDNER, W., 'The Ancient Hillfort on Moel Fenlli, Denbighshire', *Archaeologia Cambrensis*, Vol. LXXVI, 1921, pp. 237–52.

GARDNER, W. and SAVORY, H. N., *Dinorben: A Hillfort Occupied in Early Iron Age and Roman Times*, National Museum of Wales, Cardiff 1964.

HOGG, A. H. A.: I 'A Fortified Round Hut at Carreg y Llam Near Nevin', *Archaeologia Cambrensis*, Vol. CVL, 1957, pp. 46–55. II 'Garn Boduan and Tre'r Ceiri', *Archaeological Journal*, Vol. CXVII, 1960, pp. 1–39.

LETHBRIDGE, T. C. and DAVID, H. E., 'Excavation of a House-Site on Gateholm, Pembrokeshire', *Archaeologia Cambrensis*, Vol. LXXXV, 1930, pp. 366–74.

NASH-WILLIAMS, V. E., *The Early Christian Monuments of Wales*, University of Wales, Cardiff 1950.

O'NEIL, B. H. St J., 'Excavations at Breiddin Hill Camp, Montgomeryshire, 1933–35', *Archaeologia Cambrensis*, Vol. XCII, 1937, pp. 86–128.

PHILLIPS, C. W., 'The Excavation of a Hut Group at Pant-y-saer in the Parish of Llanfair-Mathafarn-Eithaf, Anglesey', *Archaeologia Cambrensis*, Vol. LXXXIX, 1934, pp. 1–36.

SAVORY, H. N.: I 'The Excavations at Dinorben Hillfort, Abergele, 1956–59'. *Transactions of the Denbighshire Historical Society*, Vol. VIII, 1959, pp. 18–39. II 'Excavations at Dinas Emrys, Beddgelert, Caernarvonshire, 1954–56', *Archaeologia Cambrensis*, Vol. CIX, 1960, pp. 13–77.

VARLEY, W. J.: I 'The Hillforts of the Welsh Marches', *Archaeological Journal*, Vol. CV, 1948, pp. 41–66. II 'Excavations of the Castle Ditch, Eddisbury, 1935–38', *Transactions of the Historic Society of Lancashire and Cheshire*, Vol. CII, 1950, pp. 1–68.

GLASTONBURY

In General Bibliography, see: CHAMBERS, E. K.; GIRALDUS CAMBRENSIS

I & II; JONES, W. A.; ROBINSON I & III. The numerous passages in other works are less directly related to the dark-age archaeology.
RADFORD, C. A. Ralegh: I 'Two Scottish Shrines—Jedburgh and St Andrews', *Archaeological Journal*, Vol. CXII, 1955, pp. 43–60.   II *Glastonbury Abbey*, Pitkin Pictorial, London 1966.

CADBURY

ALCOCK, Leslie: I 'By South Cadbury is that Camelot. . . .', *Antiquity*, Vol. XLI, March 1967, pp. 50–3.   II 'Cadbury Castle, 1967', *Antiquity*, Vol. XLII, 1968, pp. 47–51.   III 'A Reconnaissance Excavation at South Cadbury Castle, Somerset, 1966', *Antiquaries Journal*, Vol. XLVII, 1967, part I, pp. 70–6. IV 'Excavations at South Cadbury Castle, 1967, a Summary Report', *The Antiquaries Journal*, Vol. XLVIII, 1968, pp. 6–17.
Also:
BENNETT, J. A., 'Camelot', *Proceedings of the Somerset Archaeological and Natural History Society*, Vol. XXVI, 1890, pp. 1–19.
DOLLEY, R. H. M., 'The Emergency Mint at Cadbury', *British Numismatic Journal*, Vol. XXVIII, 1955–57, pp. 99–105.
GRAY, H. St George, 'Trial Excavations at Cadbury Castle, S. Somerset, 1913', *Proceedings of the Somerset Archaeological and Natural History Society*, Vol. LIX, 1913, pp. 1–24.
HARFIELD, M., 'Cadbury Castle', ibid., Vol. CVI, 1962, pp. 62–5.
JONES, T., 'A Sixteenth-Century Version of the Arthurian Cave Legend', *Studies in Language and Literature in Honour of Margaret Schlauch*, Warsaw 1966, pp. 175–85.
RADFORD, C. A. Ralegh and COX, J. A., 'Cadbury Castle, South Cadbury', *Proceedings of the Somerset Archaeological and Natural History Society*, Vols. XCIX–C, 1954–55, pp. 106–13.

COSTUME

In General Bibliography, see: COLLINGWOOD and MYRES; LINDSAY.
BOUCHER, François, *A History of Costume in the West*, Thames and Hudson, London 1965.
KÖHLER, Carl, *A History of Costume*, ed. and augmented by Emma von Sichart, Harrap, London 1928; Dover, New York 1928, new edn 1963.
LAVER, James, *Costume*, Cassell, London 1963.
QUENNELL, Marjorie and C. H. B., *Everyday Life in Anglo-Saxon, Viking and Norman Times*, 3rd edn, Batsford, London 1959.
SAYLES, George Osborne, *The Medieval Foundations of England*, Methuen, London 1948, 2nd rev. edn 1950; A. S. Barnes, Cranbury, N.J. 1961.
TENEN, I., *This England, Part I—From the Earliest Times to 1485*, Macmillan, London 1950.
TRUMAN, Nevil, *Historic Costuming*, Pitman, London and New York 1966.
YARWOOD, Doreen, *English Costume*, Batsford, London 1952; 2nd rev. edn, Dufour, Chester Springs, Pa. 1964.

List of Illustrations, Maps and Tables

The contributors and publishers are grateful to the many official bodies, institutions and individuals mentioned below for their assistance in supplying illustration material.

16 Hinton St Mary, Dorset. Floor mosaic of a Roman villa, *in situ.* Photo: by courtesy of the Trustees of the British Museum.

17 Gold *aureus* of Carausius (r. 286–93), obverse, minted in London. British Museum. Photo: Peter A. Clayton.

18 Gold *aureus* of Allectus (r. 293–96), obverse, minted in London. British Museum. Photo: Peter A. Clayton.

19 Gold medallion of Constantius Chlorus (r. 293–306) found at Arras (minted after 296). British Museum. Photo: Peter A. Clayton.

20 Stilicho; half of an ivory diptych (c. 395). Treasury, Monza Cathedral. Photo: Mansell Collection.

21 Gold *solidus* of Magnus Maximus (r. 383–88), obverse, minted in London. British Museum. Photo: Peter A. Clayton.

22 Gold *solidus* of Constantine III (r. 406–11), obverse. British Museum. Photo: Peter A. Clayton.

23 Page from the *Historia Brittonum* by Nennius, mentioning Arthur's battles. British Museum Ms. Harley 3859, fol. 187 (c. 1100). Photo: by courtesy of the Trustees of the British Museum.

24 Map showing 'Arthurian' Britain and the sites of Arthur's campaigns. Drawn by Lucinda Rodd.

25 Liddington Castle, Wiltshire. Aerial view. Photo: Aerofilms Ltd. Copyright reserved.

26 Merlin and Vortigern; from the *Chronicle* of Peter of Langtoft. British Museum Ms. Royal 20 A II, fol 3ʳ (1307). Photo: by courtesy of the Trustees of the British Museum.

27 Lancelot rescues Guinevere. Bibliothèque Nationale Ms. Fr. 342, fol. 186 (French, 1274). Photo: R. B. Fleming and Co. Ltd.

28 *Clibanarius*; from a graffito at Dura Europus (early 3rd century). After M. A. R. Colledge. *The Parthians,* London 1968.

29 Tintagel Castle, Cornwall. General view. Photo: Edwin Smith.

30 Tintagel Castle. Aerial view. Photo: J. K. St Joseph; copyright reserved, Cambridge University Collection.

31 Tintagel Castle. View to the south. Photo: Charles Woolf.

32 Tintagel Castle. Interior of inner ward. Photo: Charles Woolf.

33 Tintagel. Monastery site. Photo: Charles Woolf.

34, 35 Reconstructed east-Mediterranean vessels, Tintagel A–I and A–II ware. County Museum, Truro, Cornwall. Photo: Charles Woolf.

36 Cross-stamped sherds of Tintagel A–I ware. Photo: by courtesy of the Trustees of the British Museum.

37 Menabilly, near Fowey, Cornwall. 'Tristram's Tombstone' (6th century). Photo: Charles Woolf.

38 Lantyne, Cornwall. Church of St Sampson in St Golaute (16 century). Photo: Charles Woolf.

39 Castle Dore, Cornwall, Aerial view. Photo: J. K. St Joseph; copyright reserved, Cambridge University Collection.

40 Tintagel Castle. Plan. Drawn by Lucinda Rodd, based on the Guide book to Tintagel Castle. Reproduced with the permission of the Controller of H.M.S.O.

41 Tintagel Castle. Plan of site A and medieval chapel. Drawn by Lucinda Rodd, based on the Guide book to Tintagel Castle. Reproduced with the permission of the Controller of H.M.S.O.

42 Tintagel Castle. Plan of the 'island'. Drawn by Lucinda Rodd, based on the Guide book to Tintagel Castle. Reproduced with the permission of the Controller of H.M.S.O.

43 Tristram plays to King Mark; pictorial tile from the floor of Chertsey Abbey, Surrey (14th century). Photo: by courtesy of the Trustees of the British Museum.

44 Tara, Eire. Plan of the Banqueting Hall; after Royal Irish Academy fascimile (1880) of a drawing in the *Book of Leinster* (Irish, 12th century).

45 Dinas Emrys, Caernarvonshire. Plan. Drawn by Lucinda Rodd, after H. N. Savory.

46 Map of Wales. Drawn by Lucinda Rodd, after Leslie Alcock.

47 Degannwy Castle, Caernarvonshire. Plan of excavations, 1961–66; based on the Ordnance Survey Map, by permission of the Controller of H.M.S.O. Crown copyright reserved.

48 Dinas Powys. Plan showing putative hall and barn. Drawn by Leslie Alcock.

49 Dinas Powys, Glamorgan. General plan and southern banks. Drawn by Lucinda Rodd, after Leslie Alcock.

50 Memorial stone from the kingdom of Gwynedd. After V. E. Nash-Williams.

51 Stone of Cadman. Photo: by courtesy of the National Museum of Wales, Cardiff.

52 Voteporix's memorial stone. Carmarthen Museum. After V. E. Nash-Williams.

53 Dinas Powys. Sherds of Tintagel A pottery stamped with running leopards. Photo: Leslie Alcock.

54 Dinas Powys. Sherd of Tintagel B pottery. Photo: Leslie Alcock.

55 Dinas Powys. Glass scraps and beads. Photo: Leslie Alcock.

56 Dinas Powys. Scrap bronze and lead die. Photo: Leslie Alcock.

57 Dinas Powys. Reconstruction of brooch from the lead die. Drawn by Leslie Alcock.

58 Llangian, Caernarvonshire. Inscription from a memorial stone in the churchyard. After V. E. Nash-Williams.

59 Dinas Powys. Reconstructed crucible. After Leslie Alcock.

60 Dinas Powys. Folded strip of scrap bronze. Drawn by Leslie Alcock.

61 Dinas Powys. *Mortarium.* Drawn by Leslie Alcock.

62 Reconstruction of Tintagel A bowl. Drawn by Leslie Alcock.

63 Dinas Powys. Bone combs. After Leslie Alcock.

64 Glastonbury Abbey. General view of the abbey church, looking west down the length of the nave. Photo: Sydney W. Newberry.

65 Glastonbury Abbey. South side of the Lady Chapel and the Galilee. Photo: Glastonbury Excavation Committee.

66 Glastonbury Abbey. Excavation showing a post-hole of the wattle oratory under the paving blocks of St Dunstan's Monastery. Photo: Glastonbury Excavation Committee.

67 Glastonbury Abbey. Celtic cemetery graves lying to the south of the Lady Chapel, excavations of 1954. Photo: Glastonbury Excavation Committee.

68 Peterborough. The Hedda Stone. By courtesy of the Dean and Chapter of Peterborough Cathedral. Photo: Jarrold and Sons Ltd.

69 Bewcastle, Cumberland. The Bewcastle Cross. Photo: National Buildings Record; Crown copyright reserved.

70 Glastonbury Abbey. Tomb of King Arthur, excavated 1931. *Somerset Archaeology and National History Journal*, Vol. LXXVII, 1931. Photo: Abbot Horne.

71 Glastonbury. General view of the abbey and the town. Photo: Aerofilms Ltd. Copyright reserved.

72 Glastonbury Abbey. Plan of the Abbey. Drawn by Lucinda Rodd.

73 Glastonbury Abbey. Engraving of the lead cross from King Arthur's tomb, from *Britannia* by William Camden (1607). British Museum. Photo: John Freeman.

74 Glastonbury. Plan of the island of Glastonbury. Drawn by Philip Rahtz.

75 Glastonbury Abbey. Plan of King Ini's church. Drawn by Lucinda Rodd.

76 Glastonbury Abbey. St Joseph's Well. Photo: Glastonbury Abbey Trust.

77 Glastonbury. The Chalice Well at the foot of Tor Hill. Photo: Walter Scott.

78 Glastonbury Tor. Air view. Photo: Aerofilms Ltd. Copyright reserved.

79 Glastonbury Tor. Table showing occupation and finds. Drawn by Lucinda Rodd.

80 Glastonbury Tor. Plan of dark-age features. Drawn by Philip Rahtz.

81 Glastonbury Tor. Plan of the 'cairn'. Drawn by Philip Rahtz.

82 Glastonbury Tor. Drawing of the bronze and iron head, by Gillian Jones.

83 Glastonbury Tor. Main dark-age shelf from the east. Photo: Philip Rahtz.

84 Glastonbury Tor. Pit and grave complex. Photo: Philip Rahtz.

85 Glastonbury Tor. East-end complex from the north. Photo: Philip Rahtz.

86 Glastonbury Tor. The 'cairn'. Photo: Philip Rahtz.

87 Glastonbury Tor. East-Mediterranean pot sherds and bones *in situ*. Photo: Philip Rahtz.

88 Glastonbury Tor. Fragment of an east-Mediterranean *amphora* handle. Photo: Philip Rahtz.

89 Glastonbury Tor. Sherd of Tintagel striated B ware. Photo: Philip Rahtz.

90 Glastonbury Tor. Sherds of Tintagel B ware. Photo: Philip Rahtz.

91 Glastonbury Tor. Site of metalworking hearths. Photo: Philip Rahtz.

119 Trethevy Quoit, Cornwall. Photo: Charles Woolf.

120 Arthur's Tomb at Camelford, Cornwall. Photo: Charles Woolf.

121 Arthur's Stone, Cefn Bryn, Gower, Glamorgan. Photo: by courtesy of the National Museum of Wales, Cardiff.

122 Arthur's O'en, Stirling; engraving by Roy (18th century). Photo: by courtesy of the Royal Commission on Ancient Monuments for Scotland, Edinburgh.

123 Arthur's Seat, Edinburgh. Photo: W. A. Sharp.

124 Samson Flats, Scilly Isles, Cornwall. Ancient field-walls observed at low tide, August 1950. Photo: Paul Ashbee.

125 Llangollen, Denbighshire. The Valle Crucis Pillar, in the Abbey of Valle Crucis. Photo: by courtesy of the National Museum of Wales, Cardiff.

126 Arms of the Trevelyan family. By courtesy of *Burke's Peerage*.

127 Reconstruction of the dress of a dark-age warrior. Drawn by Charles Pickard; by courtesy of the *Observer*.

128-130 Thorsberg, Germany. Dark-age clothing. Photo: Schleswig-Holsteinischer Landsmuseum für Vor- und Frühgeschichte, Kiel.

131 Newstead, Roxburghshire. Leather shoe (Roman *c.* 2nd century). Photo: by courtesy of the National Museum of Antiquities, Edinburgh.

132 The Franks Casket (Anglian, *c.* 650–750). Photo: by courtesy of the Trustees of the British Museum.

133 Pant-y-saer, Anglesey. Penannular silver brooch, found in 1932–33 (*c.* 6th century). Photo: by courtesy of the National Museum of Wales, Cardiff.

134 St Ninian's Isle, Shetland. Brooch from St Ninian's Treasure (8th century). Photo: by courtesy of the National Museum of Antiquities, Edinburgh.

135 Snettisham, Norfolk. The Snettisham Torque; electrum (1st century BC). Photo: by courtesy of the Trustees of the British Museum.

136 Chart for calculating Easter; from the *Compendium of Science* by the monk Byrhtferth (1011). Photo: by courtesy of the Bodleian Library, Oxford.

137 Lullingstone, Kent. The Lullingstone Bowl (British, 5th–6th centuries). Photo: by courtesy of the Trustees of the British Museum.

138 Winchester. The Winchester Bowl (British, 5th–6th centuries). Photo: by courtesy of the Trustees of the British Museum.

139 Taplow, Buckinghamshire. Saxon drinking horn (6th century). Photo: by courtesy of the Trustees of the British Museum.

140 Co. Durham. The Castle Eden Vase (Rhenish, early 6th century). Photo: by courtesy of the Trustees of the British Museum.

141 Bourton-on-the-Water, Gloucestershire. Reconstruction of excavated Saxon hut. Photo: by courtesy of the Trustees of the British Museum.

142 Harmondsworth, Middlesex. Tithe barn (12th century). Photo: National Buildings Record; Crown copyright reserved.

143 Invergowrie, Angus. Pictish slab cross (8th century). Photo: by courtesy of the National Museum of Antiquities, Edinburgh.

144 The Monymusk Reliquary; considered to be that known as the Brechbennock of St Columba (c. 597). Photo: by courtesy of the National Museum of Antiquities, Edinburgh.

145 Iona. View of Martin's Cross outside the abbey (9th century). Photo: Edwin Smith.

146 Cast bronze plaque of the Crucifixion, possibly a book cover (Irish, 8th century). Photo: by courtesy of the National Museum of Ireland, Dublin.

147 Lindisfarne Priory, Holy Island. Photo: Edwin Smith.

148 The boy Arthur draws the sword from the stone; from the film *The Sword in the Stone*. Photo: Copyright Walt Disney Productions.

149 The Castle of Camelot; from the film *Camelot*. Photo: Warner Brothers.

Index